SUNSET RIDGE
973 ARM
Armstrong, Orla
The fifteen decis

D0329134

3 3335 00003 4075

THE FIFTEEN DECISIVE BATTLES
OF THE
UNITED STATES

The Fifteen Decisive Battles

of the

United States

by

O. K. ARMSTRONG

Maps by James Macdonald

LONGMANS, GREEN AND CO.

NEW YORK · LONDON · TORONTO

1961

LONGMANS, GREEN AND CO., INC.
119 WEST 40TH STREET, NEW YORK 18

LONGMANS, GREEN AND CO., LTD.
48 GROSVENOR STREET, LONDON W 1

LONGMANS, GREEN AND CO.
137 BOND STREET, TORONTO 2

THE FIFTEEN DECISIVE BATTLES OF THE UNITED STATES

COPYRIGHT © 1961

BY O. K. ARMSTRONG

ALL RIGHTS RESERVED, INCLUDING THE RIGHT TO REPRODUCE
THIS BOOK, OR ANY PORTION THEREOF, IN ANY FORM

PUBLISHED SIMULTANEOUSLY IN THE DOMINION OF CANADA BY
LONGMANS, GREEN AND CO., TORONTO

FIRST EDITION

LIBRARY OF CONGRESS CATALOG CARD NUMBER 61-9745

Printed in the United States of America

The Author's Foreword

What makes a battle, a military campaign, decisive?

That question was ably answered in the middle of the nineteenth century by Sir Edward Creasy, eminent lawyer, professor, and teacher in the University of London, in a book entitled *The Fifteen Decisive Battles of the World*. Sir Edward surveyed the long history of wars and their battles, from antiquity to the times of Napoleon Bonaparte, and announced that a battle need not be considered decisive because of its length, the numbers of warriors engaged, or the casualties suffered. The test, Dr. Creasy held, is whether the outcome of the battle so influenced the entire campaign or war that victory for one side and defeat for the other logically followed, and thereby the course of history for the nations and peoples involved, and perhaps for the entire world, was determined.

Applying that rule, Dr. Creasy found that fifteen great battles had most vitally affected the destiny of mankind, beginning with the victory of the Greeks over the Persian hordes at Marathon in 490 B.C. and ending with the victory of the Duke of Wellington over Napoleon at Waterloo in 1815. Historians and scholars have generally approved this selection. Certainly there is general agreement with Dr. Creasy's remark:

It cannot be denied that a fearful and wonderful interest is attached to these scenes of carnage. There is undeniable greatness in the disciplined courage and the love of honor which make the combatants confront agony and destruction. And the powers of the human intellect are rarely more strongly displayed than they are in the commander, who regulates, arrays and wields at his will these masses of armed disputants.

During the last hundred years, the American Civil War tested whether our Union of states could survive, the German legions conquered the French armies at Sedan, wars were fought in the Orient and in Africa, the Spanish-American War made the United States a world power, World War I led to the destruction of the old empires and kingdoms in Europe, and the beginnings of communist power; and World War II shook the world with its tremendous upheavals and its vast destruction of economic, social, and spiritual values. As these words are written, the nations and peoples of the free world find it necessary to stand formidably armed to meet the threat of communist aggression stemming from the control of this worldwide conspiracy over the peoples of the Soviet Union, Red China, and the countries of eastern Europe which became pawns in the game of power politics at the close of World War II in 1945.

When the author began the research to select the decisive battles in the wars fought upon the North American continent, and especially those in which the armed forces of the United States were involved, whether on this continent or elsewhere, World War I had receded into history by only a dozen years. I was a veteran of that war. I was firmly convinced that there would never be another great war. I held, as did my comrades of World War I generally, that our participation in the conflict in Europe transformed it into a great crusade to make the world safe for democracy—a war to end all wars. It was my purpose to honor those who had given or offered their lives for causes that they and their compatriots, from colonial days to that last great war, considered just and honorable.

I selected thirteen battles as truly decisive in shaping the course of American history. Then World War II shattered the hope for a warless world and added two battles more, both indicative of the tremendous responsibility the United States had assumed in world affairs.

The author realizes that there can be valid differences of opinion on the impact, upon national and world history, of some of the battles in this selection. Certainly some of the engagements had more far-reaching consequences than others. The defeat of the British at Yorktown, by the allied American and French forces under George Washington, insured victory for the colonies in the War for Independence and thus marked an immeasurably important step forward in mankind's quest for self-government. The high tide of Confederate strength was turned back at Gettysburg and the Union was saved. The brilliant victory of American sea power under Admiral George Dewey on Manila Bay closed forever the history of Spain as a world power. The irresistible flow of American divisions to France during 1917–18, converging upon the battle of the Aisne-Marne, sealed the doom of the German armies and made victory sure for the Allies. To some degree, each of the fifteen decisive battles I have presented irrevocably shaped the destiny of humankind.

This selection in no way reflects discredit upon the struggles in Latin American countries for independence from Spain and Portugal. The matchless energy, superb courage and brilliant leadership of Simón Bolívar rallied the forces of liberty that triumphed in his native Venezuela, in Colombia, Peru, and Bolivia, and that carried aloft the sword of freedom to sever forever the bonds of European domination in Central and South America. When the words "American history" are used, they acknowledge the part played in shaping the destiny of the Western Hemisphere by the good neighbors to the south of the United States of America.

This study is not intended to glorify only the winners and reflect dishonor upon the vanquished. There was never a war but the vast majority of the participants believed in their cause; never a battle but the officers and men on both sides were brave and gallant; never a resort to arms by governments to enforce their will by weapons in the absence of world order under law, but the people, civilian and military, hoped a just and lasting peace would follow.

I cannot claim for this work that its chapters add to the mass of historical lore with much newly discovered material. Rather, I have endeavored to catch the panorama of the great military pageants as they passed in review, throwing such spotlights upon the characters and their courageous deeds as they seem to deserve.

And Now the Greater Battle

I resumed this study after World War II had ushered in the new and terrifying era—the atomic age, which quickly mushroomed into the thermonuclear age. It is still my purpose to honor those who bore the battle, whether their cause triumphed or not; to show how the brave met the brave; how the skill of commanders, the steadfastness of officers, the courageous obedience of armed men, on land or sea, led to victory, or, by the turn of fortune, met defeat.

But another and more compelling purpose prompts me to present the accounts of the decisive battles of American arms: it affords the opportunity to point out that World War II closed the book on wars. I must call attention to the stark fact that war is now totally and completely obsolete. As a method of resolving differences between governments of sovereign nations, which today means between entire populations, war is the ultimate in futility and absurdity.

Is proof needed? Then let us reflect that the very methods of attack and defense, of advance and retreat, of skirmish and maneuver, related repeatedly in these fifteen decisive battles, belong to an age that vanished in the poisonous radiation clouds over Hiroshima and Nagasaki. Whether or not the American Civil War was the last war fought between gentlemen, it is certain that chivalry and honor in combat disap-

peared with the beginning of World War II. Whereas courage
and patriotism still live in the hearts of men and women and
would drive them again to any sacrifices in another great war,
they would have little chance to display any such heroic
qualities, and still smaller chance to survive contact with
hydrogen bomb explosions.

It is obvious that a future war between armed forces
possessing and using atomic and thermonuclear weapons would
be one vast holocaust of horrible death and utter destruction.
The author shares the profound conviction of people of good
will everywhere that the supreme task of humanity is to prevent war in the present and the future. The great challenge of
this age for those who believe in the preservation of a way of
life in which people may enjoy liberty and the pursuit of
happiness is to make war impossible. It can be done—and it
must be done. It will mean abandoning fear and appeasement
of the evil force that through the mistakes of the victorious
powers in World War II allowed the worldwide communist
conspiracy to spread from the Soviet Union to dominate the
countries of eastern Europe, all mainland China, Manchuria,
the northern parts of Korea and Vietnam, and Tibet; and to
threaten millions more peoples with its aggressive designs, in
every area of the globe.

The task will mean meeting the present challenge of a
regime based upon atheistic materialism, dedicated to stamp-
ing out all freedom of the individual citizen and his collective
liberties, with our determined announcement that this world
cannot endure half slave and half free, and that those of the
free world will never cease their efforts for human liberty
until all the world is free. It will call for the steadfast endeavors of those who can withstand discouragements and temporary defeats, and who with courage and initiative will
fashion the new tools needed to build a lasting peace.

The peace that humanity seeks must replace the international anarchy of the mid-twentieth century with order under law. It must improve upon the United Nations, reshaping that organization into an instrument whereby its high aims and objectives can be realized instead of thwarted by the enemies of peace, a forum where simple truth can prevail over vicious propaganda, a parliament whose constructive action cannot be vetoed by aggressors who thrive upon conflict and disorder.

The structure of peace that we must build, if we are not all to perish together, must be based upon these four great foundation stones: liberty and self-government for all people, equal justice under national and international law, collective security to prevent the rise of lawless aggressors, and a brotherhood of those who recognize and utilize for the common good those spiritual and moral values without which all else will fail.

If, in addition to building a protection for our own lives and for those of future generations, we desire to honor those in past years who were willing to pay their "last full measure of devotion" to the country asking this bounty of them, we will assume without delay our responsibilities in this great task.

O. K. ARMSTRONG

Springfield, Missouri

Contents

Maps

THE FIFTEEN DECISIVE BATTLES
OF THE
UNITED STATES

Dedication

These collective accounts of the battles
That have shaped the destiny
Of the United States of America
From colonial days to World War II
Are dedicated to all those in our nation
Who plan and work and pray
For a just and lasting peace
Based upon world order under law
And having as its enduring structure
Liberty—Justice—Security—Brotherhood
For all mankind

CHAPTER ONE

Oglethorpe Defends His Colony

On the morning of July 5, 1742, James Edward Oglethorpe, principal founder of the English colony of Georgia, standing on the ramparts of a fort at the southern coast of St. Simons Island, raised a long spyglass to his eye and surveyed a fearful sight. He saw upon the horizon of the languid Atlantic waters the sails of a huge flotilla of ships. Above and among these sails fluttered the gold-and-crimson banners of King Philip V of Spain. Aboard the foremost vessel was the commander of the expedition, General Don Manuel de Mantiano, governor of the Spanish colony of Florida.

Earlier that morning, as the first streaks of light were breaking over the waters, that formidable armada had been sighted by Oglethorpe's small scouting vessel, which had hurried into the harbor of St. Simons.

"The Spaniards come again!" men of its crew had shouted. "They come with hundreds of ships!"

Now as Oglethorpe scanned the Spanish flotilla, he counted —not hundreds—but thirty-six vessels; frigates, schooners, half-galleys, and sloops. Thirty-six were enough, the Georgian knew, to conquer his own small fleet, to batter down his forts and to bring disaster to his entire colony.

This engagement, Oglethorpe well understood, was to be decisive. Ever since he had brought his colonists from England and Scotland and Austria to that pleasant coastal land, his right to settlement had been challenged by the Spaniards of Florida,

1

who claimed the territory northward well into the Carolinas. Those thirty-six vessels, with their colors so defiantly unfurled to the winds, bore Spanish leaders and men determined to end once and for all the campaign they had waged for nine years against the English settlers. Victory for the proud viceroy of King Philip would mean the extension of the province of Florida far to the northward. Don Manuel was eager for battle. Upon its outcome would depend the destiny of the English colony in that area of the North American continent.

A Challenge to the Might of Spain

James Oglethorpe had come to America after a distinguished career as a member of the English Parliament. He did not come for lands or gold, but to find a place where men and their families might be free. As a member of the Committee on Prisons in the Parliament, Oglethorpe had been shocked at the deplorable conditions among those behind the bars. Many prisoners were confined for debt. Others were serving long sentences for petty misdemeanors. All were living in misery and filth.

"Men can be made better, if given a chance in freedom," Oglethorpe told his colleagues in the Parliament. They listened politely, but scorned his theories. Everyone understood that "criminals" had to be locked up and otherwise punished. But when Oglethorpe proposed taking some of the prisoners across the seas to establish a new colony of the British crown, they were willing—if only to get rid of this eccentric person, along with his wretches.

So, in 1732, Oglethorpe obtained a charter granting him authority to head a colony in America, extending southward from the Carolina grant to the Spanish possessions, including the six islands off the coast. By a curious provision of the charter, the founder and his trustees were to have full power over the colony, but were "to obtain no profit from its man-

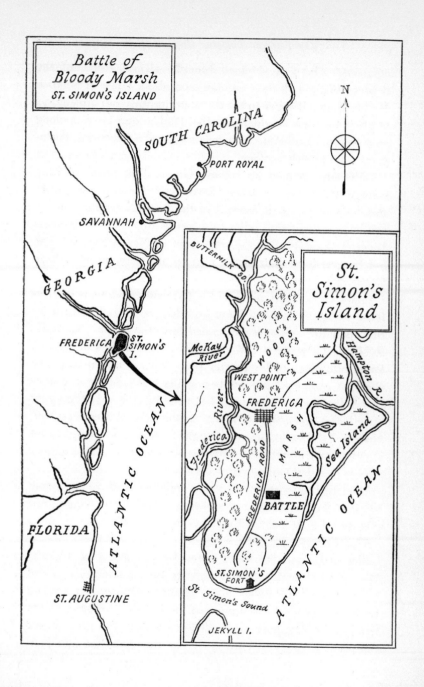

Battle of Bloody Marsh
ST. SIMON'S ISLAND

N

SOUTH CAROLINA

PORT ROYAL

SAVANNAH

GEORGIA

FREDERICA ST. SIMON'S I.

ATLANTIC OCEAN

FLORIDA

ST. AUGUSTINE

St. Simon's Island

BUTTERMILK SO.

WOODS

McKay River

WEST POINT

FREDERICA

Frederica River

Hampton R.

MARSH

Sea Island

Frederica Road

BATTLE

ST. SIMON'S FORT

St Simon's Sound

ATLANTIC OCEAN

JEKYLL I.

agement." The first shipload brought several scores of the debtors, many with their families, and also a group of Scottish Highlanders, all eager to try the opportunities and adventures of life in the New World. Soon other Highlanders arrived, along with German Lutherans from Salzburg, and a few Swiss, Portuguese, and Jewish families.

Oglethorpe named his colony "Georgia," in honor of King George II, and their town "Savannah," for the low grassy meadows of the area. Several of the Scottish families moved southward about fifty miles to a fertile area on the Altamaha River, and established the settlement of New Inverness. The Salzburgers built their homes near by and named their village Ebenezer.

James Oglethorpe was a man of sturdy convictions and intense energy. He had a long, beak-like nose, and because of this his fellow colonists nicknamed him "the Eagle." Naturally stubborn, he was not easily swayed by arguments or threats. Some provisions of his charter proved harsh and unjust. For example, each tract granted to a settler was considered a military fief, to be held for the oldest male heir; in case the estate ended, the grant was to revert to the colony. Learning that lands in the Carolina colonies could be had in fee simple, that is, with no inheritance restrictions, several of Oglethorpe's settlers deserted and moved northward.

Undisturbed by such defections, Oglethorpe drove his people to clear the wilderness, plant crops, build their villages. He placated the Indians with gifts and peace pacts.

The Georgia colonists soon discovered that theirs was a buffer area, open to harassments by the rulers of Florida. Don Manuel sent repeated protests to Oglethorpe, pointing out that his settlers were usurpers and trespassers on Spanish territory. Certain facts supported the haughty viceroy's claim. Spanish trading posts and mission houses, with chapels for the priests, had been built along the trail from the San Juan

River to the foothills of the Carolinas. Spain had never relinquished any sovereignty thus established, said the Don.

Capital of Florida, that pleasant land over which Ponce de Leon had roamed in search of a fountain of youth, was St. Augustine, oldest continuous settlement on the continent. The town was guarded by a huge fort, San Marco, and over the valor and cruelty of its walls and dungeons the flag of Spain had flown for eighty years. From this fort, Don Manuel sent his ships to seize the water commerce of the Georgia colonists and his raiders to threaten their settlements. His lieutenants carried firearms to the Indians and incited them to theft and pillage.

Oglethorpe sailed back to England in 1734, returning with one hundred and fifty militarily-trained Scottish Highlanders and their families. Some of these were relatives of the colonists, among them Lieutenant Lachlan McIntosh, later to distinguish himself as a general in the War for Independence.

Now the Eagle began building his colony's defense. He moved his home from Savannah to St. Simons, an island separated from the mainland by a coastal river that Oglethorpe named "Frederica" for Prince Frederick, eldest son of King George II. He persuaded several other families to join him, and in February 1736 they began to build Fort Frederica. In his report to the Home Office in London Oglethorpe wrote: "We immediately got up a house and thatched it with Palmettoes, dug a cellar, traced out a Fort with 4 Bastions. . . ."

When completed, Fort Frederica stood guard at a bend of the river. To defend the coast, Fort St. Simons was next constructed; then Fort William, on Jekyll Island, garrisoned by Captain William Horton and a small company of troops.

Don Manuel saw in these actions a challenge to the right and might of Spain. He stepped up his raids against the shipping of the British colonies. He sent agents into South Carolina to stir up a revolt among the Negro slaves. One day in the spring of 1737, under promises that they would be taken to Florida for a life of freedom and ease, hundreds of Negroes seized arms and ammunition in a warehouse at Stono. The insurrection was put down mercilessly by the militia under Colonel Alexander Vanderhoussen.

Oglethorpe and the Georgia trustees sent an urgent appeal to Sir Robert Walpole, Home Secretary, for help. In a letter dated June 22, 1737, they declared:

We likewise think ourselves obliged to represent to You the Situation of Carolina and Georgia, which Provinces are almost Surrounded by the French and Spaniards (who lye upon the same Continent and can march into the former through the latter by Land). The many Improvements there made, and the Harbours now discovered, Occasions these Powers to be covetous of them; and the more these Provinces improve, the stronger will be their desire of getting them, for Georgia is the key of all North America; and if they possessed these Ports, they could by cruising from thence Search all the Carolina and Virginia homeward bound Ships, and would probably confiscate many of them, since they generally bring Spanish Silver home, which is the only coin currant in America. For these reasons the Trustees humble Apprehend, that it will be Expedient for His Majesty to Order a Regiment of Seven Hundred Men to be raised, which being properly posted upon the Islands and along the Rivers; will protect both these Provinces from the Spaniards. . . . What planters will stay, much less improve under these Circumstances? A Spanish claim to all these Lands, backed by regular forces, and none to Protect them! . . .

Sir Robert's reply told the Georgia founder to do the best he could with his own resources. The best Oglethorpe could do was to replace the palmetto logs of his forts with thick, durable "tabby" made of oyster shells and mortar, wheedle some cannon and ammunition from the War Ministry in London, and build several ships for a show of defense against the Spanish raiders. He also recruited all the able-bodied men into a militia, commanded by himself as general and drilled by the Highlanders under Colonel Palmer.

By 1739 the dreaded Spanish *Guarda Costa* vessels were stopping and searching English ships at will, and coastal towns were being harassed, all the way from the San Juan (St. Johns) River in Florida to Cape Hatteras. While one ship was being boarded, its first mate, Robert Jenkins, engaged a Spanish officer in a sword duel and lost an ear. He told his story before a committee of Parliament, exhibiting his ear in a bottle. The aroused members declared war with Spain. At last the War Ministry authorized Oglethorpe to take the offensive against Don Manuel and the Spanish forces on land or sea.

The Eagle Takes a Bold Flight

As the spring of 1740 spread its flowering warmth over the Georgia fields and woodlands, Oglethorpe decided to carry the battle to the Spanish capital at St. Augustine. He would win a decisive victory and forever end the Spanish claim to the lands and islands of his colony. A spy reported that most of the vessels guarding St. Augustine had sailed for Havana for supplies. Now was the time for attack!

Colonel Vanderhoussen agreed to help, and marched to Savannah with five hundred men. General Oglethorpe requisitioned from his own small army 91 Highlanders, 310 Englishmen and Salzburgers, and a few companies of Indians. The whole force marched southward, while several sloops loaded with supplies sailed down the coast.

Below the San Juan River, the Carolina and Georgia men swooped down on two Spanish forts before the men of their small garrisons could be aroused from their siestas. Most of the Spaniards were taken prisoner, but some horsemen escaped and made this victory costly. They rode hard to St. Augustine and notified the governor of the invasion. Don

Manuel prepared to receive his enemy. He made ready all his garrison at San Marco: one hundred artillerymen, several troops of horsemen, and eight companies of musketmen. In addition, he armed about two hundred Negroes with big cutlasses and several companies of Indians with long knives. By a stroke of good fortune for the Spanish commander, six half-galleys with brass nine-pound guns, and two sloops loaded with provisions, had just come up from Havana.

The colonial allies paused several miles north of town and the English vessels dropped anchor beyond gunshot range. Through their glasses, Oglethorpe and his officers could see gray Fort San Marco, flanked by cannon ranged along the shore, like a grim-jawed she-wolf with her snarling pups by her side. It was clear that the defense was prepared, that the men of the garrison stood by their arms and that the cannon on fort and vessels were loaded and aimed. Nevertheless, for three weeks the intrepid Georgian defied the Spanish commander and his garrison to risk a battle.

Colonel Palmer and his Highlanders made up the advance force. Suddenly one night they were surprised by a column of Spaniards. Twenty Highlanders were killed and twenty-seven captured. The remainder fled for their lives, reaching the safety of Colonel Vanderhoussen's camp. The Eagle realized that his feathers had been scorched. His campaign against St. Augustine was a failure. Now racked with fever, he sadly led the expedition back to Georgia.

There could be no doubt that Don Manuel de Mantiano would move for revenge. Just when, Oglethorpe and his colonists could not guess. With a calm as leisurely as the placid breezes that rustled the palm fronds over his head, the Spanish chieftain made preparations for an invading squadron and army. He vowed to wipe out Savannah, the Scots of New Inverness, the psalm-singing Salzburgers of Ebenezer and all others of the Oglethorpe colony, then move on to conquer Port Royal and Charlestown in South Carolina.

The usual Spanish routine of eating, drinking, lovemaking, and siestas was shattered, as Don Manuel forced all hands to the tasks. There were musterings and drills. There were the sounds of repairs on the sloops. There was the *whil-r-rip!* of whips on the bare backs of English and Scottish prisoners, brought up lean and pale from the San Marco dungeons to work at the foundries and forges. Sails on frigates and lighter vessels, tacking up from Havana, swelled to formidable numbers the flotilla of the Florida viceroy. At the same time, Don Manuel ordered his captains to continue their threats and depredations by land and sea, to keep the Georgia and Carolina settlers in a state of alarm. He bribed the Indian chiefs in efforts to win them against Oglethorpe.

On May 12, 1741, Oglethorpe wrote to the War Ministry from Savannah:

I go on fortifying this Town, making magazines, and doing everything I can to defend the Province vigourously, & I hope my Endeavours will be approved of by His Majesty, since the whole aim of my life is to do the duty of a faithful subject & grateful servant. . . .

Ever since the ill-fated St. Augustine campaign, the general had suffered malarial fever. When too ill to stand, he had servants carry him about so that he could continue his arduous tasks of leadership. When a Spanish man-of-war anchored off Jekyll Island late in that summer of 1741, Oglethorpe took his schooner *Norfolk* and several sloops and made for the intruder, chasing her all the way to within sight of San Marco —which served only to enrage Don Manuel.

Although Oglethorpe must have had little hope that the home government would assist him in another offensive campaign, he wrote again to the War Ministry, outlining "two Proposals Relating to the War In Georgia and Florida"—the first setting forth his needs for another invasion of Florida and the second his needs for defense. For the latter, he declared, he should have:

Two Troops of Rangers, One Hundred Boatmen with proper Craft and two sloops that are now here: the small Garrisons that are in the Country and the Highland Company will be necessary to be continued, as also some Artillery and Ammunition to be sent. . . .

After months of delay, the reply came back. The Ministry informed Oglethorpe that he could keep the two sloops, and recruit at Crown expense the boatmen needed for them and for other craft already at his disposal. One troop of six hundred regulars, called "Rangers," would embark for Georgia soon. All else was vague and indefinite. Perhaps, Sir Robert Walpole suggested, the other colonies would help.

The general again appealed to South Carolina. Lieutenant-Governor William Bull, head of the militia, who had helped Oglethorpe lay out the town of Savannah, turned a deaf ear. He wanted no more of this impetuous neighbor's disastrous campaigns. But in due course, the ship carrying the Rangers from England came into Savannah harbor. Oglethorpe called on all available men to help strengthen the forts and to build ships, and they worked steadily at the tasks of burning shells for lime, mixing the tabby mortar, felling trees, hewing lumber, driving the wooden pegs, and mounting the cannon that the general's envoys had begged, borrowed, or bought on hurried trips to the colonies of the North.

"The Battle Must Be Fought Here!"

Don Manuel sent a force of about one thousand troops on fourteen ships to attack the Georgia colony. His purpose may have been to feel out his enemy's strength, but again he may have presumed contemptuously that only this fleet and land forces would be needed to destroy the English forts and forces. Oglethorpe dispatched Captain Horton to guard the coast while Lieutenant Dunbar remained at Fort William. The Spanish vessels made first for the fort, but Dunbar's cannoneers repulsed them. Then the invaders turned and sailed into Cumberland Sound.

On his best schooner, with two smaller ships supporting, Oglethorpe sailed bravely out to the attack. One officer proved cowardly and turned his sloop back into the sheltering waters off the mainland. Undaunted, the other two struck boldly among the Spanish ships, sending terrific cannon fire to right and left. The Spanish vessels were so entangled in position that they could hardly fire without hitting one another, and one after the other turned sail and fled. Four of the flotilla were so badly damaged that they were abandoned before they sank.

General Oglethorpe prepared for the next blow, which he knew would be all the harder. He reinforced Fort Frederica. He fitted out a large ship under Captain Thomson especially for the defense of St. Simons Fort and settlement. He requisitioned a number of private vessels and distributed the available cannon among them. He ordered all his troops to be ready to meet an attack at a moment's notice. He gave generous gifts to the Indians to guard against last minute treachery from these allies.

Now thoroughly enraged, burning for revenge and for restoration of his prestige, Don Manuel de Mantiano prepared for a massive invasion. He sent to Havana for more ships, and when they arrived he tallied with grim satisfaction a total of fifty-one sail, all well-armed and well-manned. He selected thirty-six vessels to carry his expedition and to attack the forts. His land forces numbered more than 4,000 men, armed with the best of Spanish muskets, pistols and sabres, under command of Major General Antonio di Ridondo. Don Manuel himself stood proudly on the deck of his commodore's flagship as the flotilla pointed northward from St. Augustine. It was this armada that Oglethorpe spied through his glass on that summer morning, July 5, 1742.

Approaching Jekyll Island, Don Manuel wasted no time. His commodore deployed the ships into line and the foremost made directly for the harbor. Captain Thomson's frigate, bearing twenty-two guns, including an eighteen-pounder in the stern and two nine-pound cannon in the bow, was ready for battle. The Spanish vessel loosed a salvo at close range. Captain Thomson's gunners found deadly aim, and the lighters brought their sizzling match-staffs down on the powder-holes in the breeches of the cannon with the calm bravery of veteran sea-fighters. The Spanish commodore's flagship came alongside Thomson's frigate and Spanish sailors attempted to board. Thomson's mariners and musketmen beat them off. Every vessel of the nine in Oglethorpe's tiny fleet acquitted herself with honor, but the Spanish engaged them and brushed them aside. Despite some losses from crippled sails and leaking hulks, the flotilla pushed on to the harbor. And there they triumphantly anchored. The Spanish troops landed and camped. Don Manuel was well satisfied with his progress.

General Oglethorpe called a council of war. His rugged ship captains and troop commanders assembled with him to take stock of their chances for further defense of the colony. The Eagle told them:

"We are resolved not to suffer defeat! We will rather die like Leonidas and his Spartans, if we can but protect Georgia and Carolina and the rest of the Americans from desolation!"

To all in the council, it was obvious what the Spanish commander planned to do. He would strike for St. Simons to destroy Fort Frederica and the town, then he would attack

the other forts by land and water, and move on to destroy
Savannah.

"The battle must be fought here on St. Simons," said Oglethorpe. "And because of their superior numbers, Indian tactics
must be used. Our whole force will assemble at Frederica
and use that fort as our base for attack and defense."

All agreed, and during July 6 the ships sailed into Frederica
River, bringing the Highlanders, Rangers and other troops
to the fort. Next morning they saw the Spanish columns enter
the island and camp near the settlement of St. Simons.

On the morning of July 7 a detachment of Spaniards
marched quietly out of camp toward Frederica for reconnaisance. Oglethorpe's vigilant scouts came running, and the
general sent a company of Rangers, a company of Scots and
a party of Indians to meet them. Attacking them by a sudden
sortie from the dense woods, the defenders took the Spanish
captain and some of his men prisoners.

Oglethorpe realized a general battle would follow. To meet
the main Spanish force with less than half their number would
be fatal. The only chance to save Frederica and the colony
was the plan agreed upon in the council: Indian tactics—to
fire into them and disappear, to harass them, to seize prisoners when possible, to cut down their proud gold and crimson flags one by one. The Georgia chieftain ordered his forces
to post on either side of the roadway to the fort, in the woods
and bushes that bordered the path. He remained at Fort
Frederica, where he hoped a final stand might be made if
necessary. And whatever the outcome, he knew that the valor
of the Georgia defenders would not waver.

At the Bloody Marsh

Silently, like the Indians that stalk ahead of them on moc-
casined feet, the Highlanders, the Rangers and the other
detachments move out from Frederica along the trail. Soon

they meet Captain Noble Jones of the Savannah Volunteer Company with his platoon, who have spent the night on advance guard.

"The whole Spanish camp is advancing!" Jones reports.

An Indian youth is sent on the run to tell Oglethorpe that the battle is at hand. "Hold all fire until we make an ambush," is Colonel Palmer's command. Alert as the hawks in the boughs above them, the assorted comrades-in-arms take up their march. One by one their units disappear into the woods and undergrowth. There they crouch beneath the tall pines and spreading live oaks, listening and waiting. The Highlanders move forward to an open meadowland surrounded by woods on three sides with a marsh leading to the tidewater on their left.

"Here we will make our stand," Palmer declares. "Each company will stay close together. Deploy!"

The Highlanders move into the thickets. And soon the waiting defenders, standing or lying tensely with their loaded muskets at their sides, hear in the distance the blare of trumpets and the roll of drums.

Grandly, with colorful standards flying, the Spanish column moves along the trail toward Frederica. Its officers ride at the head, on sweaty mounts, trailed by some 1,400 men. They reach the meadowland, and an order is given to halt. The flags come down. The officers dismount. The soldiers move up into the savannah, and begin to stack their arms—they are making camp. Here is an ambush made to order.

The late afternoon sun gleams on the long gray muzzles of their pieces, on the sabres of the officers, and the ornate bridles of the horses. The helmets of the soldiers clank as the men stack them in orderly piles. The commissaries are barking commands. Kettles are brought up, and meat unpacked. Sergeants are calling off details of men to forage for firewood. That means the defenders will soon be discovered. The wait-

ing grows still more tense—but the Spaniards catch not a
sound from the woods about them.

Finally Colonel Palmer nods to his aide, Lieutenant Mac-
Kay. The lieutenant places his tasseled cap upon the point of
his sword, holds it aloft and advances into the trail only a
few yards away from the nearest Spaniards. An officer's horse
tethered in the camp sees the cap waving on the sword, rears,
and whinnies.

"Fire!" shouts MacKay. "Fire upon the invaders!"

The whole battalion of Highlanders rush into the open and
fire. The withering rain of leaden balls mows down the surprised Spaniards. From the side opposite the marsh Lieutenant Sutherland closes in with his Rangers, sending in more
devastating fire. The rattle of muskets merges into a continuous roar.

Spanish officers attempt to form their men, but with no
arms their soldiers answer only one order, that of the instinct
to run. They hunt for cover in the woods and thickets, only
to die by the point-blank aim of the ambushers. Hundreds
run back along the trail toward St. Simons, but scores of these
perish at the hands of the pursuing Rangers and Indians.

Oglethorpe mounts his horse and rides toward the sounds
of battle. He comes upon a scene of carnage. The ground of
the meadowland is red with the blood of the wounded and
dead. The general warmly commends his lieutenants, and
orders:

"Take prisoners! Take more prisoners!"

Dusk draws on. The firing has ceased. Several of the defenders have sabre wounds, but none has lost his life, while
four captains, several junior officers, and about two hundred
men are counted among the slain Spaniards. Wounded prisoners are loaded into wagons and carried to Frederica for
treatment.

The Indians have completely disappeared. All night long

they straggle back to the fort, bringing in scalps. The general remonstrates: "I want prisoners!"

An Indian chieftain shrugs. "Ugh! Spanish scalps are better!" he retorts.

The Victory Is Complete

The battle by the marsh left Don Manuel de Montiano, his officers and soldiers, shaken and fearful. They were more than ever uncertain as to the strength of the Georgia defenders. Nevertheless, the Spanish commander tried desperately to stem the tide of the campaign. For two days he and the officers regrouped their companies, issuing new weapons where needed, and making plans to surround Frederica and force its surrender.

Oglethorpe countered with a clever strategy. On the night of July 9 he gathered together all his drummers and spread them through the trails and clearings of St. Simons. All night through they "beat up the Spanish camp," as he expressed it in his report, as though leading a dozen columns for an attack. And all night the Spanish soldiers anxiously stood with their arms.

Convinced now that Oglethorpe commanded a huge force, perhaps as large as his own, Don Manuel tried to take Frederica by water. He sent a large frigate and two sloops into the river to make the assault. The cannon along the banks and on the fort barked a fiery answer and the Spanish ships turned back disabled.

General Oglethorpe next undertook a night attack that he hoped would drive the enemy from the island. A French volunteer fired a shot to warn the Spaniards, and deserted to their ranks. Now the true state of the English strength would be known to the enemy. But Oglethorpe countered with a ruse. Next day he freed a Spanish prisoner, asking him to deliver a letter secretly to the French deserter. The letter told

the Frenchman to make the Spaniards believe the Georgia
forces were weak, then draw their vessels to the shore where
the "hidden batteries" could destroy them. If he succeeded,
the letter said, his "reward" would be doubled.

The ruse worked. The Spanish commanders decided to
abandon the attempt on Frederica and use Cumberland Island
as a base for future attacks. In savage anger, the Don applied
the torch to every building in St. Simons town, and loading
his troops, made for Cumberland Sound. Again the Georgia
Eagle moved too swiftly for him, landing a force to threaten
the waiting Spanish detachment. In panic, the Spaniards killed
their horses and took to their ships. Don Manuel made only
one more move before full flight. This is how Oglethorpe
described it:

The Galleys and small craft to the Number of fifteen went
through the inland Water Passages. They attempted to land near
Ft. William, but were repulsed by the Rangers; then they attacked
it with cannon and small Arms from the water for 3 Hours, but
the place was so bravely Defended by Lieutenant Alex Stuart
that they were repulsed and ran out to sea . . . they hoisted
all the sails They could and stood to the Southward. I followed
them with the Boats to Fort William, and from thence sent out
the Rangers and some Boats who followed them to Saint John's
but they went off rowing and sailing to St. Augustine.

The victory that began at the Bloody Marsh was complete.
Later threats, and later moves by Oglethorpe in retaliation,
were made, but never again were Georgia and the Carolinas
under serious threat. The San Juan (St. Johns) River, and
later the St. Marys River, were recognized as boundaries beyond which Spanish power could not pass. Instead of a buffer,
Georgia became the southern anchor of the British colonies
in America.

Today, the Georgia colony is a pleasant area of the great
state that bears its name. The six coastal islands are known

as "the Golden Isles of Georgia." To commemorate the two hundredth anniversary of the decisive battle, people of the community erected on the site a shaft of granite with a bronze plaque. All about it, in grandeur and tranquillity, stand the moss-bearded oaks and tall pines. And in the hearts of the people of the commonwealth there is honor for their founder and their forebears who on St. Simons Island made so valorous a defense.

CHAPTER TWO

Wolfe Vanquishes the French at Quebec

In February 1759, forty vessels of war set sail from England with about 8,500 English and Scottish troops, commanded by a young major general, James Wolfe. They were bound for America on a mission destined to settle whether the great Canadian provinces should remain French or become a dominion of the British Crown.

This history-making flotilla made a safe crossing and reached Cape Breton Island at the mouth of the St. Lawrence River. The ships dipped their ensigns in salute to the British flags proudly waving over the town of Louisbourg. On June 6 they weighed anchor and pointed their prows up the river, the sailors and soldiers cheering the toast:

"To the colors of England! May they fly over every French fort, garrison, and port in America!"

This expedition ended long years of struggle for supremacy on the North American continent. A few months later on the Plains of Abraham, a plateau outside Quebec, the question was finally decided. There, near that regal city on the St. Lawrence River, two brave leaders, Wolfe and General the Marquis de Montcalm, led their forces in a historic battle. The outcome of that meeting vitally affected the future of the entire New World. And in the decisive engagement, both the gallant generals lost their lives.

Long before Wolfe's expedition touched North American waters and Canadian soil, rivalry between England and France

19

over possessions and trade had flared into wars. Beginning in Europe, these conflicts inevitably spread to America. France had a just claim to a share of the New World, for her adventurous explorers were visiting the fertile northlands while the dons of Spain were carrying the banners of that empire over the regions to the south. Jacques Cartier, from St.-Malo on the coast of Brittany, made four voyages to America between 1534 and 1544. He explored the Gulf of the St. Lawrence and the coastal regions round about, raising a huge cross with the *fleur-de-lis* and the inscription: *"Vive le Roi de France."* Samuel de Champlain extended the explorations about the Great Lakes. In 1608 he fixed on a site for Quebec and brought the first settlers to his new town. Three years later he set up the trading post of Mont Royal.

In the footsteps of such men followed the trappers and traders. Montreal and other towns were built. While English settlements were being made on the Atlantic shores from Massachusetts to the Carolinas in the seventeenth century, intrepid Frenchmen charted the waters of bays, lakes, and rivers, and mapped the lands of primeval forests, mountains, and fertile valleys in the Canadian and western regions for the sovereigns of France. Illustrious are the names of Louis Joliet, and his pious companion, Pere Marquette, who explored the Mississippi, Father of Waters; Cavalier de la Salle, who pushed on to the Gulf of Mexico, taking possession of a mighty region which he named Louisiana for King Louis XIV. Forts and settlements followed. For seven decades after 1690, the campaigns for possession and supremacy went on.

A Continent at Stake

In 1702 England went to war against France and Spain to check the continued greed of the aging Louis. In the colonies the struggle was called Queen Anne's War. Expeditions fitted out in New England against the easternmost province of

New France, Acadia, resulted in the seizure of that area, which the British renamed Nova Scotia or "New Scotland." When peace was signed in 1713, Acadia, Newfoundland and the country of the Hudson Bay were ceded to England.

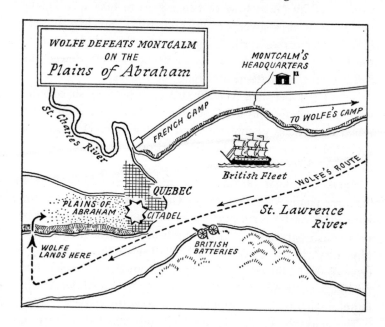

Here was a challenge to France's power in America, and that nation's leaders began vigorous moves to strengthen her New World possessions. Far down near the mouth of the Mississippi, Nouvelle Orléans was founded and made the capital of the vast Louisiana wilderness. The colony at Mobile was fortified. At the northern borders of New York colony, Forts Niagara and Crown Point were built. Numerous forts and settlements were established in the western country, as at St. Louis near the union of the Mississippi and the Missouri, Vincennes on the Wabash, and outposts on the Ohio. Control of all the waterways of the great Mississippi Valley was secured by the French during the first half of the eighteenth century.

On Cape Breton Island, commanding the mouth of the St. Lawrence, an elaborate stronghold, Fort Louisbourg, was built, surrounded by a lusty town that soon grew to 4,000 inhabitants. Quebec was thus given an outer guardian. So, like a great crescent, from the North Atlantic to the Great Lakes and to the Gulf of Mexico, the power of France overshadowed the thriving English settlements along the seaboard.

Boundaries between New France and the English colonies were not yet established, and across these uncertain areas rolled the wheels of ambition and exploitation. Dominion of the whole continent, outside the territories of Spain, became the prize at stake.

Upon the stage of this international struggle stalked a vigorous young Virginian, Major George Washington. On the basis of a charter for a huge grant of land from King George II, English patentees in 1752 established a settlement on the Monongahela River. The French challenged this move. Governor Robert Dinwiddie of Virginia claimed the French had no rights on the Monongahela, and dispatched Major Washington with a regiment of militia to protect the settlers.

The soldierly Virginian surprised and defeated a body of French troops near Fort Duquesne, then fell back to a colonial outpost, Fort Necessity. Here, Washington's companies were attacked by an overwhelming number of French and Indians and captured, then released to return home with the honors of war.

The British War Ministry now sent Major General Edward Braddock to command the forces in Virginia. With him were two regiments of regulars, well-trained in the European school of arms but totally ignorant of the tactics of pioneer and Indian warfare. Washington advised the English commander to allow his men to learn the ways of the Redskins, but Braddock, a proud and stubborn man, scornfully replied that his troops would "fight like English gentlemen."

Westward through Virginia and into Pennsylvania the Braddock expedition marched. His regulars in gleaming red-and-white uniforms, Washington, now a colonel, with his colonials in buckskins and caps. Near Fort Duquesne an ambush awaited. Surrounding the English as they reached open ground, the French and Indians attacked. The colonials fell back at once into the woods. Braddock's battalions stood and were mowed down. Washington rallied his troops and led them bravely, ordering a retreat that saved the survivors from annihilation. Braddock received a mortal wound, and was buried near the tragic field. Virginians—soldiers, planters, merchants—now knew that Colonel Washington was destined to fill a place of leadership among them.

The border struggles ebbed and flowed without formal declarations of war between England and France until May 1756, when war again became a grim reality in Europe. England joined Frederick the Great of Prussia against France, Austria, Russia, Sweden and Saxony. The Court of France decided this was the time to make a decisive challenge to the power of the English colonies in America.

Louis Joseph, Marquis de Montcalm, was selected to lead the campaign. A native of Nîmes, he entered the French army at the age of fifteen and grew up to be a dependable, accomplished officer. Montcalm embarked from Brest with about 1,500 troops. Some 1,600 had preceded him, so that with colonial militia, he mustered a force of 6,000 men. The Comte de Vaudreuil was governor at Quebec. The new commander found this official a vain and pompous man, surrounded by a swarm of corrupt aides and underlings.

Boldly and in soldierly fashion, Montcalm planned an offensive campaign. He fortified Niagara, and strengthened Fort Frontenac on Lake Ontario and Fort Ticonderoga on

Lake Champlain. In August 1756, he surprised and captured Fort Oswego.

John Campbell, Earl of Loudon, sent by the British government to command in the colonies, proved wholly incompetent. He attempted an expedition against Louisbourg, and while he was on the march toward Halifax, Montcalm sallied out of Fort Ticonderoga and captured Fort William Henry. During the next summer General James Abercrombie, Lord Loudon's chief of staff—with considerable more gallantry than Loudon ever displayed—threw 15,000 men, including several regiments of Scottish Highlanders in their picturesque dress, against Montcalm at Fort Ticonderoga. The defense of trees, logs, muskets, and cannon, however, forced the British to retire with a thousand wounded, leaving behind eight hundred slain.

Pitt Appoints a Major General

Thus, humiliation and defeat had dogged most of the British efforts against the French during the Marquis de Montcalm's leadership. Now the tide was ready to turn. The human factor most responsible for the shift of fortunes that settled the destiny of the North American continent was Prime Minister William Pitt the Elder, a statesman of character, vision and tenacity. Pitt began sweeping out corruption and graft from the government. He supplied Frederick the Great with gold to fight the war in Europe, while the British navy and armies expanded the possessions and rule of England beyond the seas.

Pitt dispatched a young, intelligent general, Jeffrey Amherst, and an even younger, equally intelligent and more daring brigadier, James Wolfe, to assist in contesting French claims at any point in the New World. Late in the spring of 1758, Admiral Edward Boscawen arrived at Halifax with a strong fleet. There he met General Amherst, and plans were made for the first major stroke toward evening up the score of Montcalm's victories—the capture of Louisbourg. Amherst commanded 12,000 men, and Admiral Boscawen's fighting ships mounted 1,650 very effective guns. They made a landing, and laid siege to the fort. The French surrendered, and Cape Breton with its large quantities of supplies fell into English hands.

Throughout this campaign, the brilliant leadership of James Wolfe was apparent. He was Amherst's eyes and ears, quick to see the advantages or defects of each move contemplated, a born commander in his true appraisal of every factor needed to win a victory.

Wolfe was a native of Kent. He grew up in frail health. At the age of fifteen he entered the army, at sixteen he was fighting in Flanders, and at twenty-two was lieutenant colonel of a regiment taking part in the campaigns against Scotland. Then to Ireland, as quartermaster with the troops. Although a stern officer with an inflammable temper, he was decisive and brave. Before leaving for America, Wolfe wrote his mother:

"All I hope is that I may be ready at all times to meet that fate which no one can avoid, and to die with grace and honour when my hour has come, whether it be soon or late."

Wolfe returned to London tingling with a plan. For several hours of many days he was closeted with Pitt, the king's first minister. Enough of this warfare against forts and frontier outposts, Wolfe said. He proposed to capture Quebec, capital city of Canada, and thus with one stroke force the whole northern dominion of New France to capitulate!

Here was a man after Pitt's heart, for Wolfe advocated bold and aggressive action, a policy every successful military leader of all ages has followed. Pitt made the thirty-two-year-old brigadier a major general. Shrewdly the British statesman realized that it would not do to replace the capable Amherst.

Wolfe must serve under the commander-in-chief, but Wolfe would have his own campaign. He could have his try at capturing Quebec.

Amherst was directed to make one more attempt to take Ticonderoga and Crown Point. Another subordinate, General John Prideaux, was ordered to march against Montreal. Win or lose, the French challenge would be accepted in America.

By the time Wolfe's formidable expedition arrived in the St. Lawrence, General Amherst had successfully moved against his objectives in the upper New York colony. The Marquis de Montcalm had definitely lost the offensive, but anticipating the move against Quebec, he had for months worked tirelessly to make the defense of the city—and of Canada—secure.

Corruption and mismanagement tarnished the government of Vaudreuil and made Montcalm's task most difficult. Civil officers looted the treasury of money needed for internal improvements as well as for the common defense. This, the general knew, was bad for a land beset with foreign enemies.

"*Quel pays!* What a country!" Montcalm wrote to a friend. "Here thieves grow rich and honest men are ruined." However, Montcalm held the respect and loyalty of the armed forces. They knew that the threat of the English was serious.

The greatest advantage to the French lay in the almost impregnable situation of their Queen City. Quebec sat grandly on a great rock-like formation on the north bank of the St. Lawrence. To the west lay a plateau, the Plains of Abraham. From the rim of the heights upon which the "upper town" perched, more than three hundred feet above the St. Lawrence, French guns frowned ominously in all directions through apertures in walls and stockades. Montcalm had fortified the northern banks of the river for miles above Quebec, while below the city his posts extended beyond the St. Charles. About 14,000 troops were available for the defense of Quebec, but only 3,500 regulars were under the personal command of Montcalm. The rest were militia, directed by the incompetent and blundering Governor Vaudreuil.

One of the most able and experienced navigators of the English Navy, Captain James Cook, guided Wolfe's squadron of men-of-war and transports over the numerous shoals and rapids to the Isle of Orleans, four miles below Quebec. Here the force landed on June 26, 1759. Wolfe quickly seized Point Levis, opposite Quebec. Posting his cannon, he started a fiery bombardment across the river. Some damage was done to the fortifications, stores, and homes, but clearly such cannon fire could never batter down the defenses of the citadel sufficiently to permit a landing and assault.

The Task Is Difficult

July went by while Wolfe and his brigadiers, with Admiral Saunders and his naval captains, considered this plan and that. One plan was actually tried, but failed dismally. On the last day of the month Wolfe made a bold attempt to land a force upon the north bank of the river not far from Montmorency. Here a height of land was well fortified with French redoubts reinforced by infantry. If the lowest artillery entrenchment could be taken, Wolfe reasoned, the French might sally down in force to regain it, and thus bring on a battle. Two regiments were assigned the attack, led by a picked battalion of grenadiers. Several brigades of the main force were posted at Montmorency, out of view, ready for action.

The cannon on the banks of this stream were made ready, the ships closed in to cover with their guns, and the transports made shore with the attacking force. The impetuous English grenadiers rushed up the slope toward the outer French redoubt. Volleys of fire from cannon and muskets met them and stopped their unsupported advance. The heavens opened and a rainstorm fell as though to match the fury of the French defense. The slope became too slippery to climb, while flint and steel could no longer fire the powder wet by the deluge.

Wolfe called back his force. The failure was a bitter dose for the commander and for the officers and men of his expedition, while the troops of Montcalm and Vaudreuil were jubilant. The French presumed the whole campaign to take Quebec would now be abandoned. The disappointment snapped Wolfe's fragile health and for some days he was critically ill. His indomitable spirit pulled him through, and while yet too weak to sit up, he began forming his plans for a new attack.

Before this unsuccessful attempt, one of the larger British ships, the *Sutherland,* ran past the batteries of the city and anchored out on the St. Lawrence. Now several other vessels made the run, and under a withering fire that partially disabled some of them, gained a position above the city. Montcalm dispatched De Bourgainville and 1,500 men to guard the northern bank. But the land force could not prevent the British vessels from cutting off supplies from Montreal and other points up the river. Food became much more difficult to obtain and rationing began.

Now the British ships sailed back and forth in an effort to bring the French out of their citadel and garrison. Wolfe hoped for an open battle, but Montcalm could not be enticed into any movements to break the siege or any tactics other than defensive. The superiority of the English fleet, he knew, would make a battle at any point near the river precarious indeed, while inside the strongholds of the city he felt entirely secure.

As the summer of that year of 1759 wore away, some of Wolfe's officers were beginning to despair. Nothing could be gained by continuing a fruitless and hopeless siege, they asserted. But the young general assured them they would have action soon, and discussed with them a new plan of attack.

He had discovered that a small cove dented the river bank just above the city. A steep pathway led directly up to the plateau, the Plains of Abraham. If an attacking party could gain and hold the Plains, Quebec could be taken.

Wolfe's staff and commanders were far from agreement that the plan was practical. How could a force reach even the cove without being discovered by the sentries who guarded every yard of the northern bank? If surprise could not be utilized, how could a force scale the heights in sufficient numbers for battle?

Wolfe answered that the attempt would be made at night. There would be a diversion by the British fleet, with a heavy bombardment from the ships, to hold the French attention and draw their forces while the landing was being made.

"The plan is difficult—yes," said the general. "And for that reason, the enemy will not expect it to be tried. So all the greater our chance for success!"

On September 3, Wolfe evacuated the force left near Montmorency. Cheers went up among the French redoubts, echoing along the river and into the city. The British were retiring at last! But Wolfe was only concentrating his men on the southern bank. At Point Levis, the main force paused. Then about 4,000 continued the march westward. To a point ten miles above the city they tramped, carrying supplies and boats. Then they rowed to the waiting British gunboats and embarked. The anxious French defenders wondered.

Every day for a week the ships drifted or sailed down opposite the Plains of Abraham and back again, while Montcalm's guarding battalions wearied themselves with marches along the banks of the St. Lawrence.

"The Paths of Glory——"

It is the evening of September 12, just before dusk of the crisp autumn day. Admiral Saunders draws up the fleet that has remained below Quebec to a point near the mouth of the St. Charles. Boats are lowered, filled with British troops as though for a landing. Suddenly the British guns boom out. All over Quebec the alarm is sounded:

"An attack! The British come!"

As Wolfe has anticipated, Montcalm hurries the major part of his force north and east toward the sounds of bombardment. The British ships are firing at the fortifications on the shore. French cannon are answering. There is little the defenders can do except await the expected attack at dawn. Montcalm's men remain at their arms through the night.

But this is a well-executed British feint. Up the river, in the black darkness of the moonless midnight, a lantern shines from the mainmast of the *Sutherland*. At the signal, the British force on the ships at anchor there begin scrambling noiselessly into flat-bottomed rowboats. By 2 o'clock in the morning, 1,750 are loaded. The tide is now ebbing, the current moving swiftly toward the city. Two lanterns are hoisted over the *Sutherland*, and at the signal the oars are dipped silently. There is little need to row, except to steer, as the current bears the force toward the cove at the foot of the Plains of Abraham.

In one of the leading boats sits General Wolfe. At his side is an aide, Lieutenant John Robinson, who will write for history a graphic account of the fateful two hours' voyage toward the scene of the decisive battle. Wolfe, in a low and dramatic tone, tells the officers about him that he has a strong premonition their desperate gamble will succeed. Then he quotes parts of Gray's "Elegy in a Country Churchyard," ending with the significant words, "The paths of glory lead but to the grave."

There is silence for a moment. Then Wolfe says, "Gentlemen, I would rather have written those lines than take Quebec!"

The boats are moving silently toward the north bank. Will they be detected? Suddenly the stillness is broken by a sharp challenge.

"*Qui vive?*"

The French sentry's equivalent of the challenge "Who goes there?" sends chills down the spines of the British soldiers huddled in their flatboats. Discovery will bring the shots of French cannon and muskets blazing out over the water, despite the diversion being created beyond the city by the British gunboats.

As though fate had carefully placed him there to meet this emergency, a Scottish Highlander of General Fraser's command, who speaks French fluently, is in the boat nearest the sentry.

"La France!" replies the Highlander instantly.

"*A quel régiment?*" ("Of what regiment?") the challenge rings out again.

"*De la Reine!*" ("The Queen's!") is the Scot's answer. The sentry's duty now is to ask for the password. For reasons that will never be known, he fails to demand it. No one in the British force knows that password!

Quietly the boats tie up near the cove. Twenty-four men, volunteers all and led by Colonel (later General) William Howe, forming the "advance of honor," first climb the narrow path. They gain the top, surprise and overpower the guard, and behind them come struggling up, two abreast, the whole attacking force. The dawn of September 13 finds the British drawn up in battle line upon the Plains of Abraham.

Again the alarm is spread, and Montcalm hurries from his all-night vigil at the St. Charles back through the city and to the plateau. He realizes the seriousness of the situation, yet calmly directs the moves that begin the engagement. Governor Vaudreuil, even in this crisis, insists upon being consulted as to plans for the battle, much to the delay of the troops and the exasperation of the capable General Montcalm. The morning wears slowly on.

Wolfe has formed his force in single rank, to gain the maximum of his soldiers' fire. Again and again he passes the word, "You must stand firm, however the attack may come. Do not fire until ordered!"

With muskets primed and at the alert stand the Redcoats and Highlanders, their officers with drawn swords ready to relay the commands. One regiment, Colonel Daniel Webb's, is held in reserve near the edge of the plateau. Colonel Ralph Burton has been waiting with a brigade directly opposite the cove, under orders to begin crossing if the morning light shows the heights have been scaled. Now his transports span the river in a line.

Silently, grimly, the British in the battleline watch the hurried assembling of Montcalm's troops. French militia and Indians are sent in an attempt to outflank the British at the left and thus cut off the pathway to the cove. Their fire is damaging, but the British stand firm. Anticipating this move, Wolfe has reinforced the left flank at an angle which rakes the attackers with effective fire. Again and again the attacks are repulsed.

Montcalm sends word for De Bourgainville to hurry to the Plains with his force. Fear that the troops under the shelter of Admiral Saunders' smoking guns will yet attempt an assault from the St. Charles side keeps Montcalm from drawing in all his regulars for the battle on the Plains.

It is almost 10 o'clock when Montcalm's main force is ready. He orders a frontal attack, with firing as the ranks advance. Stolidly the British line receives the ragged fire. When a soldier falls, those on either side move closer. A bullet pierces Wolfe's wrist. He seizes a handkerchief, binds the wound tightly, and repeats his order to hold the fire. When the advance line of the French are a bare thirty-eight yards distant, he orders: "Fire!"

The volley of sound rolls over the Plains of Abraham. The

first line of the French goes down almost to a man. Powder cartridges are placed, balls rammed home again, the locks cocked, and the fire is repeated. The French survivors stagger back.

Again the French line forms and advances. Now Wolfe orders a charge. With shouts his colonels and majors relay the command. The general flashes his sword, personally leading the battalion of Louisbourg Grenadiers. A conspicuous target! Again he feels the sting of a wound, this time in his groin. Another ball lodges in his chest—almost unnoticed by his advancing soldiers, he falls to earth.

In vain Montcalm and his officers seek to rally their troops. Retreat becomes general, and at many points it turns to panic and flight.

As Wolfe is raised to a sitting position, one of his soldiers cries, "They run! See how they run!"

"Who run?" the fallen commander asks.

"The French, sir. They give ground everywhere!"

Still the general to the last, Wolfe orders an important move:

"Go one of you, tell Colonel Burton to march Webb's regiment down to St. Charles River to cut off the enemy retreat over the bridge."

Then, as he sinks again, "Now God be praised, I will die in peace!"

Pursuing the fleeing columns over the Plains, the British take many prisoners before the gate of lower town is reached. Here the British halt to avoid a possible rally by the garrison and troops still remaining. And here a ball passes through Montcalm's body as he is swept along by his retreating guard. He is carried into the garrison. A surgeon is summoned.

Informed that his wound is mortal, Montcalm declares: "So much the better. I shall not live to see the surrender of Quebec!"

Canada Becomes British—and French

Thus the decisive battle ended. The British entrenched themselves upon the plateau that had given them victory and had cost them their leader. De Bourgainville's force joined the flight of the defenders, most of whom flanked the British lines and retreated to the town of Jacques Cartier, thirty miles up the river. Vaudreuil himself fled to Montreal, issuing a manifesto which threw the blame for the defeat upon Montcalm. The garrison in Quebec capitulated four days later, and into the city marched the Redcoats and Highlanders, unfurling the flag of England upon the citadel.

In the chapel where Montcalm's remains had been placed, the British chaplain read a service for the brave departed soldier, James Wolfe, who had joined his gallant foe in death.

The French still held Montreal. In April of the following year an able general, De Levis, attempted to retake Quebec. The British fleet came to the rescue of the land forces, and the French retired again to Montreal. General Amherst invaded this city in September, 1760, and Governor Vaudreuil surrendered.

Thus the decisive defeat at Quebec led to the loss by France of her northern American possessions. By the Treaty of Paris in 1763, Canada was formally ceded to Great Britain. The great crescent of New France, from Nouvelle Orléans to the Acadian lands, was broken.

The British colonies from New England southward were freed from the threat of French domination. In the decade that followed they grew lustily in population, in commerce, in agriculture, and most important of all, they developed a love of independence. The seeds of future self-government took firmer root.

Through two centuries the Dominion of Canada has remained British, developing from colony to commonwealth. But always the area of which Quebec was and is the proud Queen City has remained French, in speech, in manners, in grand tradition. The residents of the old French provinces hold tenaciously to their language, and both English and French are officially recognized in the Parliament and agencies of the Dominion government.

Now Canada moves forward, keeping pace with the great strides of twentieth-century progress in the development of natural and human resources, grateful that when French rule ended, a hardy race of Frenchmen remained to share the building of their country.

CHAPTER THREE

Canada Remains British

Early in 1775, in a church in Richmond, Virginia, used as the meeting place of a convention of Virginia patriots, the voice of an earnest, eloquent man was heard, urging his fellow citizens to strengthen the Virginia militia and stand firm against the oppressive acts of England, the mother country. As the members of the convention sat listening intently, Patrick Henry's speech reached a resounding climax:

"Is life so dear, or peace so sweet, as to be purchased at the price of chains and slavery? Forbid it, Almighty God! I care not what course others may take; but as for me, give me liberty, or give me death!"

History records few instances to match the gross stupidity of the ministers and advisers of King George III in their treatment of the American colonies. For two decades they had allowed British shippers to make exorbitant profits at the expense of the colonial people. They raised revenue by taxes that were unjust and irritating. They refused to grant the people of the New World a proper voice in their government. For a decade the coals of resentment had glowed, occasionally bursting into flames of active resistance. British frigates sent to collect assessments authorized by the Navigation Acts were fired upon. Men disguised as Indians threw a cargo of tea from England into the murky water of Boston harbor, showing the anger of merchants and consumers against the levies on imports.

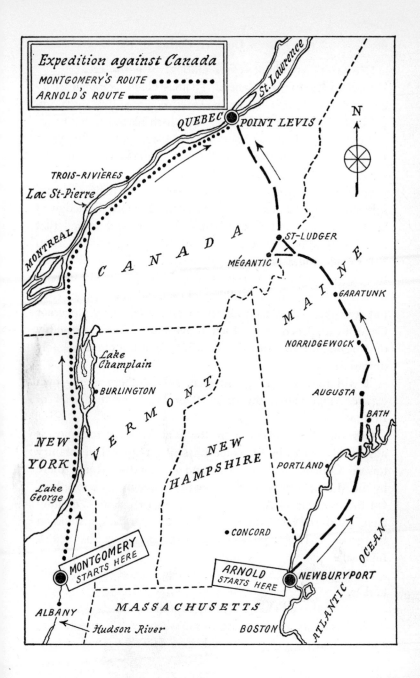

Expedition against Canada

MONTGOMERY'S ROUTE ●●●●●●●●●
ARNOLD'S ROUTE ▬ ▬ ▬ ▬

St. Lawrence

QUEBEC · POINT LEVIS

N

TROIS-RIVIÈRES

Lac St-Pierre

MONTREAL

C A N A D A

ST-LUDGER

MÉGANTIC

M A I N E

GARATUNK

NORRIDGEWOCK

Lake
Champlain

· BURLINGTON

V E R M O N T

AUGUSTA

BATH

NEW
YORK

NEW
HAMPSHIRE

PORTLAND

Lake
George

MONTGOMERY
STARTS HERE

ARNOLD
STARTS HERE

· CONCORD

NEWBURYPORT

A T L A N T I C   O C E A N

ALBANY

M A S S A C H U S E T T S

Hudson River

BOSTON

"No taxation without representation!" was the cry.

In 1774 Lieutenant General Thomas Gage, commander-in-chief of the British forces in America since 1763, was appointed governor of Massachusetts, which placed in his hands the enforcement of the import taxes. Gage put his troops in Boston on a war footing and the city virtually under martial law.

Such leaders of the colonies as Benjamin Franklin of Pennsylvania, John Adams of Massachusetts, Edward Rutledge of South Carolina, and Samuel Chase of Maryland sensed that a decision about whether to fight for independence from British rule could not longer be postponed. George Washington, now recognized as a leading citizen of Virginia in both military and civilian life, still hoped that war could be averted, but was alarmed at the military measures taken by Governor Gage. In a speech at the First Provisional General Assembly of Virginia in the summer of 1774, Washington resolutely declared:

"I will raise one thousand men, subsist them at my own expense, and march myself at their head for the relief of Boston!"

Governor Gage, ordered by the War Ministry to suppress any hostile moves by the colonists, sent a regiment of infantry toward Concord to seize arms and ammunition stored there by the Massachusetts militia. Now resistance became rebellion. On the morning of April 19, a company of colonial "minutemen," mustered hurriedly under Captain John Parker, stood on the green at Lexington and defied the march of the British Redcoats.

"If they mean to have war, let it begin here!" said Captain Parker.

"Fire on the rebels!" a British captain ordered.

That fire was answered by the muskets of the minutemen, and the War for Independence began. The shots fired at Lexington and Concord reverberated until they were "heard 'round the world." The War for American Independence lasted nearly eight years—years filled with hardship and sacrifice for those determined to carry on to final victory. There were many campaigns and battles, some of them triumphs, many of them defeats, for the American patriots. Three of the battles stand out as truly decisive. The first was a defeat for the colonial troops. Two were hard-won victories.

In June 1775, the Second Continental Congress met in Independence Hall at Philadelphia and voted funds for the army. A member then rose and said:

"Mr. Chairman, the Committee on Military Affairs has selected for nomination as Commander-in-Chief, the honorable gentleman from Virginia, George Washington."

Washington strode from the hall, to be called back in a moment by shouts from the members that the vote had been unanimous. That afternoon he mounted his horse and with his aides rode northward toward Boston. On the way, he received word of the battle on Breed's Hill, close by Bunker Hill near Boston, where outnumbered American militia had withstood British assaults until overwhelmed. By a great elm tree in Cambridge, General Washington took command of the Continental troops.

Day by day, the army was augmented by units of militia and a stream of volunteers. Captain Daniel Morgan came up from Virginia with several companies of riflemen. Brigadier General Philip Schuyler of New York arrived and pledged his state's regiments. Thousands of young men enlisted: Tom Brown, a farmer; Tim Jones, the blacksmith's helper; McIntosh, the schoolmaster; Getty, the clerk; Murphy the shipbuilder's apprentice. Leaving their work and trades, they came to the drill grounds with their muskets and powder horns.

Into General Washington's Cambridge headquarters stalked

a handsome, black-haired officer from Connecticut, who saluted and gave his name, "Colonel Benedict Arnold, sir!" He
was reporting for duty with his regiment. Washington welcomed the colonel. He knew that Benedict Arnold came from
an honored family, and that a grandfather had been colonial
governor of Rhode Island. The general saw before him an
intensely patriotic young man, eager for action.

Arnold came with more than his regiment. He brought
a plan which he placed before the commander of the Continental Army—a bold plan: he proposed an expedition into
Canada, to snatch that colony from British hands. He told
Washington that Montreal and Quebec could be taken by one
swift invasion. He urged also that he be appointed to command the expedition. Washington realized the tremendous
possibilities of the idea. If Canada could be won over to
the cause of the American colonies, its resources would be
thrown into the balance against England.

After many conferences with his officers and with members
of the Continental Congress, who visited his headquarters
during the summer, Washington approved the expedition to
capture Canada. But he decided that General Schuyler, an
officer more experienced than Colonel Arnold, should command the invasion force.

Informed by General Washington of the decision, Arnold
expressed his keen disappointment. Then he proposed that
the expedition be divided, Schuyler to command one force,
himself the other. He pointed out that there were two
routes for an invasion of Canada: one led toward Montreal,
by way of the Hudson River and Lake Champlain; the other
directly toward Quebec. General Schuyler assured the commander-in-chief that he was familiar with the route to
Montreal. But could a direct route to Quebec be found?
French settlers and British surveyors had made explorations
through the Maine wilderness, but no army had tried it.

Arnold found the answer to that question. He had secured
the maps of Captain John Montresor, an engineer who was
aide to General Edward Braddock in the French and Indian
War, served with General James Wolfe at the capture of
Quebec, and in 1761 had made a journey by the Kennebec,
and Dead and Chaudière rivers, to the St. Lawrence and
Quebec. The eager colonel insisted that where Montresor
had gone, he could go!

Washington agreed, and on August 20 wrote Schuyler that
an eastern branch of the expedition would proceed by way
of the Kennebec:

And so to Quebec by a Route ninety miles below Montreal. . . .
It would make a diversion that would distract Carleton (governor
of Montreal) and facilitate your Views. He must either break up
and follow the Party to Quebec, where he will leave you a free
passage, or he must suffer that important Place to fall into our
Hands, an Event which would have a decisive effect.

Several officers who knew the northern country advised that
no army could get through this wilderness. Even the boats
for the men and supplies would have to be carried great
distances between rivers and lakes. Paths would have to be
cut where portages did not exist, the way cleared before men
could walk even single file. But no words of caution dampened
Benedict Arnold's enthusiasm for the adventure. He promised
to get through and conquer Quebec while Schuyler was taking Montreal, and together they would annex Canada to
the American states.

Brave Men for the Expeditions

General Schuyler chose Richard Montgomery, a young Irish-
born brigadier general who lived near Albany, to be his
second in command. Montgomery was every inch a soldier
and an able officer. Like Schuyler, he had played a conspicuous part in the campaign along the Hudson and the

lakes of northern New York in the French and Indian War. Since Arnold's march was presumed to take longer, Schuyler agreed to let him have a head start while he and Montgomery made ready a picked division of something more than a thousand men for their force.

General Washington took personal interest in preparations for the expeditions. One order, signed by his adjutant, Horatio Gates, instructed Reuben Colburn, boat-maker on the Kennebec, to build "200 Batteaux of four oars each at 40 shillings lawful money" for use of Arnold's men. Washington prepared long instructions for both commanders, cautioning them that they should go as friends of the Canadian people and enemies only of the British War Ministry. He had a manifesto printed, to be distributed to the people:

> TO THE INHABITANTS OF CANADA: FRIENDS AND BRETHREN
> The unnatural Contest between the English Colonies and Great Britain has now risen to such a Height, that Arms alone must decide it.
> The Colonies, confiding in the Justice of their Cause and the purity of their intentions, have reluctantly appealed to that Being, in whose hands are all Human Events. . . . Encouraged by the advice of many Friends of Liberty among you, the Great American Congress have sent an Army into your Province, under the command of General Schuyler; not to plunder but to protect you. . . . I have detached Col. Arnold into your Country, with a part of the Army under my Command. I have enjoined upon him, and I am certain that he will consider himself, and act as in Company of his Patrons and best Friends. . . . The cause of America and of Liberty is the Cause of every virtuous American Citizen, whatever may be his religion or his descent. . . . Come ye Generous Citizens, range yourselves under the Standard of General Liberty.
> GEORGE WASHINGTON

Benedict Arnold's ambition and enthusiasm led Washington into two serious mistakes. The first was approving the route to Quebec. The second was dispatching a force entirely too small. Only about 1,100 officers and men were assigned to

Arnold, even though they were the best soldiers the colonies could afford. They included companies of musketmen from New England, in four battalions commanded by Lieutenant Colonels Christopher Greene and Roger Enos, and Majors Timothy Bigelow and Return J. Meigs; three companies of Virginia riflemen under Captain Daniel Morgan, and two companies of riflemen from Pennsylvania under Captain John Topham. Among the junior officers was a quick-witted young lieutenant from New Jersey, Aaron Burr.

Most picturesque of these hardy men were the Virginians. They wore fringed buckskin jackets and pantaloons, with powder horns and cartridge cases slung on one side and their canteens on the other, rifles on their shoulder, coonskin caps on their heads and fire in their hearts. They loudly called themselves the best marksmen in the country, if not in the world. This was hotly disputed by the Pennsylvanians, every man of whom was as expert as the firing arms of that day would permit. Men from either division had learned from boyhood to shatter such small objects as corncobs at fifty paces, and felt disgraced if they shot a wild turkey any-where but in the head. Some of the New Englanders were equally expert marksmen, and all were good woodsmen.

Newburyport on the coast of Massachusetts was the rendez-vous for taking ship for the Kennebec, and to this point the units marched, to be feted by a huge barbecue on the night of September 18. The troops feasted in a jolly mood. This would be their last meal before the steady diet of campaign fare. Ahead of them lay weeks of boating and marching, or hacking their way through forest wastes. Two of the soldiers brought their wives along, and these women shared the hardships of the entire campaign.

The force boarded the eleven small trading boats loaned by a shipper, Nathaniel Tracy, and sailed away with many a shout and wave of farewell. A fog descended and crosswinds rose, ominous forecast of the evil that dogged their whole expedition. The rich food eaten at the barbecue was nearly all given over to the waves by the seasick soldiers.

Up the Kennebec they headed, then on to Fort Western by the village of Augusta. Here the bateaus were loaded with provisions. Colonel Arnold made an inspection and designated Chaudière Pond as the next rendezvous. From there, he declared, they would push quickly on to the St. Lawrence. "Forward, men! Quebec is ours!" he ordered.

Hardy and brave as these men were, used as they were to the great outdoors, it is doubtful that one among them imagined what lay ahead. Several diaries kept by soldiers of that memorable expedition preserved the amazing record of their hardships. Arnold himself graphically painted the picture of the epic march in his fragmentary journal and his reports to General Washington.

The colonel divided his small corps into four divisions and sent them forward in order: Morgan and Topham first, Greene and Bigelow second, Meigs third and Enos last. Then he set out in a canoe to reach the head of his army. The day was September 29. The air was cool with the crispness of autumn.

The bateaus, it was soon discovered, were no bargain at the "40 shillings lawful money." They were of green lumber and they leaked. The men caulked them as best they could. Steadily those at the oars rowed, while others waded and pushed, and the men marching along the banks cut paths through the thickets. At night the campfires gleamed, the provisions were opened, the corncakes roasted, food eaten, and sleep sought under skies now turned murky and bleak. October 4 brought the head of the column to Norridgewock Falls. With great difficulty a portage of ten miles was made to the Dead River.

Then, like a battalion of watery demons lashing at intruders, the sky and the Dead River came alive. Rain fell in torrents. Wind of almost hurricane force beat on the men. The river rose and kept rising. The air became wintry cold. Boats were tossed and swung about in the swift currents: several overturned, and meat, flour, bedding, and ammunition disappeared to be swept away by the foaming, swirling eddies. Wet, almost frozen, the men tried in vain to build fires and to find comfort.

On October 13 Arnold dispatched a messenger toward Montreal with a letter for General Schuyler. Another letter he sent by an Indian runner—whom he thought could be trusted—to a friend living in Quebec, informing him of the expedition's coming. The rains slackened somewhat, but for much of the distance the forests stood in the way, and a path had to be cut, at least eight feet wide, by the straining muscles of men who swung axes and pulled and rolled the logs aside.

Since the Virginians and Pennsylvanians were bearing the heaviest load of the march, Arnold sent word back to Greene and Enos to select the strongest men and to send them with fifteen days' ration to the head of the force. Greene complied, but Enos became fearful. Next morning he abruptly ordered his companies to about-face. Back he marched them—back to Connecticut. Brave men among them begged to be relieved from their outfits to continue the expedition, but their commander's lack of spirit had killed for most of Enos' soldiers all ambition for the march.

Arnold sternly announced there would be no turning back. Yet with every hour the shortage of food grew more acute. The colonel said he would go for help himself. Selecting sixty men and loading their supplies in several of the boats he set out up the Dead River.

"Food lies just ahead!" he shouted cheerfully. "Then— Quebec is ours!"

Success for Montgomary—Hardships for Arnold

The weary marchers of the main force waited for Arnold's return in wretched misery. The rain changed to snow, and it blew against them like the shrieking of fiends. From October 29 to November 2 were the blackest days. The men killed their dogs, dear companions of these frontiersmen, and ate them. They ate their cartridge boxes, chewed the leather of their shoes, and boiled their moccasins for soup. One of the soldiers, Private John Joseph Henry, recorded:

"There is scarcely anyone who has any more than one day's provision, and that small, and a great number none at all. Some have had none for all of two days. Captain Goodrich's Co. have nothing but a large dog, which they killed and ate tonight."

On the morning of November 3, the Virginians and their comrades in the van heard the sounds of riders and the bellowing of cattle. They looked at one another blankly. Had all gone mad at once? No! There *were* riders—and cattle! There were men with carts—and provisions!

Arnold had reached Sartigan on October 30, and had hurriedly sent back several Canadians and Indians with food. All the way down the line the shout went up. "Provisions in sight!" The men could hardly wait for meat to be cooked, seizing raw chunks as the commissaries fell quickly to their tasks.

And what of General Schuyler's expedition? The march up the Hudson had started on October 10, and almost immediately Schuyler had fallen ill with rheumatic fever. Forced to his bed, he placed Richard Montgomery in command. The advance continued to the south bank of the St. Lawrence opposite Montreal. None of the severe hardships of the march through the Maine wilderness had hampered this force.

Now Montgomery was ready to challenge the defenses of Montreal. General Sir Guy Carleton, commanding the city, had only a meager garrison of little more than a hundred men and no effective artillery. He quickly abandoned Montreal and set out for Quebec with his garrison, to defend that city at all costs. Montgomery struck quickly, capturing the few small gunboats on the river. Then he took over the city without firing another shot. Soon he had recruited enough Canadians to fill two companies, principally with former soldiers of French descent who still gave no strong allegiance to the British Crown.

Arnold's ragged, weather-beaten force pulled up at Point Levis on November 9, where General Wolfe had made camp before his assault upon the Queen City in 1759. Their stomachs had resumed normal functioning, their spirits were high and their faith in their enthusiastic commander unshaken. Arnold moved his troops westward and at night crossed the river, setting up camp at Point aux Trembles, ten miles from Quebec, convenient for a juncture with the captors of Montreal.

Montgomery sent a cheerful message to Arnold, announcing he would join him shortly. But Arnold missed an important prize—the British general. Down the river came a British frigate headed for Quebec. The Americans, watching from the bank, saw the vessel pass. Some strange feeling prompted Arnold to challenge it, but an engagement by his battery from the shore did not seem practical. The gunboat drew into harbor and unloaded General Carleton and his staff. Had this vigorous leader been intercepted, the whole campaign might have turned out differently.

Montgomery left Brigadier General David Wooster—a genial, hard-drinking and quite incompetent man—in charge at Montreal and set out with three hundred troops and several pieces of artillery. Arnold sent Morgan and his riflemen to a point south of Quebec to deploy along the bank, while Captain Dearborn and his company were dispatched across the St. Charles to keep vigilant eyes upon the town. On November 30 Arnold sent another letter urging all possible haste, with this accompanying note:

"This will be handed you by Mr. Burr, a volunteer in the Army and son of the former President of New Jersey College. He is a young gentleman of much life and activity, and has acted with great spirit and resolution on our fatiguing march. . . ."

On December 1 Montgomery arrived at Point aux Trembles and was welcomed by Arnold. The soldiers of the two expeditions mingled their shouts and all hands attacked a celebration barbecue. General Montgomery assumed command. Colonel Arnold was content to serve under him, rightly presuming that the general would treat him as a co-commander in the battle before them.

The Indian messenger Arnold had sent to Quebec proved treacherous, and for a price turned over the letter dispatched during the march to Lieutenant Governor Cramache. That official appealed for more troops to strengthen the Quebec garrison. From Newfoundland came a company of 150 men, and a frigate with twenty-six guns sailed in from Nova Scotia. General Carleton was busy at the double task of making ready his defenses and winning support of the citizens. It was no secret that many of the French people, inside the city and out, were friendly to the Americans. Arnold's spies reported that the inhabitants were ready to shout *"Vive le Congrès Continental!"* if the Americans won, or *"Vive le Ministre!"* if the invasion failed.

Montgomery began circulating General Washington's Manifesto, along with a proclamation of his own which read:

MY BROTHERS AND FRIENDS

The unfortunate necessity of dislodging the Ministerial troops compels me to besiege your town. . . . I entreat you to use every exertion in your power to obtain for me a peaceful entry. . . . We profess to come to give liberty and peaceable enjoyment of property in this oppressed Province.

RICHARD MONTGOMERY

The American commanders called a council. All the officers agreed that with winter already upon them and trenches impossible to maintain, a siege of the city was impractical. A surprise attack was agreed to. All the companies were alerted and special drills began. Lieutenant Burr volunteered to teach the men to scale ladders with full equipment.

But cold weather set in. Bitter cold! No metal could be handled without fingers freezing. The eyelids of sentries froze together. And an enemy more dreadful than cold stalked among them. Smallpox! "Smallpox in camp!" Men blanched at the mention of the disease as though they had been stabbed. A score came down with the loathsome malady in a few days, and were hustled off to an improvised hospital to nurse themselves as best they could, with no medicine of any kind—or to die.

The enlistments of three New England companies were due to expire on December 31. Unrest and dissatisfaction were rife among those men. Montgomery and Arnold realized that the assault must be quickly made. On Christmas morning, Montgomery addressed his force with a moving appeal for continued loyalty and courage. He knew how anxious all were to return to their homes, but duty must hold them until the victory was won. It would be soon, he said.

Both commanders knew how fearful were the odds against them. Barely 950 effectives, including Arnold's 550, Montgomery's 300, and the two Canadian companies, faced the task of storming the walls and overpowering a garrison of about 1,000 British regulars and several hundred Canadian volunteers.

Another council completed the details of the assault: Arnold would approach the city through St. Roque, at the west, storm the barrier at Sault au Matelot, and thus gain entrance to "Lower Town." Captain Dearborn's company would make a juncture with his force at St. Roque. Montgomery would advance by the roadway that skirted Wolfe's Cove and along the bank of the St. Lawrence to Près de Ville on the opposite side of Lower Town from Arnold. Forcing his way through the barrier, he would press through Champlain Street to join Arnold at the foot of Mountain Street. The Canadian companies were to storm and burn St. John's gates and reach the Mountain Street rendezvous. Together the forces would move up the slopes of "Upper Town," Quebec proper, firing the buildings as they went, if necessary. A desperate gamble!

In Cambridge, General Washington was asking anxiously, "What are Montgomery and Arnold doing?" The commander-in-chief faced a new year heavy with the uncertainties of this struggle for independence.

"Liberty or Death!"

Now it is December 30, 1775. For the meager American force preparing to attack Quebec, the bitterly frigid days and nights have moved slowly toward the year's end, as though congealed in the ice and snow that cover their camp. This day dawns clear, but at night the snow swirls in fine, white lines, and near midnight it falls in huge flakes.

"Every man to his place!" orders Montgomery. The attack will be made. The companies are formed. Arms are inspected and cartridge papers filled with powder. Sprigs of hemlock and bands with the words "Liberty or Death!" are fastened to all the caps, so that the Americans—many wearing uniforms seized from the British—can be distinguished from their enemy. At 3:30 the officers report all in readiness.

Arnold moves forward, beside him Morgan and Greene with their battalions. Lamb's company of artillery with an eight-pound brass field piece comes next, then Captain Topham, Major Bigelow, and Major Meigs with their companies. Montgomery, with his select detachment, moves off toward Wolfe's Cove.

The night is inky dark. The storm increases to a blizzard. The snow beats against the faces of the silent marchers and drifts in white layers upon their clothing. The British within the garrison have stood by their arms for days. They have been warned that the attack might be made on the first stormy night, and now they are posted and ready. At 5 o'clock the sentries sight the attackers. Rockets cut fiery paths into the black wilderness of sky and the alarm bells clang their warnings.

"Turn out! They come!" the cry rings along the streets from Lower Town to Upper Town.

Arnold's men deploy from the woodland and skirt an open field to approach the barrier at Sault au Matelot. The snow upon them makes them moving targets, dimly visible to the defenders pressed at every fire-hole in the wall. Suddenly the British muskets blaze. Several Americans fall. Some are silent, others moan in the deep snow.

"Press forward, men! Press forward!" shouts Benedict Arnold. Then he himself sinks with a cry of pain. A ball has pierced his left leg. Officers and men rush to lift him up. It is a bad wound. He cannot continue. With his arms over the shoulders of Parson Spring and a soldier, he is almost dragged back to the shack they have used as a hospital, weeping not from his pain but from anguish over this misfortune that takes him from the battle.

Captain Morgan takes command. The hardy Virginian is

outranked by both Bigelow and Meigs, but a few brief words of assent are all he needs.

"Follow me, men! Liberty or death!" Morgan's voice rings out over the firing. He dashes for the barrier. The ladder bearers are close at his heels, and behind them the musket-men, sloshing and panting through the snow, hugging their pieces to their breasts. Again and again the fire of the defenders spits through the night, but on the Americans come, sweeping over the barrier and onto the wharf that fronts the walls of the battery. Up go the ladders. First to ascend is Morgan. Musket balls whir about his head as he pokes it over the wall—one through his cap and another through a tuft of his hair. But over he climbs, barely missing the bayonets of waiting British regulars. Next come Captain Thayer and his shouting troops.

The guards fire another round and rush for their exits. Quickly surrounded by Americans, the British throw down their muskets, leave their cannon and surrender. Morgan posts his men, placing the guards where in the gray dawning light they can pick off the British as fresh troops come to aid the defenders. Now he anxiously waits for Montgomery.

Correctly guessing the intention of the attackers, Carleton has placed the strongest of his forces at Près de Ville, and there Captain Barnsfare's artillerymen wait with loaded cannon and lighted staffs. Montgomery circles the cove, Lieutenant Burr at his side. They approach the wooden palisade. Quickly the advance guards saw and hack some of the boards away, and through these breaches all 300 men push forward. A Canadian guide takes the lead and they move toward the redoubts.

"Push on, brave men! Quebec is ours!" shouts Montgomery.

It is the general's last command. A storm of grapeshot from the battery blazes a deathly greeting. Montgomery falls, shot through the head and body. Captain McPherson, Captain

Cheeseman and the Canadian guide all fall. Consternation seizes the Americans. Under a steady rain of bullets they retreat, leaving those that have fallen where they lie.

Captain Dearborn, meanwhile, has crossed the St. Charles and is coming up to aid in the engagement at Sault au Matelot. Morgan realizes by now that General Montgomery's plans must have gone wrong. A hurried consultation with Bigelow and Meigs convinces him they will not be able to hold their ground in Lower Town, much less assault the garrison of Upper Town, with Montgomery's help.

Many of the people of Lower Town are scurrying out of range of the fighting. Several houses are burning, and beyond these the Americans dodge in and out of shelter, firing their pieces at British skirmishers when they can keep their powder dry enough. It is now clear daylight and cold, but still snowing. Increasingly the muskets become useless, as the *Snap!* of the flint on steel brings no response from the wet powder.

Suddenly a British officer, Captain Laws, springs into the garrison where Morgan and several other officers and men are preparing to retreat.

"Surrender in the name of the Crown!" Laws orders.

The Americans seize and disarm him. But at the next moment, into the room storm squads of British troops. American resistance is useless. The defenders have caught them. Morgan stands with his back to the wall and defies the Redcoats. With tears in his eyes and choking with rage, he draws his sword and defies any man—or all of them—to take it out of his hands. He is saved from this feat of rashness by a priest, who calmly walks toward him with extended hand.

"I give *you* my sword," says Morgan, "but not one of these cowards shall take it!"

Less than half of Arnold's assaulting troops escape and make their way back to camp. The evening muster of that first day of 1776 shows a loss of 419 Americans, with an additional forty-two wounded. The snow drifts give up a total of thirty killed. Many of the wounded are yet to die, while 389 are prisoners. The defenders have lost only twenty-one killed and about twenty-five seriously wounded.

How the Map Might Have Been

The battle was over. The expedition against Canada had failed. On the next morning, General Carleton came to where Captain Morgan was held prisoner. He greeted the American officer courteously and said:

"I ask you, sir, to do me the favor to come with me and identify the body of an officer." The British commander paused, then continued: "We think it is General Montgomery."

It was, indeed. The body had been found nearly buried in the snow, surrounded by others that had fallen. The brave Irish-American was given a funeral service with military honors, while the American officers and men looked on sorrowfully. Lying on his cot, his shattered leg strapped in splints, was Benedict Arnold, sorrowing most of all.

Although it was clear the expedition had failed, Colonel Arnold's proud and stubborn heart would not admit defeat for fully three months. General Wooster came up the river to take command, and daily whiled away the hours in a French tavern on the St. Lawrence. Arnold hobbled about on crutches, keeping his survivors as comfortable as possible, while he sent beseeching letters to Washington and Schuyler. If they could but send him 2,500 men, he begged, Quebec could yet be taken.

But Washington was completely engaged in besieging Boston, and other corps of the Continental force could spare none of their meager troops. The Canadian general's strength was being increased steadily. In early April he paroled the prisoners, with the understanding that they would leave Canadian soil. Back to the Hudson came the men of the expedition, casting a backward glance now and then at the Canada they had failed to win.

As a matter of strategy, the hapless expedition was partially successful, in that for a time it diverted half the British reinforcements from England to Canada, rather than to Boston and New York to oppose Washington's forces. The interlude permitted the American commander-in-chief to strengthen his units, and prepare both offensive and defensive moves that prevented quick victory.

But the dream of seizing Canada was shattered—the dream, which if realized, would have made the map of the United States embrace the whole of North America from the Rio Grande to the North Pole, from Atlantic to Pacific. Today, over the mighty northern Dominion, proudly waves the flag with its Union Jack of Great Britain and its Canadian coat of arms with the maple leaves, symbol of an industrious and peaceful people.

CHAPTER FOUR

Burgoyne Surrenders at Saratoga

Into the two-story building General George Washington was using as headquarters in the town of Cambridge, Massachusetts, near Boston, came his principal officers for a council. It was March, 1776. For weary months the commander-in-chief of the Continental Army had kept the British troops in Boston under nominal siege, while begging the officials of the state governments to send more recruits and supplies. Now the time had come to prove the fiber of the nondescript army.

At the southern edge of Boston rose Dorchester Heights. With his officers about him, Washington pointed in the direction of the hill as he proposed a question:

"Gentlemen, can we storm and capture Dorchester Heights?"

The American officers saw the significance of this proposal. Some had already discussed it. All understood the established military maxim: "He who places his artillery upon higher ground than his enemy gains the advantage."

"It is worth the try, general!" was the officers' consensus. Washington dismissed his commanders, returning their salutes and clasping the hand of each as a symbol of agreement.

The general's staff quickly completed the plan of attack and the orders were given. At the first streaks of dawn on March 16, the American infantry rushed in columns along the roadways and lanes leading up the heights. Behind them rumbled the howitzers and guns. Caught by surprise, the British guards and garrison made little defense before retreating. In consternation the British general, Sir William Howe,

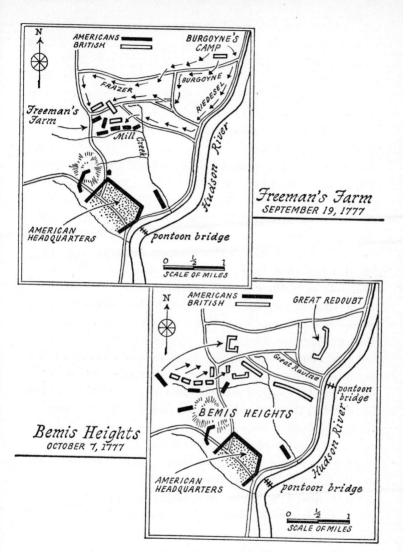

Freeman's Farm
SEPTEMBER 19, 1777

Bemis Heights
OCTOBER 7, 1777

BURGOYNE'S DEFEAT

who had replaced General Thomas Gage as commander-in-chief in Boston, saw the Continental flags go up over the ramparts of Dorchester Heights.

At last Washington's artillery commanded not only most of the city but the harbor as well. The British position was too precarious for safety. Howe sadly evacuated Boston, loaded his troops aboard waiting ships and sailed for Nova Scotia to plan a new campaign.

News of the victory heartened the colonial troops and members of the Continental Congress. In the upsurge of patriotic fervor, complete independence from England became a burning topic of conversation. Thomas Jefferson of Virginia, a tall, thin, serious-minded young delegate to the Congress, urged that the American states announce their independence. Aging but still alert Ben Franklin, shrewd Yankee John Adams and many others of the Congress heartily agreed with him.

On April 12 the Assembly of North Carolina instructed its delegates to propose a resolution of independence. The Virginia delegates in the Congress promptly endorsed the move, followed by an overwhelming majority of the members. Jefferson was appointed chairman of a committee to draft the resolution. He called it a Declaration of Independence. When he sent it to the clerk's desk for reading, he and his associates could not have known that it would prove to be the most significant document in the age-old struggle of mankind toward self-government since the Magna Carta, a brilliant lamp of liberty lighted by a people determined that they and their children should be forever free. On July 4, 1776, the stirring words of the Declaration were triumphantly announced to the people:

THE UNANIMOUS DECLARATION OF THE THIRTEEN UNITED STATES
OF AMERICA

When in the Course of human events. . . . We, therefore . . . appealing to the Supreme Judge of the world for the rectitude of our intentions . . . declare, That these United Colonies are, and of Right ought to be Free and Independent States. . . .

There could be no turning back now. "We must hang together, or surely we shall all hang separately," remarked Franklin, as he signed the historic parchment.

John Burgoyne Has a Plan

Ahead lay months of hardships and discouraging defeats for the patriots before a decisive battle brought a turn in the tide of the Revolution. While the historic events were transpiring in the capital, General Washington, anticipating that Howe's next move would be against New York, was in that city setting up a defense. He spread his thin line from the Hudson to the East River, posting the bulk of his army of 9,000 men at Brooklyn Heights, on Long Island, under General Israel Putnam.

General Howe reached New York harbor on July 5 and fixed his base on Staten Island. Within a few weeks his army of 30,000 troops had arrived, ready for action. Late in August the British commander moved to the attack, forcing Washington's poorly equipped defenders out of Long Island into New York and northward to White Plains, with heavy losses. The Redcoat general next captured Washington's two forts on the Hudson, with more than 2,500 prisoners. Then he loaded his troops on sailing transports, crossed the Hudson, scaled the Palisades, and began his march across New Jersey to capture Philadelphia and end the war.

General Washington could do little more than rally the survivors of these defeats and wait his chance. He retired through New Jersey and across the Delaware River into Pennsylvania, seeing his army almost decimated by sickness and desertions. During those dark last weeks of 1776, no one knew better than the general that some victory was badly needed to raise the morale of his soldiers and the hopes of the American people.

The advancing columns of Howe's army, made up of Hessian mercenary soldiers under Colonel Johann Rall, reached Trenton. Washington decided on a bold move. He led his force back across the Delaware on Christmas night, in small boats which the troops edged through cakes of floating ice, and in a surprise attack routed the Hessians, capturing 995 prisoners. Colonel Rall was fatally wounded. During the first week of the new year, 1777, Washington again crossed the Delaware near Trenton, overtook a British force under General Charles Cornwallis at Princeton, and by generalship of the highest order won another important victory.

These successes encouraged the people, but were only temporary gains. Washington camped at Morristown, New Jersey, and used the winter and spring to muster more men, established some order out of the haphazard system of supply, and plead with the states to support the war. "Under the common banner of liberty" was a phrase the commander-in-chief often used in his pleas.

When Howe evacuated Boston, he had under his command a strong-willed major general, John Burgoyne, a former member of Parliament and well-known as a dramatist and playwright. Burgoyne accompanied the troops to Nova Scotia, but became more and more dissatisfied with plans for suppressing the rebellious colonies and with prospects for winning glory for himself. He sailed back to England for an audience with King George.

His Majesty was eager to listen to anyone whose ideas on "the American rebellion" had some dash and vigor, and Burgoyne's scheme was both bold and logical. He proposed an offensive campaign to gain possession of the Hudson Valley by a thrust southward from Canada, cutting the four New England states from those of the middle and south; to move next upon Philadelphia and capture the Continental capital, and hold key cities from Boston to Baltimore; then to strike at American resistance wherever it might threaten.

King George and his advisers agreed that the plan was good. The War Ministry began filling in the details: Burgoyne would move south through Lake Champlain to Fort Edward, and down the Hudson to Albany; Colonel Barry St. Leger would move up the St. Lawrence River to northern New York; Howe would send Sir Henry Clinton up the Hudson toward Albany. Thus Albany was selected as the terminus for the three segments of the campaign—rendezvous for the celebration of victory. One stipulation Burgoyne firmly insisted upon:

"Your Majesty and Ministers, I must be in command. I beg you to appoint me the lieutenant general!"

His Majesty happily agreed to that detail, but his ministers privately vetoed it. They informed the ambitious commander that he would have to remain a major general until he had won a victory.

By early June, Major General John Burgoyne, at his camp near the southern Canadian border, was champing at the bit that held him to the task of making ready his troops and supplies. Finally all was in order, and the march southward began with all in gay spirits. "Gentleman Johnny" Burgoyne rode in a splendid carriage, with thirty vehicles—wagons and two-wheeled carts—carrying his personal baggage, choice foods and liquors.

"Victory by Christmas!" was the cry from officers and men. Burgoyne saw himself back in England, receiving as his reward a title of nobility and bowing to the plaudits of a grateful people. His army of 7,902 troops was the best equipped of any yet to set foot on American soil. British regulars numbered 4,135, and German troops from Braunschweig, 3,116. There were 148 Canadians and 503 Indians. The English infantry and artillerymen were the best the homeland could offer, professional troops for the most part, and veterans of many campaigns and battles. The "Brunswickers" were as good as any of those unfortunate hirelings from the German states; while they fought with no love for the cause, they were disciplined and soldierly. Major General William Phillips, Brigadier General Simon Fraser and Brigadier General Baron Frederick Adolph Riedesel were Burgoyne's principal officers, the latter commanding the Germans.

Several officers brought along their wives, and some even their children, confident that the rebellion would soon be put down and they would be rewarded with rich estates in the New World. One woman was described by Colonel James Wilkinson, Gates's adjutant, in his journal as "the amiable, the accomplished and dignified Baroness Riedesel." This German gentlewoman kept a diary and filled it with intimate details of the campaign.

The American troops preparing to defend Albany and the Hudson Valley were pitifully few, wretchedly equipped and poorly trained. General Philip Schuyler, who lived near Saratoga, twenty miles north of Albany, was in command of these Continental troops and militia hastily gathered to stand against the British. Washington ordered General Arthur St. Clair, commanding at Fort Ticonderoga, to cooperate. St. Clair made preparations to hold his fort and keep the enemy at bay while Schuyler pursued the heartbreaking task of mustering recruits and collecting supplies.

With unselfish devotion to his duty, Schuyler wrote appealing letters to the commanders and adjutants of the state militias. Apathy, delay and jealousy were all too often his only answers. General Horatio Gates, a man of mediocre military ability but overweaning personal ambition, was actively scheming to replace Schuyler in command, hoping then to replace Washington as commander-in-chief. Against such fearful odds, Schuyler went cheerfully about the business of equipping a force to meet the blow he knew would fall before the summer faded.

The Invading Army Strikes

On July 1, 1777, Burgoyne reached the rolling hills beyond Fort Ticonderoga. The Americans believed that here they held a veritable Gibraltar. Here, any British advance from Canada was to be halted. But the Redcoat general promptly prepared to attack it. His shrewd, experienced commander of artillery, General Phillips, put into practice the same principle utilized by General Washington at Boston. He seized the mountain to the north of the American stronghold, nicknamed "Sugar Loaf," which his troops promptly christened "Mount Defiance." General St. Clair decided there was nothing to do but evacuate Ticonderoga and retreat. When Schuyler received the news at the hands of a rider on July 7, he was stunned with disappointment. Consternation filled American hearts and bitter criticisms were hurled at Schuyler.

"He must have been bribed by silver bullets fired into the fort by Burgoyne," was the word passed from mouth to mouth, while John Adams rose in Congress to declare with biting sarcasm, "We shall never gain a victory until we shoot a general!"

Yet Schuyler's energy and leadership still saved the American army of the north. He effectively slowed Burgoyne's advance by felling trees, destroying bridges and removing supplies. He transferred the ordnance, including forty cannon, and provisions, from Fort George to Saratoga. He rekindled the spirit of hope in the hearts of his soldiers and quieted the feelings of panic among the people. He knew of the intrigues against him, but his loyalty to duty never wavered. He wrote to the New York Committee of Safety:

"I thank God I have fortitude enough not to sink under the load of calumny that is heaped upon me, and despite it all, I am supported by a presentiment that we shall still have a merry Christmas."

Washington, with his usual insight into the true situation, supported Schuyler firmly.

Although disappointed by the failure of Benedict Arnold's expedition into Canada, the commander-in-chief recommended that this tempestuous officer be commissioned a major general. Now Washington dispatched him, with Brigadier General John Glover and their divisions, to assist in the defense of the Hudson River area.

Gentleman Johnny crossed the Hudson and pushed on southward, reaching the town of Skenesborough on July 7, entirely confident of victory. He issued a pompous proclamation to the American people, warning them of the terror which his allies, the savage Indians, might spread among them. This only served to rally soldiers and civilians alike to the defense of their firesides and communities.

A capable military engineer from Poland, who had volunteered his services to the Continental Congress, Colonel Thaddeus Kosciusko, had built entrenchments for a camp south of Moses' Creek, and to these fortifications Schuyler withdrew his troops on July 22. Pausing for a week, he pushed on to Stillwater. Here, at "the sprouts of the Mohawk," he determined to make a stand against the invaders.

St. Leger was advancing with his British regulars, a battalion of Tories and a detachment of Indians, upon Fort Schuyler, near the village of Rome. On the sixth of August, General Nicholas Herkimer and his Tryon County Militia stood in the British path at Oriskany and fought them to a standstill. Schuyler ordered Arnold to assist and that intrepid thunderbolt sent St. Leger retreating, thus breaking Burgoyne's plan for support from the west.

On the morning of August 10, Schuyler received a note

with the words he so dreaded to read: "By order of the Continental Congress, Major General Philip Schuyler is hereby relieved of his command. . . ." He was not surprised that his successor was General Horatio Gates. He swallowed his grief, returned to Albany and announced that he would serve his country in the fight for freedom if he had to do it as the humblest private citizen.

Had he been permitted to remain, he would have found the tide turning in his favor. Daniel Morgan, now a colonel, with his companies of expert Virginia riflemen, came marching up with lusty cheers and singing. At Bennington, Vermont, detachments of Burgoyne's left wing were roundly defeated by John Stark and Seth Warner with their Green Mountain Boys. The spirits of the northern colonists revived. Recruits came riding and tramping in, muskets in hand, powder horns at their sides.

But to the south, Washington's heroic efforts failed to prevent the enemy's advance into Pennsylvania. Coming by sea from New York, Howe's army of 18,000 men landed south of Philadelphia. At Brandywine Creek on September 11, Washington led his inferior forces to the attack. The Americans fought bravely and well, but were defeated, sacrificing at least a thousand men in killed, wounded and prisoners. Washington retreated northward, while Howe marched triumphantly into Philadelphia. The Continental Congress fled to York, Pennsylvania. Three weeks later the commander-in-chief tried a surprise attack upon the British camped at Germantown, northeast of Philadelphia. All the general's skill and that of such officers as General John Sullivan and Nathanael Greene, all the dash and bravery of Colonel Anthony Wayne who led the attack, all the dogged determination of the troops, could not dislodge the invaders. Again a victory was badly needed by the American patriots.

Burgoyne's Challenge Is Accepted

Gates marched northward to meet Burgoyne's advance. He paused at Schuyler's Stillwater entrenchments, but on the advice of Colonel Kosciusko pushed on to Bemis Heights, four miles from Saratoga, fortifying his camp with earthworks and batteries. Burgoyne's army was coming forward in three columns, while a flotilla of boats kept abreast on the Hudson, carrying an assortment of material and supplies. Past Saratoga they came, and to near Bemis Heights. Here the British general camped, to consider how best to continue his victorious march to Albany.

One man could have been of great value to Gates. Philip Schuyler knew every hill, every basin, all the woodlands and roadways of that region. But Gates did not wish to share any glory of the campaign with this man, or any other man, however worthy. He was especially irked at the eagerness of Benedict Arnold, and resolved to hold this military whirlwind in check.

At the dawn of September 19, Gates's scouts reported that the British camp was breaking. That could mean only one thing: an advance into battle. Burgoyne sent Fraser's column first, moving southwestward. The commander himself advanced with his main body of troops, almost directly southward. General Phillips and Baron Riedesel started upon the road paralleling the Hudson.

"We shall await them here, gentlemen," was Gates's verbal order, passed to each of his commanders. Arnold quickly grasped the situation and protested. He pointed out that Burgoyne's actions indicated the intention to strike the American left flank, and that it would be better to make an attack to forestall the British move. Gates grudgingly permitted the units under Morgan and Dearborn to go out "to observe the enemy," ordering Arnold to stay behind.

Shortly after noon, Morgan's troops encountered Burgoyne's Canadian and Indian forces scouting ahead, and fell upon them. The scouting parties fled, with the Americans in full pursuit. At the edge of a woodland, on the farm of Isaac Freeman, Morgan came in full contact with Fraser's main body. The surprised Virginians were driven back. Fraser pushed forward to flank the Americans, while Burgoyne, stationed beyond Freeman's forest, prepared to join him.

Again Benedict Arnold had anticipated the move of the enemy and measured its alarming probabilities. He ordered his brigade forward, between Fraser and Burgoyne, and plunged into the fight. For more than an hour, the late summer's sun beat down upon a furious encounter. It was Arnold against Fraser. Back and forth from Freeman's woods and into his cleared fields the tide of Redcoats would sweep, to be followed by the countertide of nondescript uniforms of the various American Continentals and militia. Hand-to-hand fighting marked every foot of a fifteen-acre field. Several British batteries were lost and retaken as many as five times. Colonel Morgan's sharpshooters, called together by the gallant Virginian's shrill turkey whistle, rallied to the fight with their usual bravery. Many of them posted themselves in trees, picking off scores of invaders.

Gates had under his command about 16,000 troops. From his reserve he could have amply reinforced Arnold's battle-weary regiments, but timidity or jealousy restrained him, until near dusk when he sent in one brigade. Darkness halted the battle, which the proud British commander claimed as a victory. Although Riedesel's Germans had repeatedly come to the rescue during the hard-fought engagement, Burgoyne barely mentioned them in his reports, while giving glowing accounts of his own generalship.

Both sides were too exhausted to renew the fight the next day. The field was sprinkled over with the bodies of the slain from both sides. Burgoyne had lost more than five hundred men, including some of his best officers.

On that evening a letter reached the Redcoat commander from General Clinton, who said he was about to start up the Hudson to Burgoyne's aid, bringing a month's supplies. Burgoyne moved the main body of his army back upon the higher ground to the north of Bemis Heights, and built fortifications to await Clinton's arrival. On the river banks he stored his magazines and erected his hospital tents, guarded by the British 47th Regiment, veterans of every principal engagement in the north since Bunker Hill.

Only a cannon-shot distance separated the two hostile camps during three weeks of anxious waiting. Gates utilized some of the time laying in badly needed ammunition and supplies, and the rest of the time quarreling with his officers. Gates did not mention Benedict Arnold in his report of the battle of Freeman's farm, and spoke of Colonel Morgan without any commendation of the Virginian's truly effective leadership. Arnold questioned Gates as to his treatment of Morgan, and the general, in a rage, relieved Arnold of all command and ordered him to his tent.

Where was Clinton? Burgoyne wondered why he did not come. And why was Howe so indifferent to the campaign? Long after the Saratoga battle, the truth became known.

After Burgoyne's plan was approved in London, a memorandum was written for Colonial Secretary Lord George Germain to be dispatched to Howe, instructing the general to cooperate with Burgoyne in the Hudson campaign. His Lordship did not like the appearance of the clerk's script, and ordered a "fairer copy." A fox hunt was scheduled, and that social event was most important for Germain. The dispatch to Howe could wait. After the fox hunt it still waited—overlooked completely! Clinton, therefore, was acting on his own initiative in his promise to help Burgoyne. Not until October

3 did he start north, but victory marched with him. On the sixth he captured the two forts on the west bank of the Hudson that stood in his way, and soon afterward he captured or disabled the ships guarding the river. Collecting a large amount of supplies, he loaded his gunboats and pack trains, and with nearly 2,000 troops set out for Albany.

The Brave Meet the Brave

It is the clear, crisp morning of October 7. Burgoyne's supplies are running low. He faces a hard choice: immediate attack, or retreat. He decides to attack, and forms his battle lines. His plan is to force the American left, the farthest from the river, and if successful there, to compel a general retreat. His most mobile force, the 24th Infantry and the light infantry regiments, are given the right wing under General Fraser. Riedesel and Phillips with their corps are placed in the center, while most of the artillery under General Balcarres forms the British left.

Burgoyne leads about one-fourth his force—1,550 troops with twelve pieces of artillery—within striking distance of the American camp, to determine whether the American commander will accept or refuse battle. Gates's adjutant, Colonel Wilkinson, posts himself on a high knoll to observe the enemy movements. He informs Gates that apparently Burgoyne offers an engagement.

"What would you suggest?" Gates asks.

"I would indulge him, sir!" is Wilkinson's reply.

The decisive hour has come. Gates forms his troops for battle. With commendable skill he counters the invader's plan. He orders Colonel Morgan to move westward to strike the right flank of the British, while the New York and New Hampshire troops under Brigadier General Poor will assault the right. Brigadier General Learned and Colonel Dearborn will hold the center.

And Benedict Arnold? He approaches General Gates and salutes. "Allow me, sir, to serve as a volunteer in the ranks!" he begs. Gates refuses, and curtly turns away.

In perfect order the Americans advance, holding their fire until the first volley from the British infantry roars over the heights. Then they charge. Morgan rushes his men down a slope and against Fraser's lines like a tempest, crowding the Redcoats into temporary retreat. Burgoyne rides up and his units rally again. General Poor's men take one of the redoubts, while Dearborn's riflemen are hotly engaging the Germans and British of the center.

Hearing the sounds and smelling the smoke of battle, Benedict Arnold can endure idleness no longer. He dashes for his horse, rides directly into Learned's brigade, and is greeted by cheers.

"Arnold is here! General Arnold!" shout the men.

Taking command of the brigade and of other nearby detachments, he directs an assault upon the Germans, forcing a breach through which the American musketmen and cavalry pour. The Redcoat line falls back.

But Fraser rides up and rallies his men. Again it is a duel between the German general and Arnold. Where Fraser goes, German and British valor rises to the heights. Where Arnold goes, American daring knows no bounds.

While the battle is at its peak, Morgan calls three of his Virginian riflemen. "That officer on the gray horse is General Fraser," he says, pointing with his sword. "I respect him, but I order you to take station in that clump of trees and do your duty."

A few moments later, Fraser slumps from his horse, a bullet in his side. Burgoyne now takes personal charge of the battle, exposing himself fearlessly to danger. The American commander stays far back of the firing and spends considerable time cursing Arnold for disobeying his orders.

The British begin retreating, despite Burgoyne's desperate efforts. Arnold leads the pursuit, and the Americans, lifted from their weariness by his exultant spirit, carry redoubts and breastworks. Spurring his horse into the batteries of light artillery, he directs the capture of numerous cannon still smoking from their grim work. Just as dusk closes in, at the point of resistance offered by the German artillerymen, Riedesel's ablest remaining officer, Colonel Breyman, is killed. As Arnold leads his men against this position in the final assault of the day, his horse is shot under him and a ball strikes his leg, the same leg that was wounded at Quebec.

Officers and men rush to carry him away. As he lies under a tree, a dispatch is handed him by an officer whom Gates has sent chasing him here and there through the battle. It reads: "General Arnold is ordered to return to his quarters, lest he do some rash thing." This to the man whose rashness, so far, has carried the day!

Burgoyne is torn between the impulse to make another stand, even with his depleted forces and ammunition, or hurry across the Hudson and northward to safety. Gates has anticipated that his opponent might decide to retreat, and has sent General Fellows across the river to occupy an old camp at Battenkill. Now he dispatches General Bailey with a brigade of New England troops across the Hudson to strengthen Fellows in any operations to oppose Burgoyne's passage. Burgoyne decides to cross Fish Creek at his rear and fall back upon the heights of Saratoga. During the rainy, dismal night that follows, he makes the retreat, leaving many of his wounded and abandoning much of the baggage.

General Fraser dies of his wound. The brave officer has asked to be buried in the redoubt he has last defended. It is now close to the American advance guard. Late in the day a cortege, bearing the casket, files toward the battle-scarred bastion. A battery of American artillery opens fire, a shell showering mud upon the chaplain and the sorrowing procession.

"Hold the fire, men! It's General Fraser's funeral!" a soldier cries. Then, pointed skyward, over the valley booms the American gun at one-minute intervals in a solemn tribute to a gallant foeman's passing.

In her diary, Baroness Riedesel, with a liberty of straightforward comment that women of all ages have rightly appropriated, makes an entry for the ninth of October:

Toward evening, we at last came to Saratoga, which was only half an hour's march from the place where we had spent the whole day. I was wet through and through by the frequent rains, and was obliged to remain in this condition the entire night. I therefore seated myself before a good fire, and undressed my children. I asked General Phillips, who came up to where we were, why we did not continue our retreat while there was yet time, as my husband had pledged himself to cover it, and bring the army through. "Poor woman," he answered, "I am amazed at you! He halts because he is tired, and intends to spend the night here, and give us supper." In this latter achievement, especially, General Burgoyne is very fond of indulging. He spends half the nights in singing and drinking, and amusing himself with the wife of a commissary who is his mistress and who as well as he, loves champagne.

On the evening of the tenth, an American scout informs General Gates that Burgoyne is preparing to retreat toward Fort Edward. Assuming that only a small force would be left behind as a rear guard, Gates orders a general pursuit. A spy notifies Burgoyne of the American intention, and the British commander spends the latter half of that night preparing his whole army to repulse any attack. Morgan and Learned are already advancing toward the British position within a wooded tract still shrouded in the morning mist, when Colonel Wilkinson learns from a British deserter that Burgoyne has not retreated, but is ready to rout the American forces as soon as they appear. Wilkinson spurs his horse to catch Learned and begs him not to be led into a trap.

"Have you orders to that effect?" Learned demands.

"I have not, as there was no time for me to see General Gates," the colonel replies.

"Then the standing order is to attack!" Learned declares, drawing his sword and turning to give the command.

In those few moments the mist has lifted, and the startled men of the American columns see before them the main body of Burgoyne's troops in battle line. Wilkinson is right! The order for retreat is quickly passed, and thus Gates and his army are saved from possible disaster. That the American commander has exposed his force to such risk without adequate intelligence of the enemy position and strength can be explained only as due to his tragically erratic generalship.

The Noose Is Drawn

However, no fault can be found with Gates's next and decisive move. He decides to encircle the British Army and besiege it. All his commanders agree that if they can prevent Burgoyne's escape, that potent ally of all besiegers, hunger, might force surrender. On his maps, Colonel Kosciusko shows where each unit can be most effectively placed.

Quietly, under cover of darkness, the columns advance to their positions. Around the British right, toward the west, hurry Morgan and his dauntless Virginians with their recruits from the Carolinas and Georgia. They are followed by Learned's brigade and a regiment of hardy Pennsylvanians. Over the river silently row the troops of New Hampshire, Connecticut and Rhode Island to join those who have been sent in advance to prevent retreat to the north. New York, New Jersey, Maryland and Delaware troops deploy their units to cover the southern positions. Stark and his musketmen from Vermont and other New England areas are given the assignment of honor: to swing widely around the British lines and thus close the gap in the north, "the cork in the bottle of Burgoyne," the happy Yankee fighters call it.

Thus Gates commands troops from every state of the new nation, eager to test their bravery and to measure their strength of arms in this decisive hour. By nightfall of the eleventh the only question is whether Stark can close the northern gap before Burgoyne attempts to break through.

By the flickering light of candles within his tent, with tall, red-coated sentries posted stiffly outside, Burgoyne meets his generals for a council of war. Baron Riedesel is positive in his advice:

"Retreat while there is time! Move tonight northward four miles, cross the river, avoid an engagement at Fort Edward, and strike for Ticonderoga. There we can re-establish our lines of supply and communication, and advance or retreat as the occasion demands."

Burgoyne listens to the German officer's words, then sinks into a fever of indecision. It seems incredible to his proud nature that he could have maneuvered his army into critical danger. Riedesel's counsel obviously is sound. With great reluctance Burgoyne agrees, with one modification: wait until morning.

But by morning Stark is in place, the sentries of his right clasping hands with those of Morgan's corps to the west and those of his left saluting across the river their fellow New Englanders of Learned's brigade. Too late for British retreat!

But the British commander is not ready to surrender. He sets himself resolutely to find the weakest links in the chain of grim besiegers and to attempt a breakthrough at any cost. Blazing away with his artillery, he tries this point of the American line and that. But each shot fired means that much less ammunition, with no chance for replacement. And into the ranks of his soldiers, the Americans, crouched behind their hastily prepared breastworks of trees and earth, fire intermittent volleys every hour of the day and into the night. American sharpshooters watch every move and aim with deadly effect at every enemy soldier within range, while volleys from Fellow's battery thunder across the Hudson.

Water is difficult to obtain, for American riflemen pick off the British, German or Canadian soldiers who dash with their buckets to one or the other of the springs in their besieged area. Several women, wives of officers of the beleagured forces, take up the task. The Americans hold their fire.

General Riedesel has sent his wife and daughters to a large house within the lines. No official reports of the battle can surpass in simple eloquence, even in translation, the words the baroness uses in her diary to describe the hardships of the siege:

Immediately after our arrival a frightful cannonade began, principally directed against the house in which we had sought refuge, probably because the enemy believed, from seeing so many people flocking around it, that all the generals made it their headquarters. Alas! It sheltered none but wounded soldiers, or women.

We were finally obliged to take refuge in a cellar, in which I laid myself down in a corner not far from the door. My children lay down on the earth with their heads upon my lap, and in this manner we passed the entire night. A horrible stench, the cries of the children, and yet more than all this, my own anguish, prevented me from closing my eyes. On the following morning the cannonade again began, but on a different side. I advised all to go out of the cellar for a little while, during which time I would have it cleaned, otherwise all would be ill.

After they had all gone out and left me alone, I for the first time surveyed our place of refuge. It consisted of three beautiful cellars, splendidly arched. I proposed that the most dangerously wounded of the officers should be brought into one of them; that the women should remain in another; and that all the rest should stay in the third, which was nearest the entrance. I had just given the cellars a good sweeping and had fumigated them by sprinkling vinegar on burning coals, and each one had found his place prepared for him—when a fresh and terrible cannonade threw us all once more into alarm. . . . Eleven cannonballs went through the house, and we could plainly hear them rolling over our heads. One poor soldier (a British surgeon by the name of Jones) whose leg they were about to amputate, having been laid upon a table for this purpose, had the other leg taken off by another cannonball, in the midst of the operation. His comrades all ran off and when they again came back they found him in one corner of the room, where he had rolled in his anguish, scarcely breathing. . . .

I had some straw brought in and laid my bed upon it, where I slept with my children—my maids sleeping not far from us. Directly opposite us three English officers were quartered—wounded it is true, but, nevertheless resolved not to be left behind in case of a retreat. One of them was Captain Green, aide-de-camp of General Phillips, a very valuable and agreeable man. Often my husband wished to withdraw me from danger, by sending me to the Americans; but I remonstrated with him on the ground that to be with people whom I would be obliged to treat with courtesy, while perhaps my husband was being killed by them, would be even yet more painful than all I was now suffering. . . . Finally, they spoke of capitulating.

It is October 13, and Burgoyne sits with his officers in a council. There is little choice. All agree that surrender is the wisest course. A flag of truce is raised, and carried by a dust-coated British infantryman to the American lines. In carefully rehearsed language, he asks the sentries if General Gates would be so kind as to receive a field officer from General Burgoyne, "on a matter of importance to both armies." Gates sends word that he will meet the British commander's spokesman at 10 o'clock.

Major Robert Kingston bears Burgoyne's message. He is met at the crossing of a creek between the lines by Colonel Wilkinson, blindfolded and led to Gates's headquarters.

"I must ask you, sir, on what terms you will accept the surrender of the British army," he says.

"The British are to surrender as prisoners of war, and shall lay down their arms within their entrenchments at the command of their adjutant general" is Gates's reply.

For an answer, Burgoyne declares that his army will rush out and die to a man rather than accept such terms. Two days are spent in further discussions, with Gates offering the generous proposal that all officers and men will be paroled and helped to return to their homelands. Burgoyne and his staff decided to accept.

But on that night of October 15, a British spy slips through with word that General Clinton is really on the way! Burgoyne grasps at this last straw. He sends Gates a message asking for more time. Calling his officers, he inquires whether he would be justified in repudiating his agreement for surrender. The majority vote that it would not be honorable. Gates grows impatient and prepares his army to renew the siege.

Burgoyne has reached the end. He signs the historic paper, which he insists must not be called a surrender, but "Articles of Convention," on the morning of October 17.

Yankee Doodle Dandy

Thus ended the decisive engagement. Arrayed in his showiest uniform and decorations, Burgoyne rode out with his staff, escorted by Colonel Wilkinson. At the river bank he paused.

"Isn't the river fordable here?" he inquired.

"Certainly, sir," replied the American adjutant. "But do you observe our troops on the opposite bank?"

"I have observed them too long," Burgoyne said, with a note of sadness.

Colonel Wilkinson's journal records:

General Gates, advised of Burgoyne's approach, met him at the head of his camp, Burgoyne in a rich royal uniform and Gates in a plain blue frock. When they had approached nearly within sword's length they reined up and halted; I then named the gentlemen, and General Burgoyne, raising his hat most gracefully, said:

"The fortune of war, General Gates, has made me your prisoner," to which the conqueror replied, "I shall always be ready to bear testimony that it has not been through any fault of your Excellency." Major General Phillips then advanced and he and General Gates saluted and shook hands. Next the Baron Riedesel and the other officers were introduced in their turn, and as soon as the ceremony was completed I left the army and returned to the British camp.

Among those introduced, limping on a bandaged leg, was Benedict Arnold. And after the ceremony, a gray-haired, sturdy man in civilian dress stepped up to congratulate Gates on his success. It was General Philip Schuyler.

The Americans turned at once to feeding the starved British, German, Canadian and Indian troops, providing medical supplies and fraternizing amiably with their former antagonists. Only one note was sounded to remind the British of the defeat they had suffered. The song "Yankee Doodle," composed by a Tory in order to deride the uncouth rebels, had been played by British fifes and drummers whenever it could offend American ears. Now the fifers and drummers of the victorious Americans played it:

"Yankee Doodle, keep it up! Yankee Doodle Dandy!"

Burgoyne's surrender marked the turning point in the entire campaign to quash the American revolution. The American victory brought two results of tremendous importance. First, it gave heart to the patriots, encouraging their officers and men, their state and national leaders, to fight on to final victory. Second, it brought into the struggle the active support of France against Great Britain, her traditional rival for colonies, for trade and political power.

Benjamin Franklin and his fellow commissioners representing the Continental Congress had been in Paris during most of the war, working patiently to win the French court to the American cause. Now their task became easier. The crafty French monarch, Louis XVI, and his equally crafty foreign minister, Charles Gravier Vargennes, decided that the Americans could win, and that a winning horse of such future value should be backed.

In February 1778 a treaty of alliance between France and the Continental government of the United States was signed, in which the French court pledged troops and the use of its fleet against the British in American waters. Like a rainbow of promise, the new alliance shone over the clouds of the American war for independence.

CHAPTER FIVE

Washington Leads to Victory at Yorktown

"We win battles in the American colonies, but we do not win campaigns," commented Lord George Germain bitterly, after General Burgoyne's crushing defeat at Saratoga.

Well might the fox-hunting nobleman complain: Burgoyne had failed, and now some other plan of campaign had to be devised. The new plan was suggested by General Sir Henry Clinton, who succeeded General Sir William Howe in command of British forces in America, and approved by the War Ministry: to invade and conquer the southern states, weaker and less populous than those in the north, and then force decisive fighting again from Philadelphia northward. While military operations never completely ceased in the north, this plan charted the final phase of the British effort to win the war against the rebellious civilians and soldiers of the American colonies.

Revenge was doubtless in Sir Henry's mind—revenge for his earlier defeat when he attempted to invade the southern area. In June 1776 he had led a force to land at Charleston, South Carolina, and to attack the city. Gallant resistance of South Carolina and Georgia militia under General William Moultrie had turned back this invasion attempt.

At first the tide again moved heavily in British favor, but the superb generalship of Washington never allowed a British victory to become decisive. The commander-in-chief took advantage of every opportunity for some gain for his hard-pressed forces. But through what hardships the patriots had

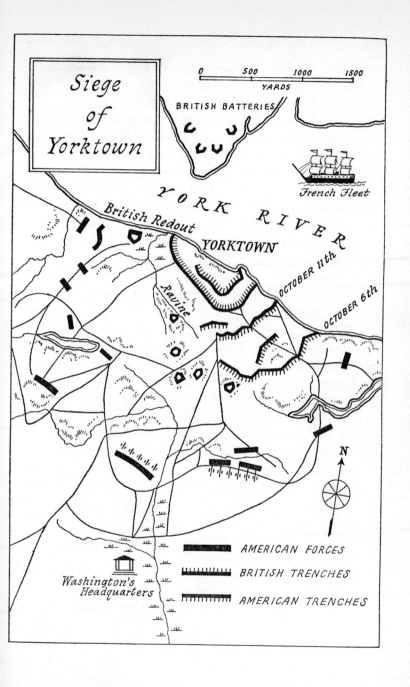

Siege
of
Yorktown

500   1000   1500
YARDS

BRITISH BATTERIES

French Fleet

YORK RIVER

British Redout

YORKTOWN

OCTOBER 11th

OCTOBER 6th

Ravine

N

Washington's
Headquarters

AMERICAN FORCES
BRITISH TRENCHES
AMERICAN TRENCHES

to march! There is no parallel for it in history. The brave fighters, on land and sea, endured cold, hunger, privation, disease and discouragement.

Washington established his winter camp at Valley Forge, Pennsylvania. His soldiers were almost destitute of uniforms, shoes and supplies. As they walked about in the snow of that bitter winter, on sentry duty or dragging up wood for fires, many shoeless feet left bloody tracks. But there was General Washington to walk among them, living symbol of faith in the cause and devotion to duty. There was Washington to kneel in the snow and ask leadership of the Omnipotent Commander.

A young French nobleman, the Marquis de Lafayette, had not waited for the official alliance to offer his service to the cause of American independence. Not yet twenty years old, he presented himself in July 1777 to the Continental Congress and was commissioned a major general. Next day he met Washington. The commander-in-chief assigned the young nobleman to duty at once, and a lifelong friendship began.

In the darkness of the Valley Forge winter, another nobleman, Baron Frederick von Steuben of Prussia, arrived and sought out General Washington. As a former aide to Frederick the Great, and an experienced military tactician, he was asked by the general to take up an important duty: to drill and discipline the American troops. This Steuben did, with Prussian thoroughness. He took a rabble of recruits and from them created an army. Kneeling on the ground with the ragged soldiers looking on, he marked with a stick the maneuvers of squads, platoons and companies.

Baron von Steuben standardized infantry drill, and cavalry and artillery movements. He laid the basis for military tactics that were still fundamental in the American armed forces a century and a half later. Day by day he personally drilled the men at Valley Forge, although he knew very little English and the soldiers could scarcely restrain their mirth at his pronunciation. When the German general was told by some American officers that drilling the troops was beneath his dignity since it was the work of sergeants, he amiably replied:

"I vass a sergeant already!"

General Clinton completed plans for an offensive and took personal charge of the new campaign. Fearing that France, the new ally of the American cause, might send a fleet to blockade the Delaware River, Clinton evacuated Philadelphia in June 1778 and started the march toward New York.

Washington drew out six brigades of his army and intercepted the British at Monmouth, New Jersey. The general's careful plan of attack was ruined when General Charles Lee, commanding the American vanguard, displayed a strange mixture of instability and cowardice and ordered a retreat at his first contact with the enemy. Washington rode up and rallied the troops. All day the battle went on, across fields, into woodlands and marshes. Weary American soldiers slept by their arms that night, expecting to resume the fighting at dawn. But daybreak found a stillness where the British had camped. The Redcoats had retreated, taking up their march toward New York. The severe engagement cost the British 260 killed, against sixty-nine of Washington's troops. Most important of all: Monmouth proved again that American soldiers could stand up to British regulars in the open field.

Moving his army northward to West Point on the Hudson, General Washington established his headquarters near by. His plan was to take personal charge of the strategic areas of the north, while the best generals he could supply would meet the enemy operations in the south.

Dark Days for the Patriots

The first move in the new British campaign was made at Savannah, late in 1778. The Redcoats landed a force of 3,500 men, defeated the defending Americans under General Robert Howe and captured this Georgia city. Washington dispatched General Benjamin Lincoln to take over command of the southern army. Under severe British pressure Lincoln moved his troops northward to Charleston. There, in April 1779, he was joined by French Admiral Charles Hector Estaing, whose fleet had been engaging the British in northern waters, and who landed a force of one thousand men.

Determined to free Savannah if possible, Lincoln and his French allies marched on the city while Admiral Estaing sailed to assault it by sea. But all the strategy and bravery of the American and French forces could not dislodge the British. The dispirited allies trudged back to Charleston. In this battle the gallant Polish volunteer, Brigadier General Casimir Pulaski, was mortally wounded. General Clinton decided the time had come to throw all his weight into the war. Sailing from New York for the South Carolina shore he landed a large force, surrounded Charleston and on May 12, 1779, forced Lincoln to surrender his defending army of nearly 5,000 men.

These disasters seriously threatened the cause of American independence. Public opinion in favor of stopping a "needless war" grew alarmingly. Support for the British, unusually strong in many parts of the south, became outspoken as Tories argued bitterly with their Whig neighbors.

With General Clinton on his southern campaign was Major General Charles Cornwallis, a British earl who had been aide-de-camp to the king and had conducted himself with bravery in the northern campaigns. A few weeks after his Charleston victory Clinton returned to New York, leaving Cornwallis to command in the south. Here was the chance for which the young, eager and capable officer had been hoping. He announced to his staff:

"We will divide the remaining rebel forces in the Carolinas, conquer each segment quickly, and end the war!"

Equally dashing and bold, and utterly ruthless into the bargain, was one of Cornwallis' brigade leaders of cavalry, Colonel Banastre Tarleton. Here and there through the Carolinas rode Tarleton and his booted and spurred Redcoats, scattering the American militia and Continentals, seizing horses and supplies, burning and looting. "Tarleton is coming!" —that cry spread terror among the Carolina patriots during the spring of 1780, as many detachments and companies of Americans were run down and defeated, and broad areas of countryside were ravaged.

Near the settlement of Waxhaw, almost on the North Carolina-South Carolina line, lived Widow Jackson and her boys, John and Andrew, aged fifteen and thirteen. Scotch-Irish and fighters to the core, loyal to the cause of independence from England, the Jackson boys joined the men of the neighborhood in resisting one of Tarleton's raiding squadrons. The boys were captured. An officer commanded Andrew to shine his boots.

The spirited country lad refused; "I am your prisoner of war, sir—not your servant!"

This so enraged the Redcoat that he brought his sword down in a wicked stroke aimed at young Jackson's neck. Andrew threw up his hand and received a bad wound upon his wrist, and an anger in his heart at the British that never died.

Only the bravery, skill and devotion of such American officers as Francis Marion and Thomas Sumter kept the fires of resistance burning in that southern area. "The Swamp Fox," as the former was dubbed by Tarleton's men because he eluded all their attempts to capture him, and "The Gamecock," as Sumter was called, continually harassed the British, swinging in to attack detachments separated from the main command.

Since his victory at Saratoga, General Horatio Gates had been clamoring for greater recognition from Washington, and at the same time plotting with his friends in the Continental Congress to replace Washington as commander-in-chief. Washington was informed of Gates's intrigues, but he allowed no personal feeling to influence his decisions as to his officers in the field. "The good of the service" was the guiding star of all his actions.

"Gates commanded at Saratoga. I shall give him his chance to repeat his success," the general informed his staff.

Gates took the command in South Carolina in July 1780. Washington dispatched 2,000 troops, principally from Maryland and Pennsylvania, to strengthen the southern theater of war. Cornwallis was at Camden, South Carolina. On August 16 Gates attempted to surprise the British there, throwing his forces, mostly raw recruits, against the seasoned and well-disciplined Redcoats. Cornwallis out-generaled Gates at every turn. Utter defeat for the Americans was the result, with loss of more than eight hundred killed and a thousand taken prisoner. General Johann de Kalb, commanding the Maryland units, fought bravely until mortally wounded. Gates helped to swell the defeat into a disgraceful rout by joining the flight of his soldiers.

General Nathanael Greene replaced Gates. He found himself at the head of a dispirited army, with the men unpaid, hungry and discouraged. But Greene was not only an experienced military tactician; he possessed keen intelligence and an unflinching courage. And he had officers to match his ability and bravery: Daniel Morgan, now a brigadier general, with his turkey whistle and his Virginians; Baron von Steuben, who came down to drill the troops; and Colonel Thaddeus Kosciusko, dispatched by Washington to take charge of engineering for the struggling southern armies.

Greene ordered Kosciusko—now affectionately called "Colonel Koski" by all the soldiers—as his first assignment to find a suitable camp. Riding night and day, with a small staff of officers and men as hardy as himself, the colonel surveyed the strange terrain and selected what he called a "camp of repose" on the Peedee River. From there Greene wrote to Washington:

"We fight, get beaten and fight again."

The Fires of Resistance Still Burn

To the beleagured patriots of the south, two items of good news had come with heartening effect. First, there was evidence that France had begun to send substantial help to the struggling American colonies, in the form of foot soldiers. On July 10, 1779, 6,000 French troops under the command of Lieutenant General Jean Baptiste Rochambeau landed at Newport, and camped under the sheltering guns of the French fleet.

At midnight on July 15 Major General Anthony Wayne, veteran of the Quebec expedition, Ticonderoga and many later battles, personally led his troops in an assault upon Stony Point on the Hudson. Scaling the walls, "Mad Anthony" Wayne and his men captured this fortress, demonstrating that courage still burned fiercely in patriot hearts.

Now, in September 1780, came news of the darkest kind— the astonishing report of the treason of General Benedict Arnold. Washington had assigned to the hero of Quebec, of the Mohawk and Saratoga, the command at West Point. Unbalanced by festering jealousies and fears, Arnold schemed to betray the fortress to the enemy. He met with a British officer, Major John André, to complete the plans. André's capture saved West Point, but Arnold escaped. When General Washington heard this shocking news, he turned to his aide, Lieutenant Colonel Alexander Hamilton, and remarked:

"Who can be trusted now!"

Such was the darkest hour before dawn in the American Revolution. On October 7, 1780, at King's Mountain on the southern border of North Carolina, occurred a battle that definitely turned the tide of the campaign in the south. Curiously enough, the engagement was fought principally between Americans. About one thousand Tory sympathizers, enlisted by the British under the banner of "Loyalists," along with a company of British Rangers commanded by Major Patrick Ferguson, were camped on the crest of the ridge. A determined force of about nine hundred backwoodsmen volunteers, under Colonels John Sevier, Isaac Shelby and James Williams, marched to the attack. Charging up the sides of the mountain they used their squirrel rifles with deadly effect. The volunteers won a smashing victory, accounting for 119 of the enemy killed, including Major Ferguson, and about half the remainder wounded or prisoners. The American backwoodsmen lost twenty-eight killed and sixty-two wounded.

Another American victory was gained the following January, when General Morgan met and defeated Tarleton's forces at Cowpens, South Carolina. Still another engagement, at Guilford Court House, North Carolina, brought Greene's main force against that of Cornwallis, in a battle that could be called a draw, since Greene retreated with his forces intact, but which cost the British commander nearly a thousand casualties.

The gains encouraged the American troops to continue the initiative against Cornwallis, and there was even hope of an early end to the war. But the British general also had plans to end the war. He withdrew northward to Wilmington, North Carolina, and then on into Virginia, with the announced intention of subduing that large and important state. He knew that his Carolina campaign could never succeed while the middle and northern colonies supplied officers and men to the south. Furthermore, Cornwallis counted on the effective part the British navy could play in his plans for the conquest of Virginia.

The sea campaign between the British and French had intensified, with vessels of what was bravely called the "Continental Navy" cooperating with the French. Intrepid Captain John Paul Jones carried the challenge to the very coasts of Britain. Operating from French harbors while the main body of the British navy was engaged elsewhere, Captain Jones raided shipping, sailed completely around the British Isles, and won a brilliant victory in his flagship *Bonhomme Richard* over the English frigate *Serapis*. But King George's ministers were now grimly determined to answer the American threat and the power of French men-of-war by sending sufficient naval strength to support the land operations and win the war.

The spring of 1781 had touched the Virginia hills and valleys with green and the planters were busy with their fields, when Lord Cornwallis started northward in his triumphal march through Virginia. On May 20 he camped on the outskirts of Petersburg, and there the bivouacs of his sentries met those of another British force which General Clinton had sent to operate in the Chesapeake region. Into Cornwallis' tent walked the two commanders of this force, to counsel with their chief of the southern operations. One was General Phillips. The other was a man whom Cornwallis must have regarded with keen and speculative interest as he stood in his red-coated uniform, wearing the epaulettes of a British brigadier general. It was Benedict Arnold—ill at ease and obviously unhappy.

Cornwallis was disturbed to find that Clinton had sent these two officers with orders to harass Virginia while Cornwallis himself was expected to continue his operations in the Carolinas, and to learn that the British commander-in-chief did not choose to risk a major engagement that might result in defeat. However, Cornwallis confidently outlined his plan to operate in Virginia. He would have only victories, he said. The ambitious general knew that victories are always the proper answer to any questions concerning a commander's actions in the field.

And victories he proceeded to win, as he moved steadily northward to Fredericksburg. Tarleton was sent to overrun the central part of the colony. Making a sudden swoop upon Charlottesville, he almost captured a most noted Virginia rebel, the author of the Declaration of Independence and now the governor of the commonwealth—Thomas Jefferson.

There was little opposition, except that furnished by the corps of Generals Anthony Wayne and Lafayette. With a combined French and American force, these commanders maneuvered to delay the British advance as best they could. In July 1781 Lafayette made a daring attack upon the invaders at Green Spring, but was severely defeated, barely saving his force by a hasty retreat.

Cornwallis now set up his headquarters at Yorktown, situated on a peninsula formed by the James and York rivers. Here the distance from river to river was but eight miles. Cornwallis' scheme was to fortify himself about the village, and command the peninsula, secure in the belief that the British fleet would give him ample protection from the sea.

The Battle of the Chesapeake Capes

General Washington, informed of this situation, studied his maps intently. He knew the Virginia tidewater section intimately. He had his own army in camp at White Plains, New York, and not far away, in Rhode Island, he had available the French army of 6,000 troops under General Rochambeau. For a year these forces had remained in virtual idleness. If the French fleet could only hold off the British from the Chesapeake Bay, Cornwallis could be bottled up and his refuge become a trap.

On May 10 the French Commodore Barras de St. Laurent sailed into Newport harbor with several fighting ships to reinforce the squadron on guard. The commodore brought to Rochambeau the news that Rear Admiral François de Grasse was under orders to sail from Haitian waters, where he had been operating, to engage the British fleet off the American coast at any place of the admiral's choosing. Rochambeau galloped to Washington's headquarters with this welcome information.

"Where should my country's fleet meet the enemy?" Rochambeau asked.

"The navy must have the deciding vote," Washington replied.

The French frigate *La Concorde* was dispatched with a message begging Admiral de Grasse to move with all possible speed and to bring all the troops that the Haiti garrison could spare. *La Concorde* returned to Newport on August 12, with the admiral's word that he would bring around 3,000 troops under General St. Simon and would make for the Chesapeake capes.

Now Washington made one of the most important decisions of the entire War for Independence: to combine all possible forces against Cornwallis at Yorktown. He and Rochambeau would join Greene, Lafayette and all the southern units, and if the French fleet could control the waters off Virginia, the victory could be won. An immediate problem for the commander-in-chief was to withdraw his forces without arousing too great suspicion on the part of the British, and this he accomplished by a ruse. He wrote a letter to General Lafayette, in which he said:

I am greatly pleased with the probability that Earl Cornwallis will fortify either Portsmouth or Old Point Comfort, for, were he to fix upon Yorktown, from its great capabilities for defense, he might remain there snugly and unharmed, until a superior British fleet would relieve him with a strong reinforcement, or embark him altogether.

This letter was intercepted by the British, by the simple device of the messenger seeing to it that he was captured by some Redcoat sentries. Placed in General Clinton's hands, it had the desired effect of quieting any fears regarding an attack upon Cornwallis at Yorktown.

"*En avant!*" came Rochambeau's order. "Forward!"

With cheers and singing the French troops sallied forth from their stagnation and joined Washington's army on the Hudson. Then, in high spirits, the combined forces started one of the most important marches of history. Southward the long columns tramped, through New Jersey and into Pennsylvania. On the last day of August, Washington and his staff, at the head of their columns, reached Philadelphia, where several days were spent in rest and loading supplies. On September 5 the commander-in-chief reached Chester, and there a French rider gave him a dispatch from Lafayette with the joyful news that Admiral de Grasse's fleet had arrived off the Chesapeake.

On that very day the great naval battle was fought. Rear Admiral Thomas Graves had led his squadron down from New York to meet Admiral de Grasse. The French ships were unloading St. Simon's 3,000 troops off Cape Henry, Virginia, when sighted by the British. From his flagship *Ville de Paris*, De Grasse gave the order to bear out to sea. By excellent seamanship the French sailors were able to tack out of the channel and into open water before Graves gave his command:

"Bear down all, and engage!"

In late afternoon the first British salvos were loosed upon the French fleet. For two hours the vessels fought at close range, churning and roiling the waves off the Chesapeake capes. Admiral de Grasse gained the advantage in position and his cannon disabled several British men-of-war, including Admiral Graves's flagship *Princessa*. Several of the French ships were also crippled, but all remained afloat and all could be sailed after repairs.

At dusk Graves signaled the end of the battle and his wounded fleet hove northward, making toward New York, the nearest port of repair. While slowly en route, Graves lost two more frigates, captured by De Grasse's alert men-of-war.

At Elkton, Maryland, the marching French and American armies were loaded on ships, and started down the bay toward Yorktown. Washington stopped for three days at his home on the Potomac, entertaining Rochambeau and several other French and American officers. The commander-in-chief then rode ahead with his staff to Williamsburg, Virginia. At the edge of the town, waiting to escort him in honor, were the French generals Lafayette and St. Simon, who gave him the welcome news of the French naval victory. The commander-in-chief dispatched a message of congratulations to Admiral de Grasse, declaring that the victory gave the allies "the happiest Presages of the most compleat Success, in our combined Operations on this Bay."

So far, Providence had indeed smiled on Washington's plan for the joint naval-land campaign against Cornwallis. With the strong French fleet guarding the capes and the British fleet too crippled to attack again for some weeks, the troops at Yorktown could be invested with no hope of support or escape by sea. Furthermore, French Admiral St. Laurent came in from Newport with several big siege guns. At last, with both infantry and artillery superior to the enemy in numbers and firepower, the American and French commanders faced the final phase of the war with high confidence.

The Quarry Is at Bay

It is the afternoon of September 13, 1781. The 8,300 British officers and men, waiting behind the two lines of redoubts that almost circle Yorktown, watch the approaching columns of American and French troops. The Americans swing to the right, the French to the left, forming a semicircle about the town with each wing resting upon the York River.

Washington's principal American generals are Benjamin Lincoln and Henry Knox, and their forces number about 8,000. The French commanders, Rochambeau, Lafayette and St. Simon, hold in their combined corps a number about equal to the Americans. All are elated at the success of the plan of concentration, and all agree that an attack should not be forced until British resistance has been worn down by a siege. For three weeks the Allied forces make secure their investment of Yorktown, while French vessels patrol the Chesapeake to make sure no British naval aid can break through.

On the night of October 6 Washington gives the order for action. The besiegers move to within six hundred yards of the British lines, and in the darkness, as silently as possible, they break ground for breastworks. At daybreak the British discover the forward move, but the trenches and emplacements are so far along that the Redcoat artillery and musket fire do little damage. At the day's end, the redoubts are completed. French and American cannon begin to bark back their answers.

For three days the attacking guns single out the batteries of the British and pound them into near silence. Those nearest to the river throw red-hot balls into the frigate *Sharon* riding at anchor and into several transports, setting them afire. On the night of October 11 the second advance is made, this time to within three hundred yards of the British lines. Cornwallis tries desperately to stop the building of the nearer redoubts, but again his fire is ineffective.

There are more days and nights of waiting, and it is time to storm the British outer defenses. The move has been carefully planned by Washington and his generals. The commander-in-chief gives to Lafayette the honor of commanding the American detachment, while Baron de Vioment will lead the French. He selects the intelligent and ambitious officer, Alexander Hamilton, who for four years has been his private military secretary, for an honor all his own: Hamilton will command the battalion of light infantry leading the assault. Eagerly he makes ready his companies.

Now Washington's tall figure is the center of the eyes of all the troops ready for the charge upon the enemy redoubts. Their officers stand, swords drawn, ready to relay the order of their commanding general.

"Forward!"

"Forward the battalion!" shouts Hamilton.

"En avant!" echoes Vioment.

With closed ranks, in doubletime, the Americans and French advance. Hamilton's companies strike so suddenly that his infantrymen overwhelm the British works while the Redcoats are firing only a few shots. Colonel Laurens leads a column to the rear and prevents the retreat of those in the outer garrison. Meanwhile, the redoubts attacked by the French are offering strong resistance. With considerable loss on both sides they are finally taken.

General Washington stands where he can survey the movements through his glass. When the redoubts are taken, he draws a long breath, turns to General Knox and remarks:

"The work is done, and *well* done!"

Mounting his white charger, Nelson, the general stays in the saddle for hours, contacting all the commanders to make sure no weak links develop in the chain encircling Cornwallis.

The British commander is stunned with surprise and grief at the trap into which he has fallen, and enraged that help has not come. Where is Sir Henry Clinton, to whom he has been sending such glowing reports of his Carolina and Virginia victories? Why has Clinton not come to help? Why has the British fleet failed at this one moment when the fate of the war hangs by the thread of a battle?

In a council with his officers, Cornwallis sees one desperate chance remaining: to cross the York River under cover of darkness, reach Gloucester Point, elude the blockading French ships, seize whatever horses they can find and dash for the north. It means leaving all the sick and the wounded behind, and abandoning the supplies. But it will save the disgrace of surrender, and that to Cornwallis is paramount.

The British general attempts the escape. A few boats reach the opposite shore safely, when the very elements turn ally to the cause of American independence. A rain and wind storm rises, making it impossible to control the boats. The tempest continues until morning, when those who have crossed are glad to return to their lines.

For Cornwallis this spells the end. His ammunition is exhausted and his food almost gone. He tells his generals and staff that he would rather die than surrender. They leave him alone in the room of the house that has served as his headquarters. On that afternoon, October 17, Cornwallis sends a flag of truce, asking for an end to hostilities for twenty-four hours. Washington and his commanders fear the British fleet might be returning full force to break the siege. They allow Cornwallis only two hours to transmit his proposals.

"Proclaim Liberty!"

Thus ended the siege and the battle of Yorktown. There was little to agree upon among the opposing commanders except for the terms of the parole of the troops under unconditional surrender. At noon on October 19, 1781, the Allied armies were drawn up in two lines more than a mile in length, the Americans on the right and the French on the left. Standing proudly in the line of commanding officers were Lafayette, Baron von Steuben, and Kosciusko—still a colonel. The

French troops were resplendent in their blue-gray uniforms with crimson trimmings, presenting quite a contrast to the worn, hard-bitten appearance of the American soldiers, some of whom had carried their muskets for more than six years of fighting. But all stood with soldierly bearing, the feel of victory in their hearts.

This was the end, the American officers and men well knew. The war would soon be over. The British could never again muster and send over an army after such a defeat as this, and after the French alliance had thrown such odds in the new nation's favor.

Washington and his staff rode out. A veritable storm of cheering broke out, as men placed their hats upon the ends of their muskets and raised them aloft, shouting their tributes to their beloved commander.

Cornwallis, sick at heart, sent General Charles O'Hara forward to give over his sword. Washington asked General Lincoln to receive this trophy of surrender. Lincoln took the sword and without hesitation handed it back.

The next day was Sunday, and Washington ordered a special divine service to be read in each brigade of the American army. He also called upon his fellow citizens to be grateful for the divine leadership that had brought them through the hardships of the revolution. In a general order announcing the victory, Washington expressed his thanks to the French for their gallant assistance on land and sea.

"Cornwallis has surrendered!" The news spread by courier and post through all the land. Washington dispatched one of his aides to Philadelphia to inform the Congress. The rider reached the city while it was wrapt in the silence of midnight, but he pressed on to the house of Delegate Thomas McKean, president of the Continental body.

"Cornwallis is taken, sir!" His words awoke the sleeping chairman, who ordered that all the watchmen be notified.

"One o'clock, and Cornwallis has surrendered!" they cried. The old bellman was awakened, and hurrying to the Hall, he pulled the rope that sent the vibrant tones ringing over the city, every peal seeming to say again, as on July 4, 1776, the words inscribed upon that bell:

"Proclaim liberty throughout all the land and to all the inhabitants thereof."

CHAPTER SIX

Perry Meets the Enemy on Lake Erie

On the morning of June 22, 1807, the thirty-eight-gun American naval frigate *Chesapeake* set sail from the bay for which she was named, heading out across the Atlantic for the Mediterranean, with Commodore James Barron aboard. Her lookouts saw that their ship was being followed by the British frigate *Leopard,* of fifty-two guns. Britain and France were at war, and vessels of the British navy were patrolling American waters in search of their enemy—and also in search of deserters from British ships.

At 3:30, when the *Chesapeake* and her British pursuer were about ten miles southeast of Cape Henry, the master of the *Leopard,* Captain S. P. Humphreys, hailed the American ship and asked to send over a message. Both ships trimmed sail and a British officer was rowed over to the *Chesapeake.* In terse language, the message demanded that the master of the *Chesapeake* permit a British boarding party to search the ship to see if there were any deserting British seamen among the crew. Commodore Barron wrote a reply:

"I know of no such men you describe. The officers that were on the recruiting service for this ship were particularly instructed by my Government, through me, not to enter any deserters from His Britannic Majesty's ships, nor do I know of any being here. . . ."

Anxiously officers and crewmen of the American frigate

saw that the British crew stood by their guns at battle stations, but it seemed unthinkable that the *Leopard* had orders to commit an act of war against a neutral ship. As the *Leopard* spread sail and edged closer, a shot from one of its guns roared over the *Chesapeake's* bow. Captain Humphreys, standing at the rail of his ship, shouted:

"Commodore Barron, you must be aware of the necessity I am under of complying with the orders of my commander-in-chief!"

Only then did the men of the *Chesapeake*, scattered from their stations and unprepared for action, realize that they faced an attack. At an order from Humphreys, a full broadside thundered from the *Leopard*, its solid shot and canister striking the *Chesapeake* point-blank at 175 feet. Two more broadsides from the British vessel completed the destruction of many of the masts, stays and other equipage of the hapless frigate. Only one shot from the *Chesapeake* answered, fired by a lieutenant who carried a live coal from the galley to his gun. As Barron struck his flag in surrender, the Americans counted three of their crew killed and eighteen wounded. The British boarding party seized four seamen—three of them American citizens and only one a British subject.

. "My country will hear of this outrage, sir!" shouted the commodore. The United States did hear of it, and there was high indignation. The event was only one in a long list of impressments of seamen from American bases and ships, often done without regard to proof of either British citizenship or desertion, in that first decade of the nineteenth century. In her war with France, England was challenging the power of Napoleon Bonaparte. Her major task was to cut off French shipping and thus "reduce the emperor's head by shrinking his waistline," as one British minister put it. This meant an embargo on trade from the United States and other neutral countries.

Napoleon was equally scornful of the rights of neutral peoples. He cared nothing for the friendship that Americans extended to the French for help in winning independence. He issued the notorious "Milan Decree" which said in effect, "Any neutral vessel that permits itself to be searched by a British gunboat shall be considered as British, and become the lawful prize of any French vessel."

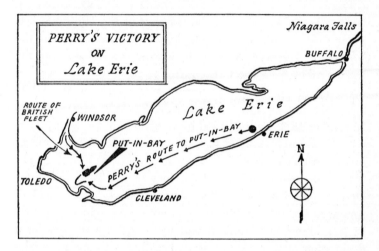

To make this crossfire worse for the United States, the British navy badly needed sailors, and was not too particular where it found them. "This man is suspected of desertion; we must take him!" was a frequent formula for impressment of a seaman. To an American, freedom included freedom of the seas. It meant that the oceanways of commerce must be free from molestation of persons and property, subject only to the well-defined rules of blockade in time of war. "Free bottoms make free goods and free sailors" was the motto.

President Jefferson sincerely believed that an embargo act, prohibiting commerce with both Britain and France, would maintain neutrality with these two belligerents. It only served to choke off what little trade remained, and President Madison was glad to sign its repeal.

Contributing to the tension between the United States and Great Britain was the land greed of many political leaders and citizens of the northwestern states and territories. Many "expansionists" openly advocated the annexation of Canada, with or without war.

From Canadian bases, British military leaders stirred up Indians to make war upon the frontiers of the United States. Their best recruit was an intelligent Shawnee chief in the Northwest Territory, Tecumseh, who attempted to rally the Indian tribes from the Great Lakes to the Gulf of Mexico in a confederation to oppose further settlements by the white men. His campaign met defeat at the Battle of Tippecanoe in November 1811, by forces led by General William Henry Harrison. Tecumseh escaped to Canada and was made an officer in the British service.

By the early months of 1812, files of the War and Navy Departments listed more than 6,000 cases of impressment of American seamen and illegal seizure of property by the British. In June, President Madison sent to Congress a request for a declaration of war, in a message bristling with specific violations of American rights.

The Unique War Begins

British statesmen had never considered the new nation on the North American continent as more than a collection of uncouth, imprudent backwoodsmen. Now they were to see the Young Giant of the West gather himself for an effort toward national greatness.

Still, the people of the United States were never united in support of this second war with Great Britain. Those who hoped to revive trade as usual, as in the New England states, actively opposed the war. The conflict was quite unique in other respects: the United States ground troops suffered about as many defeats as they won victories; although the nation had practically no navy at the start, the war's most decisive battle was a naval engagement, well-planned and bravely fought—on the fresh waters of Lake Erie; the British captured Washington, burned the capitol and the President's Mansion, but still failed to win the war; the second decisive battle—General Andrew Jackson's victory at New Orleans—was fought after peace terms had been signed. And finally, the peace treaty itself aroused storms of criticism on the part of officials of both governments, yet proved to be the most just, profitable and lasting peace of modern times.

It was certain that the war would be fought on both land and sea. Although heavily engaged in the Napoleonic wars, the British could muster the veterans of many a European campaign to add to their Canadian forces. Against them would be little more than bands of American militia and a small, poorly equipped regular army.

On the sea, the contrast was even more startling. The United States had barely begun to build a navy. There were only sixteen ships of war, of all classes, including eight light sloops of from one to ten guns, and eight brigs and frigates, the heaviest of 1,576 tons and thirty-eight guns. Opposing this puny strength, the British numbered the greatest navy of the world, more than a thousand sail of all sizes, a veritable armada of fighting power and strength.

Theodore Roosevelt wrote, from long study of the naval actions of this second war with Britain:

During the early years of this century England's naval power stood at a height never reached before or since by that of any other nation. On every sea her navies rode, not only triumphant, but with none to dispute their sway. The Island Folk had long claimed the mastery of the ocean, and they had certainly succeeded in making their claim completely good during the time of bloody warfare that followed the breaking out of the French Revolution.

And with its traditions of valor, of invincibility, and of the defeat of the Spanish Armada in 1588—when the might of Spain foundered beneath Sir Francis Drake's skillful attack in the English Channel—the Island Kingdom's rule had grown more powerful every year. Since 1792 every major European nation had felt the mighty force of England's naval blows: Sir Samuel Hood had vanquished the Russians in the Baltic; Sir Hyde Parker had defeated the entire Danish Navy at Copenhagen; Lord Duncan had shattered the Dutch fleet at Camperdown. And Horatio Nelson, mightiest of the naval commanders to fly the colors of Britain in the closing years of the old century and the opening years of the new, had established the British Navy's supremacy in the Mediterranean, and in his dying moments at Trafalgar had decisively defeated the combined navies of Spain and France.

But it must be remembered that the United States Navy, young and weak as it was, had some compensating assets. There was the inspiring memory of John Paul Jones and his refusal to admit defeat though his ship was sinking beneath him. Several engagements with French frigates in the West Indies in 1800 had proved that American seamen, given experience, could hold their own in combat. Then, in 1804–1805, it was the United States Navy that had broken the oppression of the Tripolitan pirates of the Barbary Coast, when their black-handed demands for "tribute or fight" were met by fight—carried to their very reeking harbors by such gallant commanders as Stephen Decatur.

American sailors were of the same race as the English, with the same traditions of free men, and with the distinct advantage of being all volunteers. No impressment of sailors sullied the records of the young navy, and the cruelty of a stern and unbending discipline, pride of the British admiral's heart, was happily unknown on the ships of the United States. Many sailor-boys enlisted at twelve and thirteen, and in contrast to their British cousins could grow to robust young manhood beneath the masts flying the American flag without their spirits broken or their backs covered with the welts of frequent floggings.

During the early months of the war, several individual naval battles brought to the Americans the thrilling news of victory. Near Newfoundland, Captain Isaac Hull of the American frigate *Constitution* met the British *Guerrière* and won a smashing triumph, with the loss of only fourteen men against eighty-one for the enemy. Off the North Carolina coast the American *Wasp* outfought the British *Macedonian*. Again the *Constitution's* flag fluttered in victory as the British ship *Java* was made to strike. The British admiralty was humiliated by these defeats.

"Annex Canada!" was the cry of some patriots, especially in the great Northwest Territory. General William Hull, governor of Michigan Territory, set out from Detroit with about twenty-five hundred troops to launch such a campaign. He was met by a force of Canadians, British and Indians under General Isaac Brock and severely defeated. Detroit fell to British hands, and with it the control of Lake Erie.

A Young Officer Builds a Fleet

Commodore Isaac Chauncey was in command of the American squadron on Lake Ontario. His ships were few but his foresight was great. He proposed to the Navy Department that the British threat to the Northwest Territory be met by purchasing and building enough ships to regain Lake Erie, to the west. Already he had ordered the construction of two brigs at Presque Isle on this lake, near Erie Harbor. Many more vessels would be needed, and quickly. The commodore cast about for the man to superintend the plan, and decided upon a twenty-six-year-old Navy lieutenant, Oliver Hazard Perry.

"You are the very person I want for a service in which you may gain reputation for yourself and honor for your country," Chauncey wrote the young officer.

Lieutenant Perry came naturally by his love of ships and the sea, for his father was a Rhode Island naval captain and enlisted Oliver at fourteen as a midshipman. When he was seventeen young Perry sailed with the ships fighting the Barbary pirates. Now he was in command of a small squadron of gunboats at Newport, guarding the coastal waters from Narragansett Bay to New York Harbor. His superiors considered him a highly intelligent, daring officer, his almost effeminate beauty masking a stern and decisive nature.

Lieutenant Perry accepted the commodore's assignment— and the accompanying commission as commander—with alacrity. Here was the promise of the kind of adventure the young seadog craved. Volunteering to go with him were 149 fellow Rhode Islanders, including his twelve-year-old brother, Alexander. On February 22, 1813, Commander Perry set out for Commodore Chauncey's headquarters on Lake Ontario; and there the plan to bolster Lake Erie was nearly wrecked by the man who conceived it. Chauncey feared that an attack might be made upon his own base and ships, and held Perry and his men for two weeks before issuing the restless young officer his orders to proceed.

Tucking away in his luggage his new brevet captain's commission, Oliver Hazard Perry led his men to Buffalo, thence ninety miles farther west across the frozen lake to Erie, on the Pennsylvania shore. Here was a thriving town of about 450 population, important center for supplies for the great Northwest Territory. Not an American ship remained on Lake Erie, as all had been captured when Hull surrendered Detroit. Half a dozen British ships were under sail, determined to prevent the building of an American fleet.

Chauncey had selected Presque Isle for the shipbuilding

because the shallow water and sandy bars afforded protection from enemy vessels. Perry found that Shipwright Brown, appropriately christened Noah, had laid the keels and the oaken ribs for two brigs. The captain threw his boundless energy into supervising the work. He hired the best carpenters and blacksmiths he could find. The keels of four schooners were also laid. From the Ohio and Pennsylvania forests were hewed the ribs, stays, planking and trim, out of stalwart growths of oak, hickory, chestnut and pine. Most of the material for equipage —rope, sails, cannon, ammunition and the like—had to be hauled from Albany by way of Buffalo, or from Philadelphia by way of Pittsburgh, weary distances that stretched nearly 400 miles over winding, muddy roads.

"Bring it up! Bring it up! Hurry!" was Captain Perry's constant urging. Spring had come, summer would soon be on them, and the British would be trying an invasion across the lakes. Already their ships cruised threateningly, observing the work at Presque Isle.

General Daniel Mead of the Pennsylvania militia cooperated by bringing a regiment of troops and camping in the woods close by the water. Whenever the British ships appeared, the general would call out his troops for a review, and in plain view of the British sea fighters the regiment would parade upon the beach and back into the woods, each company hurrying around while out of sight to join the procession again. Peering through their spyglasses, British officers wondered at the mighty army the Americans seemed to have assembled there.

Late in May, hearing that Chauncey planned to attack Fort George, the British stronghold on the northern bank of the Niagara River, Perry went to Buffalo and helped to lead the successful assault. General Brock was forced to abandon the Niagara frontier, and of tremendous importance to Perry, five American ships were released that had been bottled up by Canadian guns covering the river. They were the *Caledonia*, captured by Lieutenant Jesse D. Elliot early in the war, and the *Amelia*, *Tripp*, *Somers* and *Ohio*, purchased months previously by the navy. On June 18 Perry brought his ships triumphantly into the harbor of Erie.

Soon afterward, there occurred a battle near Boston Harbor that gave Perry a motto and the United States Navy a proud tradition. The *Chesapeake*, now commanded by Captain James Lawrence, set out to encounter the British frigate *Shannon*, which was cruising menacingly off the coast. Lawrence luffed up within fifty yards of the crew of the enemy ship and a sharp battle began. Both the guns and the crew of the *Shannon* proved the better. The *Chesapeake*'s rigging was shot away and many of her guns disabled. Captain Lawrence, standing bravely on deck in view of enemy marksmen, was mortally wounded. "Don't give up the ship!" were his last words.

Fired by such gallantry, Captain Perry gained permission from the navy to name one of his brigs the *Lawrence*. This was to be his flagship. The other brig was named *Niagara*, and the schooners *Ariel*, *Scorpion*, *Porcupine* and *Tigress*.

British Commodore R. H. Barclay brought his squadron and dropped anchor off Presque Isle, clearly intent upon preventing the launching of the new vessels. Barclay was a veteran naval officer, shrewd, capable, thoroughly experienced. He had served with Nelson at Trafalgar, and his greatest pride was that he had lost an arm in this historic engagement, as the British admiral had lost one previously. He was anxious to meet this young American whipper-snapper at the first opportunity.

Undaunted, Perry begged Chauncey for seamen, soldiers, marines—anybody to man his craft and put up a fight: "Think of my Situation—the enemy within striking distance, my vessels ready, and I am obliged to bite my fingers with vexation for want of men!" Chauncey sent all the men he felt it was safe to spare.

On Sunday, July 18, two itinerant preachers, described by Perry as "respectable missionaries," came on board the *Lawrence*, and prayed at great length for the success of the young captain's impending venture at arms.

— On August 1 the British squadron, tired of idle watching, sailed away. Perry seized the opportunity. The schooners were launched, passing the bars easily. But the *Lawrence* and the *Niagara* drew too much water. For four days Perry and his men worked feverishly, unloading the cannon on the shore and chaining large casks, called "camels," beneath the waterline. Enough buoyancy was thus obtained to lift the keels over the sand. While this was in progress, several of Barclay's ships returned, but General Mead paraded his regiment again and sent a ball from his biggest cannon whirring out over the water. Barclay withdrew his ships and assembled them at Malden, near the western end of the lake.

Chauncey dispatched Elliot, now a captain, to take command of the *Niagara* and with him six officers and eighty men. General Harrison sent one hundred men from his army, many of them expert gunners and some experienced at sea. Perry's force now totaled 490, about 125 of which were seamen or soldiers from Rhode Island. There was a platoon of Kentucky sharpshooters and a detachment of free Negroes recruited by the commodore with the promise of action on Lake Erie. On August 6, with shouts from the crews of all the ships, Perry's squadron set sail and anchored at Sandusky Bay on the southern shore of the lake about thirty-five miles from Toledo and thirty miles south of the British squadron at Malden.

Perry had under his command nine vessels: his flagship *Lawrence*, of twenty guns; the *Niagara*, Captain Elliot, twenty guns; the *Caledonia*, Lieutenant David Turner, three guns;

the schooner *Ariel,* Lieutenant John H. Packet, four guns; the schooner *Somers,* Lieutenant A. H. M. Conklin, two guns and two swivels; the schooner *Scorpion,* Sailing-Master Stephen Champlin, two guns; and the schooners *Tigress,* Sailing-Master Thomas C. Almy, and *Porcupine,* Sailing-Master George Serrat, and the sloop *Tripp,* Lieutenant Thomas Holdup, one gun each.

In manpower the British commodore had slightly more than 500 men, including 150 of the Royal Navy, 240 regular soldiers, 80 Canadian sailors, and a few Canadian militia and Indians. In Barclay's squadron were his flagship, the *Detroit,* nineteen guns and two howitzers; the frigate *Queen Charlotte,* seventeen guns; the brig *Hunter,* ten guns; the schooner *Lady Prevost,* thirteen guns and two howitzers; the schooner *Chippewa,* three guns; and the sloop *Little Belt,* three guns. While Perry outnumbered his antagonist in ships and total tonnage, Barclay had sixty-three guns to Perry's fifty-four, and thirty-five of the British guns were cannon of long range, against eighteen such guns on the American ships. Perry had a greater number of carronades (short, wide-mouthed guns made at the famous Carron iron works in Scotland), very effective at close range, while Barclay's long-range guns gave the commodore an advantage at a distance.

The British commander had still another advantage. As August wore on, at least one hundred of the American force were in sick bay with what Dr. Usher Parsons, the squadron's surgeon and Perry's most trusted friend, called "lake fever."

General Harrison came up to visit the squadron and to offer suggestions to the youthful navy captain. The hero of Tippecanoe advised Perry to move to a sheltered cove called Put-in-Bay. He doubtless discussed also the importance of the impending battle. The British were awaiting only a victory on Lake Erie to make a bold expedition to annex the whole Northwest Territory to Canada.

Perry knew that the eyes of the nation were upon him as he faced a battle by which, in the expressive words of the historian George Bancroft:

the defeat of the Americans would yield to the British the superiority in arms on the land, bare the shores of the Ohio to ruthless havoc and ravage, leave Detroit and the far West in the power of the English king, let loose the savage with his tomahawk on every family of emigrants along the border, and dishonor the star-spangled banner on the continent and on the lakes.

From Put-in-Bay, on September 6, Perry reconnoitered Malden and found the entire British squadron in battle array, the ships freshly painted, with canvas and rigging in trim and decks cleared for action. Returning to base he found a delegation of ladies from Erie, escorted by their gentlemen, waiting to make a presentation. As Captain Perry, backed by his staff, stood stiffly at attention, one of the ladies stepped forward, and with a pleasant little speech placed in his hands a folded ensign.

"Fly this from your flagship, Captain Perry," she said.

It was blue, and in letters of white were stitched the words "DON'T GIVE UP THE SHIP."

On September 9 Perry called the commanders and first officers of all his ships to the deck of the *Lawrence*. With them was Surgeon Parsons, to whom posterity is indebted for a vivid account of activities both before and during the battle.

"Our navy is young, gentlemen, but we shall soon have an opportunity to establish its glory," said the captain. "I shall take the lead. Watch closely my orders, and keep the lines intact." The fight must be at close quarters, Perry continued, and each of the British ships must be engaged by one or more of those of the American squadron. Perry called for his brother Alexander, and the lad brought out the ensign, "DON'T GIVE UP THE SHIP."

"When this standard is hoisted at the mainyard, it shall be your signal for going into action," the captain said.

The officers cheered, and the cheer was caught up by the men on all the ships.

"To the Battle Stations!"

It is a rosy dawn of September 10, and the American ships make out from shore northwestward. Near midmorning the lookouts call "Sail Ho! Enemy in sight!"

"Enemy in sight! All hands make ready!" rings the command.

The British vessels bear down grandly with the wind, prows cutting spray, red ensigns fluttering and guns grimly nosing from the stations. Again Perry calls the commanders to his deck, and his crisp words repeat the orders of yesterday. Noting that the *Chippewa* is ahead, followed by the *Detroit*, then the *Hunter, Queen Charlotte, Lady Prevost* and the *Little Belt,* Perry directs the schooners *Ariel* and *Scorpion* to range ahead on the larboard bow of the *Lawrence* to engage the *Chippewa,* while his flagship will engage that of the British commodore, and Captain Elliot, second in command in the squadron, will bring the other ships into line of action. Perry shakes hands with each officer, and they hurriedly take to their boats. Up goes the blue ensign on the flagship.

"All hands to the battle stations!" is the command, echoing from ship to ship. Now the decks are sprinkled with sand, to prevent them becoming slippery with blood during the battle. The sails are set and the ships make into line.

The three small "Sister Islands" lie between the two squadrons, and Perry's first objective is to beat to the windward of them, thus gaining the weather gauge, and to bear down upon his foe with the wind. This he commands Sailing-Master Taylor to do, but the wind is light, and slackening. The ships make little headway.

"Run the ship to the leeward of the islands!" Perry orders.

"But we should have to engage the enemy from the leeward!" Taylor responds.

"No matter now! To the leeward, or windward, they shall fight today!" the captain calls.

With the good fortune that often rewards audacity, Perry finds the wind suddenly shifting from the southeast. Thus he gains the weather gauge. The ships come slowly on the moderate breeze. It is 11 o'clock. The usual noonday grog is served early to all hands.

Perry gives Surgeon Parsons the papers he is to throw overboard in case of defeat and sends him below to his operating room. Six men are detailed to carry the wounded below and attend the dressings. Lieutenant Yarnall and Alexander Perry are close beside the captain as he goes from gun to gun on his final inspection. The men have all bound handkerchiefs over their heads and tied their sashes tightly about their waists. Perry cordially greets a number of sailors who have served on the *Constitution*. The Rhode Islanders from Newport give him a special cheer. The gunners stand to their pieces, the huge matches ready to light, while the loaders stand with balls, powder cartridges or swabs in their hands. The Kentucky marksmen have taken the places of honor they rightly deserve, up in the rigging where the give and take of battle will be most exciting.

"Are you ready, boys?" Perry calls out.

"Aye, all ready, sir!"

The challengers of the line are about one mile apart. There is tense silence until 11:45, when a bugle sounds on the *Detroit*, and the first blast of fire from the British flagship shatters the autumn calm. The ball falls short of the *Lawrence*. The second shot crashes squarely into the side of the American ship. A gun on the *Scorpion* answers. British long-range guns come freely into play, all trained on the *Lawrence*. Not one of Perry's guns as yet can match this range. For fifteen minutes his ship receives that fire as she advances. Several shots take severe effect. Finally, gaining range and favorable position, the *Lawrence* opens fire, followed by all the longer guns of the squadron. A few minutes later the carronades open, at first falling short, then gaining the range.

Still the shot rains upon the American flagship, piercing her sides, cutting her rigging, killing and wounding many of the crew. The British plan now is clear: to destroy the American ships separately. All in Barclay's squadron are blazing away at the *Lawrence*. One shot knocks a gunner's candle into the magazine. The gunner rushes to seize the sputtering tallow, extinguishing the flame just in time to prevent an explosion that would blow the ship to pieces. This man is never identified, and remains an unknown hero whose one timely act saves the day for his ship—and for the embattled fleet.

So rapidly are the guns of the American flagship disabled that within half an hour only three of the larger cannon can be brought to bear upon the enemy. But stern discipline prevails. The men detailed to assist the surgeon carry the wounded below to the dressing room as quickly as possible. Others of the crew step up to fill the places of the disabled at the aiming sights, the swabs, the loading tongs and the touch-holes.

"We Have Met the Enemy——"

Meanwhile, the *Caledonia* and the *Somers* are firing at the *Queen Charlotte*, the *Hunter* and the British flagship; the three smaller vessels are engaging the *Lady Prevost* and *Little Belt*. The *Niagara* is firing, principally at the *Queen Charlotte*, but has not come into good range. Despite the fire upon his vessel, Perry signals the ships to close in. All except the *Niagara* respond at once, and the firing grows to full fury. Although carrying the second officer in command and some of the most experienced seamen, the *Niagara* lags astern. Through fear, or from jealousy of his acting commodore, Captain Elliot fails to carry out the order to come into close action.

The carnage on the *Lawrence* is frightful. The sand on her decks is red with blood, and the dead and wounded are littering the stations and companionways. All the sharpshooters in the rigging have fallen, killed or wounded. Lieutenant Yarnall, his head bandaged for a bad scalp wound, still gives orders and renders superb support to his chief.

The flagship is running perilously short of effective men. Some who have been below, sick in their bunks, come to the decks to take their places wherever they can be used. Dr. Parsons relates in his account:

When the battle had raged an hour and a half, I heard a call for me at the small skylight, and stepping toward it, I saw it was the commodore, whose countenance was calm and placid as if on ordinary duty. "Doctor," he said, "send me one of your men,"— meaning one of the six that were to assist me; which was done instantly. In five minutes the call was repeated and obeyed; and at the seventh call, I told him he had them all. He asked if any could pull a rope, when two or three of the wounded crawled upon the deck to lend a feeble hand in pulling at the last guns.

Two of the wounded are killed before the surgeon's eyes by cannon balls that barely miss him. He stoops to lift a sailor with a shattered arm just before a shot passes where his head has been. On the floor, fatally wounded, is Lieutenant John Brooks, son of the governor of Massachusetts, who keeps asking how the battle is going.

The deadly fire of the American ships is having its effect. Captain Finnis and Lieutenant Stokes of the *Queen Charlotte* are both killed. Still the ship, under command of Second Lieutenant Irvine, vigorously engages the *Lawrence*. Lieutenant Garland of the *Detroit* falls mortally wounded. At 2 o'clock Perry observes a lull in the *Detroit*'s firing, not knowing at the time that Commodore Barclay himself is severely wounded and has been carried below. The command of the British flagship falls to Second Lieutenant Inglis, at a time when seamanship of the highest order is needed to maintain the vessel's position for effective fire.

The *Lawrence* now becomes completely unmanageable. Every brace is shot away, the canvas and rigging in tatters. The *Niagara* is seen at last closing up. Apparently Elliot weighs the probability that Perry has been disabled and decides that he can assume command of the squadron.

Suddenly, Perry makes a momentous decision. He signals the *Niagara*, now half a mile distant to the larboard, to stand by. Then he hauls down his blue ensign. Supposing that the American commander is making ready to surrender and that they have won the battle, British crewmen raise a cheer. But no —the American flag is not lowered from the shot-splintered mast. Turning the command of the *Lawrence* over to Lieutenant Yarnall, Perry selects four oarsmen and swings down into a boat. His brother Alexander follows him.

Standing in full view of friend and foe alike, the intrepid commodore, his ensign under his arm, is rowed to the *Niagara*, to the cheers of the smoke-blackened Americans on all their ships—in the rigging, on the decks, at the lines and the firing stations. Shot falls all about the boat and many a British marksman tries his skill in vain at this choice moving target. Yarnall now runs down his colors, as the *Lawrence* is completely out of action.

Perry takes command of the *Niagara*. Up goes his banner— DON'T GIVE UP THE SHIP. The astonished Elliot is ordered to signal up the smaller vessels into closer action. They come into line and their guns and carronades boom and blast with telling effect. Perry brings the *Niagara* to the windward of the

Lady Prevost and rakes the British schooner with deadly fire. For the first time, the American commander's fire is completely effective, and the *Lady Prevost* is silenced. The *Caledonia* follows closely, and both American frigates give raking fire to the foremost ships of the British line, while the small vessels rain grape and canister. A gun on the *Ariel* explodes, and a carronade on the *Scorpion,* overloaded by inexperienced gunners, recoils from its position and falls overboard. Despite such mishaps, every American commander gives gallant account of himself, and the same must be said of the British. In this battle, brave men are fighting the brave.

Perry now makes a bold and decisive stroke—such an action as characterizes many battles that have turned upon one courageous move. Fortunately, the comparative inaction of the *Niagara* has left her fresh and almost uninjured. Signaling the *Caledonia* to maintain close distance, Perry veers his ship squarely to cut the British line. The *Niagara* makes between the *Detroit, Queen Charlotte,* and *Hunter* on her starboard quarter, and the *Chippewa, Little Belt* and *Lady Prevost* on her port. Crewmen on the *Detroit* pull at her sails, trying to bring the vessel around broadside to the passing *Niagara,* but in the movement their flagship runs afoul of the disabled *Queen Charlotte.* Both broadsides of the *Niagara* now roar and thunder their shot, raking the *Detroit* and *Queen Charlotte* from bows to sterns, and literally splintering the sides and decks of the smaller ships.

At 3:30 a lieutenant on the *Queen Charlotte* waves a white handkerchief on the end of a pike, as the ship's colors come down. Next the *Detroit's* flags are lowered in surrender. Further resistance is useless, and in quick succession the flags of *Hunter* and *Lady Prevost* are struck. The *Little Belt* and *Chippewa* trim sail for flight and make out into the lake, but Sailing-Master Champlin in the *Scorpion* and Lieutenant

Holdup in the *Tripp* set out in pursuit. The last shot of the battle is fired by Champlin as the schooner and sloop overtake and capture the fugitives.

"And They Are Ours!"

Thus the battle ended, and thus for the first time in history an entire squadron of the proud British navy was captured.

Perry was rowed again to the *Lawrence,* and on its blood-soaked deck he wrote this brief, historic report to General Harrison: "We have met the enemy, and they are ours: Two Ships, two Brigs, one Schooner and one Sloop."

To the Honorable William Jones, Secretary of the Navy, the victorious captain penned a somewhat longer account. Then he called the surviving British officers, and those not too badly wounded, to assemble on deck the *Lawrence,* where they gave up their swords in surrender. Alarmed that he could not locate his brother Alexander, Perry dispatched a hunting party who found the boy in his bunk, fast asleep.

That evening the seamen on both sides who had given their lives in battle were consigned to the waters of the lake, and next day a funeral service was held for both the American and the British officers, with burial together on the shore.

The victory cost the Americans twenty-seven killed and three more who died of wounds, and ninety-three others wounded. Of these, the *Lawrence* furnished twenty-two of the dead and sixty-one wounded. The British losses were even greater in killed, numbering forty-one, with 110 wounded. Commodore Barclay's wound cost him his remaining arm and hastened his death.

The victory filled American hearts with hope and confidence. Harrison moved quickly to recover the territory held by the British in Ohio, and pursued their force into Canada. On October 5 he won a signal victory on the Thames. During the engagement, the Indian Chief Tecumseh was killed. Detroit was freed, and the war in the whole Northwest came to an end.

The steadfast courage of a youthful naval captain in the face of almost certain defeat inspired his squadron to victory and added a glorious chapter to the story of the new navy of a young and indomitable nation.

CHAPTER SEVEN

Jackson Defeats the British at New Orleans

American patriots hoped that the victory on Lake Erie and General William Henry Harrison's successes that followed would bring this second war with Britain to an end. But they were doomed to disappointment. British vessels, patrolling the Atlantic coast, tightened their blockades against American shipping from Maine to the Gulf. During the winter and spring of 1814, the United States' trade with the world was almost cut off.

In the late summer the British shifted the war to Washington, the capital. Their fleet, commanded by Admiral George Cockburn, defiantly sailed up Chesapeake Bay and disembarked on Maryland soil about 5,000 troops under General Robert Ross. On the evening of August 23 the vanguard of this army reached Bladensburg, near the District of Columbia line.

Washington was supposed to be defended by about 7,000 troops, including several squadrons of sailors, but most of the units were poorly equipped and wretchedly lacking in discipline. Citizens of the capital spent an anxious night.

As anxious as the rest was President James Madison, who sent his wife Dorothy (called "Dolly" by her husband and her friends) in a carriage to Virginia to be out of danger, and at early dawn met with his Cabinet at the Navy Yard to decide what to do next. All available troops had assembled south and west of Bladensburg. Soon after noon the British began

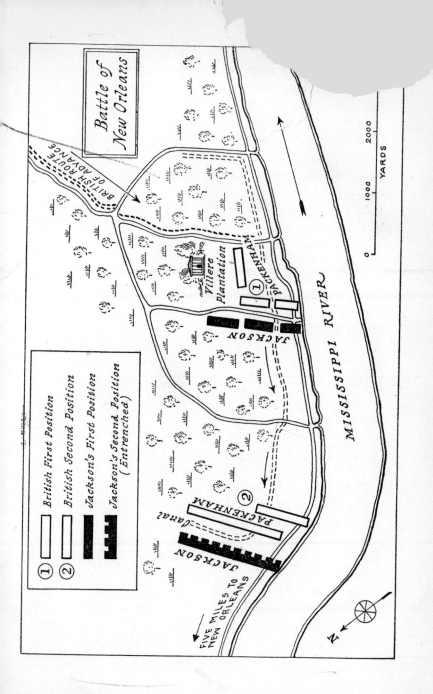

Battle of
New Orleans

BRITISH ROUTE
OF ADVANCE

Villere
Plantation

PACKENHAM

JACKSON

PACKENHAM

JACKSON

Canal

MISSISSIPPI RIVER

FIVE MILES TO
NEW ORLEANS

N

British First Position

British Second Position

Jackson's First Position

Jackson's Second Position
(Entrenched)

① ②

0   1000   2000

YARDS

th no plan of battle and no firm leadership, the Americans broke and ran when the firing grew hot. The sailors put up the best resistance, but when their support fell away, they too beat a retreat. The President and his Cabinet members rode to the scene, just in time to be swept along by the tide of fleeing soldiers. The inglorious retreat moved westward, north of Washington, and into the roadways of Maryland.

As the first columns of victorious Redcoats neared the northeast edge of the wooded park in front of the capitol building, a shot rang out from a house bordering the street and Ross's horse fell beneath him. Enraged at this hostile act, the general vowed vengeance upon the whole city—which he had already decided upon in retaliation for the burning of some buildings by the Americans at York and Queenstown in Canada.

Admiral Cockburn also wanted to wreak vengeance upon Washington, for the *National Intelligencer*, patriotic newspaper of the capital city, had repeatedly denounced him as an invader and plunderer. Hardly had the British troops made camp in the capitol park, when Cockburn led several hundred of them into the unguarded government building. Mounting a desk, the admiral made a little speech:

"Men, shall this harbor of Yankee democracy be burned?"

"Aye, sir! Aye!" shouted the soldiers.

The tables, chairs and other furnishings of the senators, representatives and Supreme Court judges were piled in heaps, and soon the flames were roaring their destruction. Cockburn next led a force to the office of the *National Intelligencer* and personally directed the wrecking of its presses. "Be sure that all the C's are destroyed, so that the rascals can not any longer abuse my name," he ordered.

Meanwhile, General Ross was directing the burning of the President's Mansion, and at nightfall James Madison and his

Cabinet looked back upon the flames and black smoke of these conflagrations. Next day all other government buildings but one were burned.

General Ross led his victorious Redcoats northward toward Baltimore, while Admiral Cockburn sailed his naval squadron up Chesapeake Bay and into the Patapsco River to support the attack upon this city. American regulars and Maryland militia put up a more spirited defense of Baltimore than was made at Washington, and the British were repulsed. During the battle, General Ross, exposing himself as he directed his columns, was killed by a sharpshooter's bullet. The American forces withdrew to safer ground, but the British, lacking their leader, failed to press their advantage.

The British fleet prepared to bombard Fort McHenry, principal stronghold at the water's edge south of Baltimore. A Maryland lawyer, Francis Scott Key, was permitted to board a British gunboat to discuss the possible release of a friend held prisoner by the Redcoat commander. Toward evening the fleet began bombarding the fort. Key was forced to remain on board all night, but through the mist of the morning he saw that the Star-Spangled Banner was still waving over Fort McHenry. Seizing paper and pen he wrote the words that became the national anthem of the people of the United States:

Oh say, can you see by the dawn's early light
  What so proudly we hailed at the twilight's last gleaming?
Whose broad stripes and bright stars, through the perilous night,
  O'er the ramparts we watched, were so gallantly streaming?

* * *

The capture of Washington and the senseless destruction of the public buildings accomplished nothing for the British except to inflame public feeling against them. However, some influential citizens clamored to end the war on almost any terms. At a convention of disgruntled New Englanders at Hartford, Connecticut, resolutions were adopted condemning the government for continuing the conflict, and some even suggested breaking up the Union.

"Old Hickory" Takes Command

Andrew Jackson, who as a lad had been wounded by a British officer's saber during the Revolution, was now a rugged frontiersman living on a big farm which he called the "Hermitage," near Nashville, Tennessee, and serving as commander of his state's militia. When General Jackson heard about the Hartford convention he declared that its leaders should be hanged as traitors, and added:

"I would like nothing better than to redeem the honor of my country by striking a blow at the invaders!"

"Andy" Jackson had studied law, practiced briefly in Salisbury, North Carolina, and as a young man of twenty-one had pushed westward with a band of Carolina immigrants into Tennessee Territory. Helping to hew from the wilderness a community of law and order, young Jackson had served as public attorney for the territory, was a delegate to the convention that created Tennessee as the sixteenth state of the Union, had served as its first representative in Congress and a brief period as senator, then for several years as judge of the state Supreme Court. Fearless, quick-tempered and headstrong, he had been embroiled in many quarrels and had fought several duels.

When this second war with Great Britain was declared, General Jackson proposed that his militia be used to defend Louisiana. President Madison accepted the offer, and in January 1813 the general mobilized two regiments of infantry and one regiment of cavalry in the public square of Nashville and started them on the way toward New Orleans. When the force reached Natchez, Mississippi, Jackson received notice from the War Department that the British threat to that region no

longer existed, and he was ordered to disband his men on the
spot. The spirited commander disobeyed this obviously unfair
order and accompanied his troops back to Tennessee. It was
on this useless expedition that Jackson's men, in honor of his
tough, rugged disposition, nicknamed him "Old Hickory."

Late that year and in early 1814 he led his troops again, this
time in a successful campaign to subdue the rebellious Creek
Indians in Alabama and Mississippi. In recognition of this service he was appointed major general in the United States Army
and given command of the Seventh Military Department,
which included Tennessee, Mississippi and the Louisiana Territory.

In London the ministers of His Britannic Majesty, contem-
plating the failure of their forces in America to win decisive
victories, now agreed upon a new campaign: to conquer and
annex the Louisiana Territory. French in population and tradition, this region west of the Mississippi had been ceded to Spain
in 1769, back again to France in 1800, and in 1803 sold to the
United States by Emperor Napoleon Bonaparte, with the remark that he was creating a worthy rival for England. British
statesmen had never recognized the transfer of Louisiana to
the United States as legal, and besides, they were anxious to
wipe out the insult of Napoleon's remark.

Jamaica, a British possession in the West Indies, was named
the rendezvous of the naval and land forces for the campaign.
Through the autumn of 1814 ships and troops gathered, rested,
and prepared their weapons. The threat was known in Washington, but peace negotiations had been opened between British and American representatives at Ghent, in the United
Netherlands, and a false sense of security added to the general
confusion of the United States government.

One man was not misled nor confused. Andrew Jackson was
sure that the British politicians throwing the dice of destiny
at Ghent would welcome the capture of Louisiana, and that

they would try to keep the territory as the fruit of conquest or as payment for ending the war. The general wrote President Madison, urging in terse backwoods language that he be ordered to proceed at once to protect the southern country against British attack. The President was hesitant, and James Monroe, newly appointed Secretary of War and continuing his duties as Secretary of State, was busy, and both delayed issuing any positive order. But Jackson, recognizing his duty when he saw it, left the Hermitage for Mobile, Alabama, to be ready for the defense of the United States wherever the invasion might strike. While he was en route, on September 15, three British ships under Captain William H. Percy attacked Fort Bowyer at Mobile Harbor. The spirited defense of the fort led by Major Lawrence and his force repulsed the attack.

Jackson learned that the British squadron had been fitted at Pensacola, in Spanish territory. He was angry at this breach of neutrality and in good Tennessee language declared: "Spain is fixing to lose Florida!" He wrote to Don Gonzales Manriquez, governor of West Florida, saying that he would not tolerate violation of Spanish neutrality by England. He ordered his close friend, General John Coffee, to bring a force of about 3,000 men, including 1,800 Tennessee mounted riflemen, to Mobile. Then the general violated his own order of neutrality, by moving into Florida on November 3 and forcing the surrender of Fort Michael, north of Pensacola. The British took to their ships.

Jackson returned to Mobile, convinced that the British attack would be made there. Governor William Claiborne of Louisiana thought differently. He told the general that Jean Lafitte, colorful leader of a band of smugglers and pirates who used Lake Barataria near New Orleans as its home base, had come in with news that the British expedition forming at Jamaica would head directly for New Orleans. Lafitte was as notorious a liar as he was a pirate, and Claiborne held about a hundred of his men in prison as outlaws, but in this instance the governor believed him. Jackson ordered General Coffee to bring his force to New Orleans with all speed, and with his staff hurried on ahead.

The New Orleans that Andrew Jackson reached on December 2, 1814, was as different from the pioneer surroundings of his home community as Nashville was different from any European city. The 70,000 inhabitants were principally Creoles—descendants of the original French, mixed with the blood of Spanish officials and traders. Here was a center of commerce, culture and hearty living. All the strength and virtues, together with the vices of the intermingled races, made the life of the city exciting.

Jackson found the citizens complacent, almost indifferent, to the British threat. The legislature, in session at the time and composed of men of the old "ruling classes," was actually hostile to this Tennessee general. But Claiborne loyally supported Jackson and took every occasion to bring him into contact with the leading planters, shippers and bankers of the city. The general's tall, slender figure became familiar among these new Americans he had come to defend, and whether they liked him or not, they saw character written in the long, pale face with flashing light-blue eyes, and they heard determination in his forthright, if often ungrammatical, speech.

The military forces at hand to defend New Orleans were quite meager: two half-filled regiments of regular infantry, and the remainder for the most part Louisiana militia. United States Navy Master-Commander (called by Jackson "Commodore") Daniel T. Patterson had two gunboats on the river below the city—a frigate appropriately named *Louisiana* and the schooner *Carolina,* while Lieutenant Thomas A. Catesby Jones was patrolling Lake Borgne, southeast of New Orleans, with five small ships. But reinforcements were on the way. In addition to General Coffee's brigade of mounted riflemen, volunteer units had been promised from Mississippi, Tennessee and Kentucky.

On the general's newly formed staff was Edward Livingston, prominent lawyer of New Orleans, who served as secretary, translator and confidential adviser. Major William O. Butler, later major general, was another aide. He left a vivid account of Jackson's movements and verbatim sayings during the tense weeks of preparation for the defense of New Orleans and the decisive battle itself.

The general was fortunate to find as his chief engineer officer Major Lacarrière Latour, who knew intimately every area of the lower Mississippi, and together they surveyed the terrain south of New Orleans. Latour advised, and Jackson agreed, that the British army would never attempt to come up the winding, shallow river, but would proceed from the Gulf into Lake Borgne, its western shore only seven miles from the city. From this lake the British could come through adjoining Lake Pontchartrain and attack the city by the Bayou St. John, or through swampland to the Bienvenue road leading to the river, eight miles below New Orleans. The latter route would bring the invaders squarely to the big sugar plantation of Jacques Phillipe de Villère, major general of the Louisiana militia; thence they could move northward over the harvested sugar-cane fields of other plantations, called the Chalmette plain.

General Jackson posted his military units to guard all approaches into the city. He set some of his militia and Negro laborers to felling trees to block the roadways leading from Lake Borgne. He requisitioned all the cannon in the city, finding a remarkable collection of guns of various sizes and calibers. He agreed with Governor Claiborne that the skills learned by Jean Lafitte and his pirates in their tarnished calling, especially their ability with cannon, should be used. The Baratarians were released from prison, and in return Lafitte promised that his best cannoneer, Dominique You, who had become quite expert in hitting Spanish ships in the Caribbean, would command a battery of artillery.

Now General Jackson stunned the complacent and pleasure-loving citizens with a proclamation of martial law. He commandeered horses, wagons, tools and arms, as well as the food which was stored in abundance due to lack of shipping. New Orleans people knew that a leader of firm and decisive action had come among them.

"They Shall Fight Tonight!"

Meanwhile at Negril Bay on the coast of the languid island of Jamaica, the fifty ships of the British fleet, under command of Admiral Sir Alexander Cochrane, made ready to transport the army for the invasion of Louisiana. On November 24, 1814, they raised their colors and stood by for final inspection. The decks were covered with red-coated officers and men, likewise arrayed for inspection, under command of General John Keane, lately arrived from England. In the force were four regiments, totaling 3,100 troops, veterans of the war in the northern states, victors of the battle at Bladensburg, captors of Washington; four more regiments which Keane had brought with him, many of them veterans of the Battle of Waterloo, followers of their great hero, the Duke of Wellington, in the campaigns of France and Spain; the 93d Highland Regiment, which had made the long voyage from the Cape of Good Hope to be in the campaign; and two regiments of colonial troops from the West Indies, about half of whom were Negroes. The ships bore a total army force of about 7,450 men, and in addition had aboard 1,500 marines equipped for land duty. As James Parton, biographer of General Jackson, observed:

Here was a force . . . commanded by officers some of whom had grown gray in victory . . . Indeed, there was not a regiment of those which had come from England which had not won brilliant distinction in strongly contested fields. The *elite* of England's army and navy were afloat on that bright day of November when the last review took place.

Beating at headwinds that retarded their progress, the heavily loaded British ships made up from the Caribbean. On December 7 they stood off Pensacola in a storm, then turned westward, too far out to be seen from the coast until they neared Cat Island, at the entrance to Lake Borgne, in the dawn of December 14.

"Gentlemen, we shall eat Christmas dinner in New Orleans!" Admiral Cochrane announced to his staff.

Such was the setting for the decisive battle for New Orleans. The battle was, in fact a *campaign* of five distinct engagements, involving the United States Army, Navy, a unit of the Marines, state militias; men of the white, Negro and Indian races; pirates and wealthy planters and businessmen speaking French fighting by the side of backswoodsmen speaking frontier English, as strange an assortment as ever fought for the American flag under one command—all welded together by the indomitable will of Old Hickory, General Andrew Jackson.

First Engagement: "Clear the lake!" To control the approaches to the city, Admiral Cochrane realized he would have to dispose of the tiny American naval squadron, and sent Captain Charles Lockyer with several gunboats to blow the five schooners to the bottom. Lieutenant Jones could expect no help from his commander, Commodore Patterson. He had barely two hundred men in his force, but the plucky officer ordered them to clear decks for action. Bravely the guns of his vessels answered the British fire, until masts were shot away, decks and hulls were splintered and guns blown into the water. Jones lost six of his crew killed, but escaped with his survivors, twenty-five of whom were wounded. The British burned his disabled ships.

New Orleans at last awoke to the fact that invasion was at hand and that all Louisiana might be seized by the British. Three deserters, Irishmen who had no stomach to fight for King George against Americans, informed Jackson of the enemy strength. They also reported that many of the officers' wives were on board the fleet, eager to see the sacking of New Orleans with the promise that when the spoils of victory were divided each would become mistress of some wealthy plantation. This information helped to spur a tide of enlistments at Jackson's recruiting offices. Among these was an old warrior, Garrique Flauzac, former major general of artillery in Napoleon's army, who had come to the New World a decade before.

To encourage the morale of troops and citizens, on Sunday December 18 Jackson staged a "grand review" of all the local volunteer units, all marching proudly in their new uniforms and saluting Governor Claiborne and Generals Jackson and Villère. At the Place d'Armes there were speeches, and bands played "Yankee Doodle" and, of course, *La Marseillaise.*

Not knowing the actual strength of the American forces, General Keane moved with caution, waiting until December 22 to begin landing his troops. The delay proved priceless for Jackson, gaining time for General Coffee to come in with his Tennesseeans. These hardy backswoodsmen had ridden from Baton Rouge, 135 miles, in the last three days. Their unshaven faces, coonskin caps and homespun pantaloons created considerable amusement among the proper ladies and gentlemen of New Orleans, but their presence boosted Jackson's sense of security. He knew that these men could shoot! Hard on the heels of the Tennesseeans came the battalion of cavalry from Mississippi under command of Colonel Thomas Hinds, every man of them an expert marksman.

Second Engagement: The battle at night. Near noon on December 23, two officers rode at a gallop to General Jackson's headquarters on Royal Street. The general, ill with dysentery and fever, got up from his couch to greet Colonel Pierre de la Ronde, whose plantation joined General Villère's on the north, and Major Gabriel Villère, son of the militia general. Breathlessly in French, the major poured out his story. Translated, it brought the startling news that the British had marched along the Bienvenue road and reached the Villère plantation. An attack upon New Orleans could come at any time. Jackson's eyes blazed with the fire that his friends—and his enemies—knew so well.

"By the Eternal, they shall not sleep on our soil!" the general exclaimed.

More and better news reached the general. At that moment, flatboats were at the wharf unloading the expected General William Carroll and his 2,000 Tennessee volunteers. Jackson posted these troops to guard New Orleans and ordered the rest of his force to the Chalmette plain. Stationing himself with his staff near the edge of town, Jackson reviewed his small army as it hurried by: the regulars, the militia, the battalion of Negroes, a company of United States Marines, another of Choctaw Indians, and finally, a grim-looking outfit of men in bright red shirts and three-cornered hats—Lafitte's men dressed in apparel from some luckless merchant ship, all eager for battle.

Scouts brought in copies of a proclamation the British had distributed to nearby plantations. In French and Spanish, it read: "Louisianians! Remain quiet in your homes. Your slaves shall be preserved to you, and your property respected. We make war only against Americans!"

At dusk Jackson sent Colonel Hinds's horsemen to reconnoiter the British. The dragoons reported that campfires gleamed at Villère's plantation and along the levee. The British were bivouacking for the night. Clearly, they were awaiting reinforcements and intended to attack at daybreak.

"We must fight them tonight!" was the general's order.

At Versailles, a plantation home barely half a mile from the enemy bivouacs, Jackson arranged his force for battle. He ordered the *Carolina* to drop down quietly opposite the British camp. With Commodore Patterson aboard, the two-masted schooner, heavy with a battery of ten six-pound guns in broadside and two twelve-pound pivot guns, came to anchor. It was still light enough to distinguish the forms of the enemy soldiers when Jackson signaled "Fire!"

The guns of the American ship roared. Over the riverbank swept the storm of grape and six-pound shot. Then another broadside, and another. Consternation seized the Redcoats, as they gathered up their wounded. Their officers could hardly believe that this audacious bombardment meant a general attack upon their post—at night. They had been assured that Andrew Jackson's troops were no better than those they had met and put to flight in the campaign about Washington, and that resistance would quickly crumble. What did this mad Jackson hope to do?

Seven broadsides, deliberately aimed and fired in thirty minutes, completed the *Carolina*'s task. Up soared her rocket signals of red, white and blue. Jackson, watching on the levee with his staff, ordered:

"Forward all the line! Keep touch! Forward!"

Hinds's Mississippi dragoons struck first, near the British center, followed by the marines and the two regiments of infantry. Coffee with his men and the Choctaw Indians rode hard to the left, circling the enemy flank and forcing the Redcoats to retreat. The *Louisiana* sent her shells screaming into the British howitzer positions, ably helped by a battery of long-range guns on the bank close by the vessel, under command of Captain Charles Humphrey. At intervals all night the American artillery roared, and the troops kept up their steady attacks. During the light of early morning General Keane withdrew from all his positions, most of his artillery disabled by the accurate fire of Jackson's cannoneers. He had failed again! One of the Redcoat lieutenants, who wrote a full account of the New Orleans campaign and signed it "The Subaltern," expressed the chagrin of his comrades:

It was a sad day for men who, a year before, had marched through France from the Pyrennees to the Sea . . . We retired, disheartened and discontented. We knew that with small arms the Americans were foemen worthy of our steel, but we did not expect them to get the best of our artillery combat . . . Candor compells the admission that the accuracy of their practice, both for range and pointing, was unexpected.

Behind the Rodriguez Ditch

With the insight of a true commander, General Jackson rightly guessed that the next move of the enemy would be an assault in full force. Realizing his inferior strength in men and weapons, the American leader could not hope for victory in an open battle. He decided to fortify his small army behind breastworks at the narrowest point between swamplands and the river, and await the British attack. That point, Major Latour pointed out, was the Rodriguez Canal, an old dry millrace about four miles below New Orleans. Four days and nights, including Christmas Day, were filled with feverish work by the troops and slaves, to deepen and widen what the soldiers referred to as "the ditch" and to throw up breastworks upon its bank. Shovels and wheelbarrows took the place of rifles.

All the cannon collected in the city were rushed into position. The general, inspecting the works with his aides, suggested that cotton bales take the place of gabions (wicker cylinders filled with earth and stones) for the artillery.

"The experiment has never been tried, General," Latour responded. "The books on fieldworks do not mention it."

"Never mind about the books, Major. We'll make a book of our own. There are plenty of cotton bales!" answered Jackson. Soon wagonloads of the fleecy staple were rumbling from the warehouses toward the breastworks.

On Christmas morning, British guns boomed a salute to a new commander, General Sir Edward Pakenham, who landed at Cat Island directly from England. With him was Major General Samuel Gibbs and a staff of experienced officers. The thirty-seven-year-old Pakenham was the brother-in-law of the Duke of Wellington, highly respected both for his military skill and personal bravery. His army looked to him for quick victory over this uncouth American leader. Sir Edward had in his papers a commission as Governor-General of Louisiana—to become effective after his conquest had succeeded.

Admiral Cochrane urged a speedy attack upon the crude American fortifications, chiding General Pakenham with the remark, "I can take 2,000 of my marines and sailors armed with cutlasses and pistols and capture Jackson's mudworks!" General Keane, smarting under the defeat of a few days before, urged caution. Jackson had some sharpshooters behind those mudworks, he said.

Third Engagement: "Destroy the gunboats!" Pakenham did order the immediate destruction of the two irritating American gunboats on the river. On the morning of December 27, British cannon on the levee poured red-hot shot into the *Carolina*. The schooner answered the fire, joined by the *Louisiana* farther up the river, but in half an hour the *Carolina* was so badly damaged that her captain ordered her abandoned—just before her magazine blew up with a roar that rattled windows in New Orleans. The British guns turned on the *Louisiana*, but the frigate was able to pull upstream to safety.

Early on December 28 Pakenham began a reconnaissance in force, with a view to a general attack. Again the *Louisiana* swung into action. Commodore Patterson turned his ship broadside and personally directed the firing of shot and grape into the column nearest the river, while Captain Humphrey's artillery blasted away at the other. The British general hurriedly called back his troops.

Fourth Engagement: Greetings to the New Year! The last three days of 1814 ebbed away, filled with intense preparations on both sides. British sailors unloaded thirty of the fleet's biggest guns and placed them for bombarding the American lines. Observing that the Americans were using cotton bales for bastions, Pakenham raided all the nearby plantations and rounded up several hundred hogsheads of sugar as ramparts for his cannon. On the night of December 31 the Redcoat general brought 4,000 of his troops forward to within half a mile of the Rodriguez ditch.

A heavy fog obscured the stage of action on the early morning of New Year's Day, 1815. At 10:30 the misty curtain lifted for the drama of battle to begin. The British guns spoke first, and at the salvo, American troops rushed to their positions and soon fire was answering fire. The sugar casks proved worthless, as American cannon balls tore through them. The cotton bales were hardly more effective. Realizing that his force again met its match in artillery combat, the British general ended the duel.

Jackson ordered the cotton bales replaced by palmetto logs, chinked with mud. Working hard in relays, the soldiers sawed and laid the logs in place, daubed the mucky soil between them and rolled the artillery pieces back into place.

On January 2 a ship bearing two more regiments of British infantry, the 7th and 43d, totaling 1,700 men under the command of General John Lambert, dropped anchor off Lake Borgne. Almost at that hour, a dispatch reached Jackson from Baton Rouge. A brigade of Kentucky volunteers under Generals John Adair and Philemon Thomas had reached there, and their flatboats were on the way to New Orleans. But, the dispatch said, most of these men had no weapons. General Jackson declared:

"I don't believe it! I have never seen a Kentuckian without a gun and a pack of cards, in my life!"

Next day the Kentuckians strode off their boats at New Orleans. It was true: only about one in three had rifles. Secretary Monroe had ordered the guns sent from Pittsburgh, but they had failed to come. Furthermore, these men were so ragged that many held their jackets and pantaloons together as they marched. New Orleans citizens quickly gathered up clothes for them, fed them heartily and started another search for guns. Several hundred old Spanish flintlocks were found in an arsenal and made ready.

Now thoroughly angered at the repulses his men had suffered, General Sir Edward Pakenham, dressed in his splendid uniform of red with its gold and white trimmings, called in his top commanders for a council of war. There were Generals Gibbs, Keane and Lambert; Colonel William Thornton and Lieutenant Colonel Thomas Mullens, and Admiral Cochrane. They filled the spacious drawing-room of the plantation house. General Villère's slaves kept fires going and with correct dignity served hot toddy to these enemy gentlemen planning to throw their army against half its number under General Jackson.

This scheme of attack was agreed to: Colonel Thornton would lead a force across the river to assault the small American units there and to sink the pesky *Louisiana*. The main force would attack and dislodge the Americans behind the old canal. Ladders would be carried for scaling the breastworks. Pakenham made it clear that he expected the troops to maintain their ranks in the traditional British manner, regardless of casualties, and by sheer weight of numbers to overwhelm the nondescript American army.

Some misgivings remained for General Keane and Colonel

Mullens, but General Gibbs remarked, "I have no patience with anyone who argues that the men who stormed Cuidad Rodrigo and Badajoz can be halted by—much less repulsed from—a low log breastwork manned by a backwoods rabble!" Little did this officer from England know how accurate was the aim of those backswoodsmen, and how thoroughly their general had inspired them with the will to win.

General Pakenham settled the matter:

"Gentlemen, the movements will begin before daylight on January 8. By early morning the Americans will be in full flight and by noon we shall occupy New Orleans. Join me there for a celebration dinner!"

Getting arms and men across the river required the British to widen and deepen an old canal from the *Bayou de Catiline,* and to this task men were impressed in turns. Jackson had sent General David Morgan with 550 Louisiana militia to guard the west bank of the river. Commodore Patterson, helping Morgan mount cannon upon the levee, reported that clearly the enemy intended an attack from the west side as well as from the Chalmette fields. Jackson sent 200 Kentuckians across the river to reinforce Morgan.

Late on Saturday night the fatigued American commander and his aides lay down in their clothes, in the Macarte plantation house near their lines, and were up at one o'clock on that historic morning of January 8, 1815.

"Fire! Load—Aim—Fire!"

The air is crisp and chill, and the fog hangs heavy over river and lowlands. It is 3:30 o'clock, and in the darkness General Jackson and his staff begin the final inspection of their battle line. Into the narrow space of 750 yards from the river's edge across the Chalmette plain and the 600 yards more into the swampy woodland are crowded the 4,000 men upon whose valor depends the salvation of New Orleans and

Louisiana. Old Hickory rides first to the woodland, dismounts and greets his old comrade-at-arms, General Coffee, whose men have for days borne the task of working in ooze and muck. Jackson repeats his order for the battle:

"When the British advance, our artillery will fire first. All rifles are to hold their fire until range is so close that every shot can count. Under no circumstances shall any unit risk an open engagement by advancing from the breastworks."

Jackson now stalks along the line with Wilkinson, Butler and Commodore Patterson, an orderly leading his gray horse. He gives the same order to the commander of every unit. Everywhere the troops are preparing and eating their breakfasts of bacon, cornbread and sweet potatoes, to which the Creoles have added strong black coffee. At every point the general greets the officers and men pleasantly, many of them by name, as they spring to attention on seeing his tall form in his dark cloak, a wide hat with an officer's cord and muddy black boots. He spends several minutes with his friend General "Billy" Carroll, where the Tennesseeans are taking their places behind the breastworks, supported by Adair's Kentuckians with Hinds's Mississippi riflemen in the rear. On toward the river the general goes, greeting in order the officers and men of the 44th Infantry, the Negro battalion commanded by Major Pierre Daquin, the battalions of New Orleans volunteers under their own Creole Captains Lacoste and Plauche, flanked on their right by the 7th Infantry which holds the important place next to the river. Fronting the 7th is a bastion extending several yards forward, held by a company of the 7th and Captain Beale's New Orleans rifles.

Here Jackson warmly greets Captain Humphrey, commanding Number One Battery of the line, as he has greeted all seven others of his amazing collection of artillery chiefs: Navy Lieutenants Norris and Crawley with guns from the disabled *Carolina,* Colonel Perry and Lieutenant Spotts of the regular artillery, a corporal from Carroll's brigade, while next to the corporal stands old General Flauzac; and in front of the Creole companies, Dominique You with his red-shirted cannoneers, who gives "Zheneral" Jackson a cup of black coffee with assurances that Lafitte's men are indeed ready.

In the foggy darkness of 4 o'clock, General Pakenham stands on the river bank, fretting because Colonel Thornton has found the water in the canal too low to get all the transports through. He cannot know that the boats which have crossed, with only four hundred men, were carried by the swift current far below their supposed landing point. The Redcoat general turns impatiently to his staff and declares:

"We can wait no longer. Prepare all for attack!"

In the chill morning air the British lines form. Commands are given and obeyed by hardy veterans, heroes of many battles, officers and men praised by the Duke of Wellington as "able to go anywhere and do anything!" Now they stand with arms ready, peering into the murky fog. At 6 o'clock Pakenham orders:

"Send up the signal rockets for the artillery!"

A battery of long guns, moved up to about a mile of the American line, shatters the early stillness with its salvo. General Flauzac is given the honor of firing the first answering shot. Several other batteries join, but aim can be taken only by flashes from the British guns, and Jackson orders that no powder be wasted.

At 7 o'clock the mist lifts somewhat and a British trumpet sounds "Forward the line!" The main force under General Gibbs moves forward, in column of companies in double files, about fifty men abreast. Colonel Mullens' 44th Regiment is in the lead, and swings obliquely to the right to assault the American line near the wood. Their advance will bring them directly to the entrenchments held by Carroll's Tennesseeans. The British left, led by Colonel Rennie's regiment, marches hard by the river bank in column of squads, every fourth man carrying a scaling ladder.

Lieutenant Spotts, peering over his battery's parapet shouts: "They come! Fire the long gun!"

His long gun thunders its greeting. Two other batteries fire. Then fog shuts out the view. After moments that seem hours the fog lifts, and Gibbs' red-coated men of the 44th, 4th and 7th are but three hundred yards away. They march grandly with colors flying, their officers mounted and waving their swords, the morning light glinting from bayonets and buckles. Cheers roll from the throats of the American soldiers at this glorious chance to test their aim.

Now the guns along the breastworks open again. Into their compact marching targets roar the balls and shot, tearing great holes in the ranks of Redcoats. Jackson, watching through a spyglass he has borrowed from Patterson, utters an admiring word on how the British soldiers move up to fill the gaps without loss of step. General Gibbs, riding splendidly at the side of his leading column on a prancing black stallion, cries an order. His men start forward on the double-quick.

Jackson springs down from the parapet. "Now hold the artillery fire!" he commands. General Carroll needs no further order. The British are so close that the American riflemen are drawing beads upon their foreheads. Carroll turns to a soldier.

"Bring down that mounted officer leading the column!" he says. The rifle cracks and the officer, Major Whitaker, falls from his mount. Then—

"Fire!" General Carroll shouts. "Fire!" the officers of the whole brigade repeat. The sheet of flame literally sweeps to the ground the front ranks of the British column. In a moment the rifles of the whole line are firing. There are four lines in each unit behind that log-and-mud entrenchment. While the men of the first line fire, the second stand ready to step into place, and the third and fourth are reloading.

"Fire! Load—aim—fire!" The commands are shouted over the continuous roar of musketry. Before those blazing rifles the British fall in heaps. General Gibbs makes frantic efforts to rally his men, as those still standing reel back, aghast, bewildered at that rain of lead which the "backwoods rabble" throws into their ranks.

Meanwhile Colonel Rennie's column, about 900 strong, comes at double-quick toward the levee, driving the American outposts before them. As the latter scramble over the breastworks, Humphrey lets go with his battery point-blank upon the heads of the advancing Redcoats. Then the rifles of the Louisiana militia and the 7th United States Infantry blaze in unison. Hardly can the British troops in the rear move forward for the bodies of the wounded and the slain. Brave Colonel Rennie survives to leap clear over the breastwork, followed by two other officers and several of his Marines. But death meets them as they leap.

At sight of Rennie's column, Carroll sends two companies of his riflemen to support the right of the American line. The Tennesseeans spring to their places among the Creoles, and add to the slaughter near the river bank. The attacking units fall back—many in disorderly retreat.

Gallantly, recklessly, Gibbs rides among his men and urges them to form ranks. The survivors of the 44th are in flight. Some units of the 7th and 4th are being rallied by the officers still on their feet, but for the most part, all is confusion. Pakenham rides forward, waving his hat. Gibbs calls out to his general the most tragic words a commander in battle can report:

"I am sorry, sir! The troops no longer obey me!"

But Keane, who commands the first reserve, is coming up. Stationed so that he might support either Gibbs or Rennie, he now orders his whole force obliquely to the right. In front are the tall, splendid Highlanders, led by Colonel Dale. Just as that fatal march begins, Dale hands his watch and papers to his regimental surgeon. "Give them to my wife. I shall die at the head of my regiment," he says.

The first sheet of flame that rolls from the parapet into that column fulfills the colonel's prediction, and brings low his leading ranks to a man. In another moment General Keane falls, badly wounded. The bewildered Scots halt. When two-thirds of their number have fallen, most of the survivors turn and run despite the shouts of Pakenham, who now rides among them. General Coffee sends a company of his riflemen and the Choctaw Indians through the wood to attack from the flank.

One British officer, Major Wilkinson, followed by several men, reaches that deadly Rodriguez ditch. The major gains the top and falls, mortally wounded. A grimy Kentucky sergeant shouts "Kivver him with a flag, boys! He's a brave 'un!" The body is carried to the rear and an American flag is placed over it.

General Pakenham's right arm is shattered by a ball. The next instant his horse falls beneath him. His arm is hurriedly bound and he mounts the horse of an aide. Another shot pierces his body. He is carried away.

"Tell Lambert to throw in the reserve!" is the general's last command.

The intrepid Gibbs has formed a third column of the Fusiliers and the 43d Infantry. He rides to the head again, and starts to lead an oblique around the remnants of the Highlanders when a ball brings down his big black steed. As the horse stumbles, four balls strike the general, in head, neck, chest and groin, and he is quickly carried to the rear. General Lambert, now the commander of the field, halts the reserve. He decides against further butchery and calls for general retreat.

All during the moments of valiant conflict the band of the Louisiana militia, stationed back of the Creoles, plays its martial tunes. Now it strikes up "Yankee Doodle," and Jackson and his officers can hardly hold back the eager soldiers from leaping over the breastworks to pursue the retreating enemy. The Americans are still outnumbered, and the general knows that to contest the open field might lose the victory his strategy of defense has gained.

It is one hour from the beginning of the British advance, and the Americans behind their ditch have no more targets. Before them stretches a carpet of wounded and dead, the uniforms making patterns of red and white, awful in the morning light. And from among them, when the firing has ceased, at least three hundred uninjured Redcoats rise and come forward to give themselves up as prisoners. A British bugler-boy, about fourteen years old, who has sat on the limb of a tree near the levee blowing "Charge!" through all the battle, unscathed although shot has zoomed all about him, is helped down by admiring Creoles and led back of the line, a bewildered hero.

But what of Morgan's men across the river? The flashes of British rifles move northward. The Americans, Jackson can see, are being forced back. The battle cannot be completely won if Colonel Thornton's attack succeeds. The poorly armed Kentuckians and Louisiana militia resist feebly. Commodore Patterson spikes his guns, fearing they will fall into enemy hands.

But Lambert decides that another attack, even to follow the advantage gained on the west bank, would be useless. He sends an aide to call Thornton back.

They Won a Lasting Peace

A civilian attached to General Gibbs' staff left a vivid account of that withering fire with which the muskets of Jackson's soldiers greeted the British invaders:

Instantly the whole American line, from the swamp to a point pasts its centre toward its right, was fairly ablaze. In less time than one can write it, the Forty-Fourth Foot was literally swept from the face of the earth. In the wreck and confusion that ensued within five minutes the regiment seemed to vanish from sight—except the half of it that lay stricken on the ground! Every mounted officer was down at the first fire. No such execution by small arms had ever been seen or heard of. Then the destruction smote the Fourth Foot and the Seventh Fusiliers . . . Never before had British veterans quailed. But it would be silly to deny that they did so now. There was something in that leaden torrent that no men on earth could face.

According to terms of the truce, American soldiers gathered up the dead of their vanquished foemen and delivered them to the British camp. The wounded were given treatment, and the more serious casualties, at least twelve hundred officers and men, were taken into New Orleans where churches and homes were turned into hospitals for their care. Final British records show that the crushing defeat of January 8, 1815, cost them 858 killed or died of wounds and 2,468 others wounded. The American defenders lost eight killed and thirteen wounded! Of all major battles, these losses are most unequal.

General Gibbs lived in agony until the following morning, cursing his fate and his general. General Keane's wound was not mortal. He and Lambert, and the survivors of their command, wanted only to quit the shores they had so confidently invaded. For ten days they maintained their camp—ten anxious days for Jackson and his victorious men, for they did not know the British intentions and scouts reported even more troops arriving from England. On January 18 the British broke camp and began the movement back toward Lake Borgne, bearing the widow of General Pakenham, and to others who had high hopes of the conquest, the tragic evidences of the defeat. The fleet moved away from American shores.

As news of the victory spread to Washington, church bells rang and citizens gathered to give thanks. In the capital there were soirees, orations and toasts to the Tennessee general and his men.

The Treaty of Ghent had been signed on December 24. The news reached Washington on February 13. By the best riders and fastest horses the tidings were dispatched to General Jackson at New Orleans. The treaty of peace proved a just and lasting basis for friendship between the growing empire of the British peoples, and the new nation that had won, then maintained, its independence by blood and sacrifices.

The Battle of New Orleans settled definitely the question as to the sovereignty of the United States over Louisiana. It proved to European rulers that American generalship, as typified by Andrew Jackson, and American soldiers such as stood between New Orleans and the British, were equal to any emergency, a match for the best armies the Old World could muster. It brought such prestige to the United States that James Monroe, who next succeeded to the Presidency, could issue unchallenged his famous doctrine that the areas of the Western Hemisphere were no longer open to colonization by European powers.

The decisive victory also helped to weld more closely to their country loyalties of the people of French and Spanish descent at the lower Mississippi, and to turn the eyes of the people of the eastern states more understandingly, and sympathetically, toward the frontiersmen of the west. Not only their eyes were turned to the west! With Louisiana secure, the great migration to the lands beyond the Mississippi began.

CHAPTER EIGHT

Houston Wins Independence for Texas

In February 1836, Antonio Lopez de Santa Anna, President of Mexico by title and absolute dictator in reality, general-in-chief of his country's army, moved northward across the Rio Grande at the head of a force of one thousand men with several cannon. On February 23 he led his troops into the town of San Antonio de Bexar. His scouts had informed him that a battalion of Texans was stationed there, in an old Spanish fort enclosed by walls, called the Alamo. El Presidente was determined to stamp out, ruthlessly and finally, the rebellion of Texas settlers against his rule.

Commanding the force of 183 Texans was a brave but headstrong officer, Lieutenant Colonel William B. Travis. General Sam Houston, commander of the Texas forces opposing Mexican rule, had sent word to Travis to blow up the Alamo and fall back to the town of San Felipe de Austin, where he would be reinforced. But Travis, not knowing that Santa Anna was coming with heavy force, preferred to make a stand at San Antonio and ignored Houston's order.

"Besiege the rebels in the Alamo!" ordered Santa Anna. "Trap the men—let no one escape!"

The shouting Mexican troops surged about the Alamo walls. Two men did escape—the first slipping out the following day with a letter from Travis, a message destined to take its place among the heroic documents of American arms:

COMMANDANCY OF THE ALAMO, BEXAR
Feb. 24th, 1836

TO THE PEOPLE OF TEXAS AND ALL AMERICANS IN THE WORLD:
Fellow Citizens and Compatriots—I am besieged by a thousand or more of the Mexicans under Santa Anna— I have sustained a continued Bombardment and cannonade for 24 hours and have not lost a man. The enemy has demanded a surrender at descretion, otherwise, the garrison are to be put to the sword, if the fort is taken— I have answered the command with a cannon shot and our flag still waves proudly from the walls. I shall never surrender nor retreat.

Then, I call on you in the name of Liberty, of patriotism, and everything dear to the American character, to come to our aid, with all despatch— The enemy is receiving reinforcements daily and will no doubt increase to three or four thousand in four or five days. If this call is neglected, I am determined to sustain myself as long as possible and die like a soldier who never forgets what is due his own honor and that of his country—*Victory* or *Death*.

WILLIAM BARRET TRAVIS, *Lt. Col. Comdt.*

For eleven days Santa Anna, true to his cruel nature, prolonged his siege. He was in no hurry. He would blast away with his cannon, then permit a lull of some hours. He knew that relief for the Texans trapped behind those old mortar walls was impossible. By another soldier who slipped through the Mexican guards, Travis sent his last pleading message, addressed to a convention of citizens meeting at Washington-on-the-Brazos:

"The spirits of my men are still high. . . . I hope your honorable body will hasten on reinforcements. . . . Our supply of ammunition is limited."

Santa Anna chose Sunday, March 6, as his day of victory.

"Let there be no prisoners!" El Presidente orated. A lone Mexican bugle blew "No Quarter." The waves of grayish uniforms began rolling over the Alamo walls.

"I shall never surrender nor retreat," Travis had said. Not

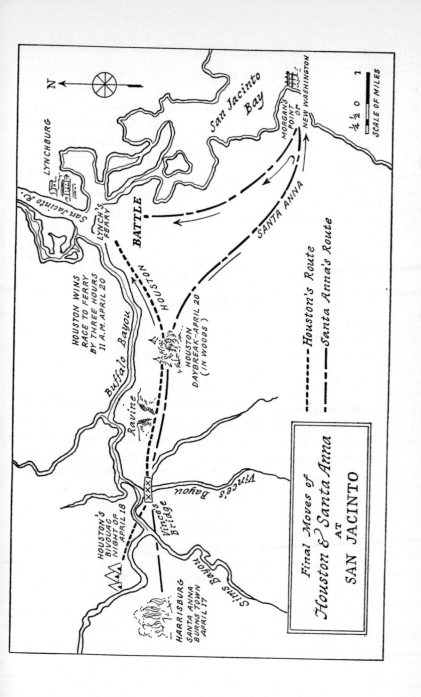

Final Moves of
Houston & Santa Anna
AT
SAN JACINTO

one Texas soldier in the Alamo lived to tell the story of what happened. Mexican soldiers in the attack told vivid tales of how dearly the defenders sold their lives. They told of David Crockett, firing his musket as calmly as though he were at some frontier celebration, pausing now and then to hoist some wounded comrade upon his massive shoulders and carry him to a spot of temporary safety. They related how Jim Bowie, ill and on a cot when the attackers swarmed in, sat there and fired to the end. Lieutenant A. M. Dickinson's faithful wife had stubbornly insisted on staying inside the walls, with their infant daughter Angelina, when Santa Anna's army closed about them. Dickinson pushed them inside the chapel of the old fort, kissed them and rushed to his place of battle. Only these two, and Travis' Negro servant Joe, were spared. The Sabbath night fell on the calm of death.

"Burn the bodies!" ordered Santa Anna, next morning. Quickly the Texas soil received the ashes of its heroes.

The Lone Star Republic Is Formed

At the time of the massacre at the Alamo, the convention at Washington-on-the-Brazos, some 150 miles northwest of San Antonio de Bexar, was drafting a declaration of independence for Texas and also a constitution for the new republic. Although a part of the Province of Coahuila under the Mexican flag, since 1820 Texas had been settled principally by immigrants from the United States. Moses Austin, a Yankee soldier of fortune, had obtained a charter to plant a colony, and had left his son Stephen to found the settlement of Americans on the Brazos River at San Felipe de Austin.

Into the great, balmy open spaces came the settlers, mostly from Virginia, Kentucky, Tennessee, Mississippi and Louisiana. The wind that blew across the prairies called its greeting, the boundless miles of bluebonnets nodded their welcome, the purple haze of the faraway horizons flung its age-old challenge. Men and women with bronzed faces and calloused hands dreamed, and came, and stayed. Like all the pioneers who knew that just ahead lay a better land, they came to Texas. They came on horseback, in great covered wagons called "prairie schooners," and on foot.

It is true that some immigrants came running ahead of the sheriffs and posses of law and order from the more settled states. There were rogues and criminals. There were those who came only for profit or adventure. Such men met the contempt or the summary justice of the true colonizers.

In 1830 the government of Mexico tried to halt all further colonization of the great region, for officials had learned that the settlers from the United States could not be controlled as were peons in the other provinces. Passports were required for those entering Texas, and passports were almost impossible to get. Taxation became oppressive, and the worst scoundrels in the government generally were sent to collect the levies.

President Andrew Jackson was keenly interested in developments in this far-western region, the more so since he received periodic reports from his good friend Sam Houston, a former Tennesseean. Houston had run away from home as a lad and lived for three years among the Cherokee Indians of eastern Tennessee. During the War of 1812 he served under General Jackson in a campaign against the Creek Indians. Jackson developed a strong attachment for this robust, hard-riding and blunt-speaking younger man. Houston practiced law in Lebanon, Tennessee, and went through the political turmoil for which the Volunteer State was even then noted, serving two terms in Congress and a term as governor. Embittered when, in 1829, his bride of three months left him, Houston resigned the governorship and went to live again among the Cherokees —this time at the reservation in western Arkansas to which most of the tribe had been removed. A strange, primitive instinct made this rugged character feel at home among the Redmen. They made him an honorary chief and named him "the Raven."

But more exciting adventures beckoned. Sam Houston rode westward occasionally, among the Texas settlers. He heard their sharp criticisms of Mexican rule, and sensed that Texas was ripening for revolution. He made the long trip to Washington and asked Jackson to send him into Texas as the President's "official observer." Jackson agreed that Sam Houston was just the man "to look the situation over."

And this Sam Houston did, on a horseback ride that covered 2,550 miles. On a spirited stallion, with saddle and bridle gleaming with Mexican silver, with huge silver spurs on his boots, a buckskin suit, pistol and knife at his belt and a long feather in his enormous hat, Houston rode to the principal settlements of Texas—to Nacogdoches, to Austin, to San Antonio de Bexar and other communities of this raw frontier. He saw the great distances, those windswept plains watered by streams coursing southeastward to the Gulf, awaiting more people, ready for the plow and the cattle herd. He talked to the settlers, telling them that Texas should be free.

Houston set up a house and law office in Nacogdoches. He established the Galveston Bay and Texas Land Company, principally to cover his activities in behalf of independence of Texas. He helped to sponsor a convention of settlers meeting at Austin on April 1, 1833, at which a strong resolution favoring local government for Texas was adopted.

Stephen Austin went to Mexico City to beg for home rule under the Mexican government, and was imprisoned for two years for his pains. Shrewd Andy Jackson had toyed with the idea of buying Texas from Mexico. Now Houston wrote his sharp-faced friend in the President's Mansion that it would not be necessary to buy Texas. The people were about ready to shake off "foreign rule," he wrote.

Antonio Lopez de Santa Anna was a pompous little man, vain and crafty, fancying himself a great military leader and styling himself "the Napoleon of the West." Promising the people of Mexico various "reforms," Santa Anna was elected president, only to set about making himself dictator. He abolished the parliament, dissolved the provinces, created military districts for local rule with hand-picked generals as governors. He donned a brilliant blue-and-gold uniform of field marshal and began his campaigns of cruel oppression.

One order of the dictator, intended to quash resistance in Texas, only hastened open rebellion: "All people of the Department of Coahuila living in Texas must surrender their private arms." For the frontiersman, this was equivalent to surrendering life itself, for weapons not only meant some insurance of personal safety against marauders, whether hostile Indians or roving outlaws, but also the means for procuring game for food. In every community of Texas, the 18,000 settlers openly declared they would resist this edict to the end.

Santa Anna sent his brother-in-law, Martin Perfecto Cos, whom he had appointed a general—a man as heartless and cunning as himself—to enforce martial rule north of the Rio Grande. In October 1835, Cos dispatched a detail of troops to Gonzales to seize the four-pounder cannon used by the citizens to scare off attacks by Indian bands. Men of the town, armed with rifles, pistols and the ever-present hunting knives, rushed the soldiers and drove them away. Word spread among the far-flung settlements to send representatives to a meeting at Austin, where plans would be made for the common defense. At this convention in October 1835, Sam Houston was appointed commander of all military forces raised to fight Mexican oppression.

Now with his title of general, Sam Houston sent out an appeal for recruits. Like ripples on a lake from a stone striking its surface, the appeal spread over the United States. Recruits came in from communities far and near—from the southern states, from cities as distant as St. Louis, Louisville and Cincinnati. Many rode their horses, and all brought their weapons, their muskets, rifles, pistols and hunting knives. One company of infantry, the New Orleans Grays, came marching to Nacogdoches on "loan" from the governor of Louisiana.

Houston spent the winter months equipping his nondescript army and selecting officers who could maintain some sort of military discipline over these adventurers. He appointed his close friend, Colonel James Fannin, a former slave trader, as his aide. He dispatched Jim Bowie, another adventurer whose exploits with the hunting knife to which he gave his name had become legend, with a company of cavalry, to meet General Cos and his Mexicans. Bowie's rough riders sent Cos's cavalry hurrying southward to San Antonio de Bexar.

Ben Milam, rugged old Indian fighter, volunteered to lead a battalion of three hundred men to drive the Mexicans over the Rio Grande. He stormed Bexar, won a complete victory over Cos's 1,400 troops, but was killed by a ball as the battle ended. His lieutenant, Colonel Francis Johnson, took charge of the Mexican general and the prisoners, disarmed them, paroled them and sent them on the march southward under promises not to bear arms against Texas again.

Not one of Santa Anna's soldiers now remained north of the Rio Grande. But Houston and his Texans knew that this situation could not last. El Presidente would seek revenge. And the first item of that revenge the Mexican chieftain found at the Alamo.

Now thoroughly determined to subjugate the rebellious Texans, Santa Anna called up the bulk of his forces, numbering about 5,000 officers and men. He ordered General José Urrea with 2,000 cavalry to move northward from Matamoros along the coast, as the right column of his campaign. From Bexar he dispatched General Antonio Gaona toward Washington-on-the-Brazos, hoping to trap the civilian leaders of the rebellion. He himself moved eastward toward Gonzales, to track down the principal quarry, Sam Houston and his army of Texans and adventurers. With Santa Anna was General Cos and his corps—in contemptuous violation of the parole agreement.

On February 27 Urrea surprised Colonel Johnson at Agua Dulce, killing or capturing the Texas force of about a hundred men. On March 7 he swooped upon Captain Grant and his company at San Patricio; Grant was killed, and his survivors made prisoners. On March 16 Urrea found Captain King and his company at Refugio, preparing to join Fannin, and wiped out the entire detachment.

It is difficult to explain why the meager American forces were so scattered as to make these disasters possible, unless the nature of Sam Houston is kept in mind. He possessed a curiously mixed mysticism and stubbornness. He had periods of moody indecision. He shrank from delegating or sharing authority. He was not only the commander-in-chief of the Texas forces but the whole general staff.

During February 1836, Houston was engrossed in the task of assembling the convention of leading citizens to make his dream of independence for Texas come true. On March 1 the convention met, in a big store building. On the next day the first who had escaped from the Alamo rushed into the room, bearing Colonel Travis' urgent message. It was Sam Houston's birthday, and the delegates were preparing to adjourn to honor their leader with a barbecue, but now they dispensed with celebrations to get on with business. A declaration of independence was adopted, proclaiming that Texas was a sovereign republic. Houston was "confirmed" as general of the Texas army. He had left his main force at Gonzales, and now, like a huge hound eager for the chase, he set out with his aides to join it. He sent an order to Colonel Fannin, waiting with a regiment at Goliad, to meet him. They would march to the relief of the men in the Alamo. They would again send the Mexicans flying toward the Rio Grande.

"The Only Chance of Saving Texas"

At Washington-on-the-Brazos the convention moved painfully along in the difficult job of composing a constitution for the new republic. Most of the sections had been drafted on March 6, when Travis' final message reached the delegates. On March 16 another messenger, sweaty, dusty and grim, brought the tragic news that the defenders at the Alamo had been wiped out. Several panic-stricken delegates at once dashed for their horses and rode away. Some wanted to adjourn the convention. Big, gruff David G. Burnett from Gonzales jumped upon the speaker's table and bellowed:

"This convention will not adjourn until we adopt a constitution!"

At 10 o'clock that night, the draft of the constitution was ready. At midnight Burnett was sworn in as the republic's provisional President. For Vice-President the convention chose Lorenzo de Zavala, a Mexican who had served in many high offices in his government, now a refugee from Santa Anna's tyranny. During the early hours of that March 17, 1836, the delegates assisted Burnett in selecting a Cabinet—which included as Secretary of War Colonel Thomas J. Rusk, who had gone with Houston to join the troops. At 4 A.M. those of the Cabinet who were present were sworn in. At 5 o'clock all hands adjourned for breakfast. Burnett and his "government" decided to establish their capital at Harrisburg on the Buffalo Bayou. There, they assumed, they would be safe from attack.

When Houston reached Gonzales, he learned of the disaster at San Antonio de Bexar. Many wives of the massacred soldiers were at Gonzales, and news of the tragedy covered them with a pall of grief.

Now with furious energy Houston began barking his orders. "Send word to Fannin to destroy Goliad and fall back to Victoria!" He commanded everyone to leave Gonzales. "Fire the town!" The houses and barns were soon ablaze. The retreat began, with the men of the army helping push the heavy wagons loaded with the goods of the settlers, back toward the northeast. Houston made no explanation of his plans; only that he would join Fannin and together they would round up the rest of his fighting men and somewhere take a stand.

But still another tragedy fell upon the Texans. Colonel Fannin seemed not to understand the urgency of Houston's order to retreat. Suddenly he found his force surrounded by a ring of General Urrea's cavalry, through which only twenty of his men escaped. Fannin surrendered with his 370 men, on agreement that all would be given "honorable treatment accorded prisoners of war." The Mexican general pledged that lives and property of the prisoners would be safe.

Santa Anna was white with fury. "I have said that every rebellious gringo in Texas must be killed!" he declared.

Urrea mildly protested—then did as he was ordered. The unarmed prisoners were commanded to fall into groups of fifty. In different directions they were led away. Not until the order had been given to halt, and another command for the Mexican guards to aim, could the defenseless men believe they were to be massacred. Some rushed barehanded and raging upon their captors. Others folded their arms and stood in helpless defiance. The volleys rang out—and again. . . . There were scattered shots—the *coups de grace*—and the trampled grass and bluebonnets ran red with blood.

Now the people of Texas were thoroughly alarmed. All over the region they began loading their wagons and hurrying toward Louisiana. Many joined the wagon train traveling under protection of Houston's troops. Others organized their own bands of defenders carrying rifles and knives. There was bitter grumbling. Why had they come to this accursed country? They would all be slaughtered. Even Sam Houston was retreating, and not saying whether he would make a stand. Was Texas to be abandoned to this devil Santa Anna?

At Harrisburg, President Burnett was raging against the general for not making a more effective defense. Even some of Houston's officers, attempting to keep up the morale of their weary and rain-soaked soldiers, were openly critical. Why did the general not tell them of his plans? Why did he not call a council of war? He never consulted them. He only retreated.

Under all bludgeonings, Sam Houston remained grim and silent. He had formulated his plan. He would fall back and draw Santa Anna into Texas as far as he could. He would lead him away from his supporting columns, and make a stand. But he told no one. He merely said, "Ten to one outnumbered—but we'll beat them when the time comes!"

Near the Brazos River the general replenished his commissary, dried out his troops, made the fugitives under his protection as comfortable as possible, and received the very welcome gift of two cannon, bought by popular subscription in Cincinnati and shipped to him by the long water route. These were right good five-inch pieces, and gave him what he so badly needed—a battery of artillery. His men christened them the "Twin Sisters," and set about cutting up old horseshoes to use for cannon shot.

When Santa Anna reached Harrisburg, he found that the officials of the new government had fled. He burned the town and pushed on toward the San Jacinto River. Now Houston became the pursuer. On the day after the Mexican general left Harrisburg, the Texans reached the smoking ruins, and camped. Erastus "Deaf" (pronounced Deef) Smith, one of Houston's best scouts, came in with some prisoners, and from them it was learned that Santa Anna had left Cos's corps behind in his eagerness to reach Harrisburg. Santa Anna would have with him only about one thousand men.

General Houston pondered this situation. He quietly studied his worn maps. The time had come to make a stand, before Cos and his corps could join the Mexican leader. He called an aide and laboriously dictated a "Manifest to the Army," dated April 29, which said:

This morning we are in preparation to meet Santa Anna. It is the only chance of saving Texas. From time to time I have looked for reinforcements in vain. We will have only about 700 men to march with, besides the camp guard. We go to conquer. It is wisdom growing out of necessity to meet the enemy now; every consideration enforces it. No previous occasion would justify it. . . . I leave the results in the hands of a wise God, I rely upon his Providence. My country will do justice to those who serve her. The rights for which we fight will be secured, and Texas Freed.

SAM HOUSTON

That night the general left a guard for his sick and the baggage, ferried his small army over the Buffalo Bayou, then across Vince's Bayou on a narrow wooden bridge, and on eastward through mud and darkness—following the same route Santa Anna's force had taken twenty-four hours before. At 2 o'clock a halt was made for rest. At 3 o'clock reveille sounded and the Texans pressed on, their hard-riding scouts on tough mustang horses ranging ahead and on the flanks. Houston was determined to find the Mexican force and surprise it if possible. At midmorning Houston's hungry, fatigued men came upon some cattle and were slaughtering the beeves when scouts brought word that Santa Anna had reached San Jacinto Bay and was marching toward Lynch's Ferry, six miles away.

"March at once!" Houston ordered, and the breakfastless men tramped forward. The Texans reached Lynch's Ferry, and gained the shelter of a wood hard by the bank of the San

Jacinto River. Again beeves were found and slaughtered, but before mess was ready, Santa Anna's force was sighted, deploying for battle.

Though he had hoped to surprise his enemy, Houston could do little but stand and fight. He ordered Lieutenant Colonel Joe Neill, commanding the Twin Sisters, to drag these guns forward from the wood—guns that had never been fired even in practice—and to aim them at the advancing line. He held his other troops at the edge of the wood. Forward the Mexicans came, infantry to the right, cavalry to the left, the lone cannon—a brass twelve-pounder—in the center. At three hundred yards the line halted.

"First battery, fire!" shouted Neill, and the first Twin Sister roared her scrap-iron missiles across the grassy terrain. Through the smoke the Texans could see that several men and horses were wounded, and that the enemy gun carriage was disabled. The second "battery" blazed away—with more Mexican casualties. Then—BOOM! came the roar of the Mexican cannon, its shot going over the heads of the Texans and into the branches of the trees. Several more rounds were fired on both sides, but no effective aim could be taken with the disabled Mexican gun.

Colonel Neill became a most costly casualty, badly wounded in the hip by a musket ball. Houston ordered his infantry to fire, and with the blast, a row of the enemy sank to the grass. The Mexican line reeled back. Santa Anna ordered a hasty withdrawal. Lieutenant Colonel Sidney Sherman, an eager Kentuckian commanding a battalion of infantry, led a squadron of cavalry in an attempt to capture the enemy fieldpiece. Sharp resistance from a squadron of Mexican dragoons thwarted the move, and Sherman retired with two men and several horses wounded.

Santa Anna gathered up his dead and wounded, and made camp near the bank of the San Jacinto, three-quarters of a mile from the Texans. General Houston, greatly relieved, pulled his men back into the shelter of the wood, and the first meal of the day was eaten.

Near sunset the general reluctantly allowed Lamar and a squadron to ride out to reconnoiter the enemy camp. Mexican cavalry met them and in the engagement two more Texans were wounded. Lieutenant Colonel Henry Millard advanced with an infantry battalion to aid Lamar's retreat. The men spent the night in the first full rest they had enjoyed in five days, yet with the knowledge that the battle would be resumed in earnest next day.

At dusk Santa Anna's scouts informed him that Cos and his force were only an all-night distance away. The Mexican general went to sleep entirely satisfied with his prospects for victory in the morning.

"Remember the Alamo!"

It is far from daybreak of that morning of April 21, 1836, but Sam Houston is dressed and walking alone under the stars. He is making his plan of battle. He directs an orderly to wake his principal officers. At 4 o'clock the general himself sounds reveille by beating on a bass drum. He breakfasts on jerked beef, hard biscuits and coffee, with his officers. He gives them his orders for the battle line, then calmly lies down under a tree and goes to sleep again.

It is broad daylight when Houston rouses himself, stretches and remarks, "The sun of Austerlitz has risen again!"

The general of the Texas armies puts on his fringed buckskin coat, buckles his belt with its pistol and hunting knife, claps on his hat with its feather, mounts his big white stallion and rides along to inspect the preparations for battle. Beyond the wood that screens his small but resolute army, between him and the Mexican camp, lies an almost level prairie, covered with deep grass. At his left is the riverbank, and there stand the men of the 2d Regiment under Lieutenant Colonel Sherman. Next is the 1st Regiment under Colonel Edward Burleson, with the New Orleans Grays—only company in the whole line to display anything like similar uniforms. Behind these regiments, in reserve, are the companies of Colonel Rusk, the Secretary of War. The Twin Sisters, heartily loved by the men of the hard-bitten army for their effective work the day before, are waiting near the edge of the wood, ready to wheel into the center of the line. Watching over them solicitously are the wounded Neill's replacement, Colonel George Hockley, his two artillery captains, two lieutenants, two sergeants and four privates. On the right are the fifty-three mounted men, proudly calling themselves the "cavalry brigade," under command of Mirabeau Bonaparte Lamar—a former private, who had so impressed Houston during the campaign that the general promoted him in one jump to colonel.

The Texas general can count only 783 men under his command, but he counts also upon the desperate bravery of the Americans, driven to this last stand to secure the independence of Texas, and upon the strategy of battle which he with his Indian cunning had decided to use against his vengeful adversary.

Mexican bugles have sounded and Santa Anna has arranged his troops. The infantry regiment of his right wing is lined up along the low bank of the placid river. For nearly two hundred yards his line of infantry and cavalry extend, with the lone fieldpiece in the center. His men of the left wing erect some barricades of lumber and bring up their wagons, piled with baggage, behind them.

At 8:30 of the sunny morning, a cloud of dust signals the approach of Cos and his men, 540 strong. Half an hour later Santa Anna is embracing his brother-in-law, while cheers of the new arrivals mingle with those of the main force. Silently, with tightened lips and grim faces, the American sentries

watch these reinforcements enter the Mexican camp. Santa
Anna now counts more than 1,500 soldiers at his command,
outnumbering the Americans almost two to one.

All the rest of the morning General Houston calmly waits,
squatting under a tree or lolling in the shade inside his small
tent, with a nonchalance that irks his officers and men. The
soldiers rest in their places, anxious and wondering. Houston's
silence is broken only by an occasional shouted order.

It is noon. "Feed the men!" The food is rationed and eaten.
"Fill the canteens!" Water is ladled out. "Water the mounts!"
The horses are watered.

Houston summons his chief commissary, John Forbes, and
orders him to fetch two axes. These he hands to Deaf Smith
and an orderly, quietly giving them some word of instruction.
Smith and his companion dash across the prairie and disappear.

The sun moves warmly toward 2 o'clock. All is quiet in the
Mexican camp, where most of the soldiers have stacked their
arms and are lying down. It is siesta time. The sentries sit
sleepily or lean indolently on their muskets.

At 3:30 Houston pops his huge watch back into a pocket and
says to an aide:

"Pass the order quietly to form for parade!"

Quickly the officers pass the order from company to company. Eagerly the men seize their pieces, and reform the lines.
The Twin Sisters are gorged with powder and scrap iron. The
cavalry companies mount. By 4 P.M. all is in readiness. The
only flag displayed by this little army of Americans from a
score or more of states fighting as Texans is a white silk banner
with the figure of a woman's head, labeled "Liberty," hoisted
by a company of Sherman's Kentuckians. Beneath it, the glove
of an officer's sweetheart bravely flutters.

Houston mounts his stallion. He commands the whole force
to move forward under cover of the wood until ordered to

debouch, then to advance directly toward the Mexican line. All are to hold their fire until the general gives the word. This advance is made. Then, turning his big frame in his saddle, Houston calls out:

"Remember the Alamo, men! Forward!"

At that moment Deaf Smith and the orderly charge back into the wood, their horses flecked with foam and dust. "We've chopped down Vince's bridge!" bellows the old scout, waving his axe. "Now fight for your lives—and remember the Alamo!"

"Remember the Alamo!" shout the bronzed men as they stride or ride over the grass of the plain. Mexican sentinels cry the alarm, but no lines are ready to form. Lamar's cavalry swings wide to the right, but no enemy cavalry answers the movement. Even Santa Anna's horses are at siesta, unsaddled.

At about two hundred yards from the enemy line, Houston orders the cannon to halt and fire. The men pulling at the ropes wheel about.

"Boom! B-L-OOM!" roar the Twin Sisters, the jagged shot tearing great gaps in the flimsy breastworks of lumber, wagons and baggage. Quickly the cannon are loaded and fired again. And again.

Now across the open terrain the Americans come at a jog trot. Some Mexican troops are at the barricades and firing, but most of their bullets whine harmlessly overhead. Through gaps made by the Twin Sisters, soldiers can be seen rushing this way and that. Some are wounded and writhing among the shattered wagons.

"Hold your fire, men!" is Houston's call with every few paces, as the general rides grandly in front of the line, prominent as an equestrian statue overtopping the shrubs in a park. Suddenly his big horse staggers and falls, shot through the chest. Houston is unhurt. Scrambling to his feet, he runs to mount a small brown steed of one of the officers. The tone of his voice never changes: "Hold the fire until I command!"

On they advance, so near that Houston's men wonder if he will let them walk into the muzzles of the Mexican rifles. At about fifty yards he orders:

"Charge, men! Charge—and fire!"

Through the boards of the barricades, over the tops of the wagons, into the Mexican camp the Texans swarm. Before them is a scene of utmost confusion. Officers are shouting commands, but commotion and panic are more conspicuous than military order. Most of Cos's men have been sleeping after their all-night march, and now they stagger from their small tents, unarmed. Taking deadly aim, Houston's sharp-shooters send a storm of leaden hail into their targets, the thunder of their pieces rolling over the prairie. Mexican soldiers flee in crowds, tossing away their arms. Those who show more courage and offer resistance are clubbed or stabbed. One brave Mexican officer forms a line on the right, only to see his men fall or run from the withering fire of the attackers. Grimly the Texans reload their rifles and pick their targets, and with almost every shot an enemy falls.

"Remember the Alamo!" shout the Texans, and even the enemy troops who understand little English know the terrible significance of that battle cry. In terror many kneel and beg:

"Me no Alamo! Me no Alamo!" Most of these were rounded up as prisoners of war.

The Twin Sisters have been wheeled up, but they can no longer be fired because of the melee of fighting men. Colonel Lamar circles his cavalry back of the camp. Closing in, his riders help to put the remaining Mexican force to rout. Lamar then sends Captain Henry Karnes with most of the cavalry in pursuit of the enemy who have mounted and fled.

From the first minute of the attack, Houston has felt a sharp pain just above his right ankle. He knows he is wounded, but ignores the pain through the tension of the battle. As the firing dies away he glances at the blood oozing from a hole in his boot. He rides up to where Colonel Hockley is standing and falls unconscious into that officer's arms.

All the rest of the afternoon and into the darkness, the chase for Santa Anna's fleeing soldiers goes on. All night the prisoners are brought in. The general has recovered sufficiently to lie on a pallet, with leg bandaged, and issue a few orders. He endures his wound stoically, knowing that by the "River of Saint Hyacinth" he and his brave men have won the independence of Texas.

"When the Time Comes——"

Before taps sounded that night, the victorious Texans counted their casualties: six killed and twenty-five wounded; two of the wounded later died. The Mexican loss totaled 632 killed, including one general, four colonels, two lieutenant colonels, five captains, twelve lieutenants; there were 208 wounded, officers and men. Very few of the remaining 730 escaped. General Almonte, Santa Anna's chief of staff, and nearly four hundred of his corps were captured in a body. The booty taken totaled in round figures nine hundred English muskets, three hundred sabers, two hundred pistols, four hundred mules and horses, along with ammunition, tents and provisions. Captured also were 24,000 silver pesos which Santa Anna expected to use to pay his troops after victory.

The slain general was neither Santa Anna nor Cos. Where were they? Late in the afternoon of the day after the battle an American soldier brought in a prisoner, a small man dressed in a lounging robe with felt slippers on his feet. The soldier had found the man trying to hide in the grass, near where Vince's bridge had been destroyed, and close by was a black horse with a fine saddle. The guard was about to turn the captive loose among the herds of prisoners, when several Mexicans stepped forward and greeted the man almost reverently: "El Presidente." It was Santa Anna.

The defeated leader was brought before Sam Houston as the general lay on his blanket. Despite Santa Anna's ridiculous appearance—the battle having interrupted his siesta—he resumed his imperial manner. He demanded an interpreter. Houston waved an arm, and a young Mexican stepped forward. Santa Anna was startled to recognize him as Lorenzo de Zavala, Jr., son of El Presidente's old political enemy. With a formal bow Santa Anna told General Houston (in words that historians of that period may have translated too heroically):

"That man may consider himself born to no common destiny who has conquered the Napoleon of the West!"

Bracing himself on an elbow, Houston upbraided his captive severely for the massacres at the Alamo and Goliad. Santa Anna blandly assured Houston that he was acting "under orders of my government."

"A dictator has no government but his own!" roared Sam Houston. After more heated conversation, Santa Anna proposed an armistice. Houston dictated the terms: Immediate evacuation of Texas by all Mexican forces. Knowing he had met his Waterloo, the Napoleon of the West agreed.

Two days later Cos was brought in. Urrea reached the Brazos River, heard of the crushing defeat of his countrymen and fled southward, trailed by the other Mexican forces that had followed Santa Anna's route as far as Austin.

During the weeks that followed, most of the settlers, rejoicing at the news of victory, returned to their ranches and homes. Houston's wound slowly healed, while he debated what to do with his chief prisoner, Santa Anna. A message from his friend Andy Jackson brought Houston's decision. On May 14 he sent El Presidente to Vera Cruz, keeping him hostage there until he signed a treaty by which Mexico agreed to withdraw all claims to territory north of the Rio Grande. Houston then released Santa Anna, an act praised as generous by some and cursed as foolish and dangerous by others.

Thus was the independence of Texas won, and secured. In a general election of the citizens on September 1, 1836, Sam Houston became President of the Republic. A flag was adopted, with its lone star symbolizing the single grandeur of the vast area. President Jackson was happy, freely predicting that "when the time comes" Texas would be a part of the United States. That time came in 1845, when Texas was admitted to the Union. Houston served as one of its first two senators.

Until the admission of Alaska, Texas was the biggest state in the Union. Its proud citizens occasionally remind themselves—and others—that it is still "the biggest glacier-free state."

Truly, Texas is big with the boundless spirit of American progress and growth. It has grown to be an economic, social and political empire, whose people can never forget that the Lone Star Republic was formed and preserved by men and women whose spirits were bold with adventure and whose hearts were strong in the love of freedom. Lest any forget, a fitting monument stands at the site of the decisive battle near the bank of the San Jacinto.

CHAPTER NINE

Taylor Stands Fast near Buena Vista

On a mid-July day in 1845, a rugged American career soldier, Zachary Taylor, commanding the Department of the Southwest with headquarters at Baton Rouge, Louisiana, received a very welcome order from President James K. Polk, through Secretary of War William L. Marcy, which began:

"In order to safeguard the rights and honor of the United States, Brigadier General Z. Taylor will proceed at once from his headquarters on the Mississippi, moving the main body of his regulars into Texas." The order stipulated that the commander and his troops were to proceed to the mouth of the Nueces River and be in readiness for action if Mexican armed forces made aggressive moves.

General Taylor loaded his tiny army of two infantry and one cavalry regiments on sailing vessels, headed down the Mississippi and out over the green waters of the Gulf of Mexico to the small town of Corpus Christi on the Nueces—and to a rendezvous with destiny that increased the size of the United States by more than one-third, opening up vast regions to permanent settlement.

Since the defeat of their forces under Santa Anna in 1836, Mexican leaders, with British encouragement, had plotted the reconquest of Texas, and were especially hostile to annexation by the United States. Officially, they claimed that the southern border of Texas was the Nueces River—not the Rio Grande.

Early in 1844 Andrew Jackson, enjoying the honors of a former President and retired national hero at his Tennessee farm home, wrote Polk's predecessor, President Tyler:

"The present golden moment to obtain Texas must not be lost, or Texas might from necessity be thrown into the arms of England and be forever lost to the United States."

Tyler agreed with "Old Hickory." Before turning the President's Mansion over to Polk, he secured a joint resolution of Congress calling for annexation of Texas. On June 18, 1845, the Texas Congress and President Sam Houston formally approved this resolution, and on July 4 the Lone Star was added to the flag of the Stars and Stripes.

Already, the great westward movement of pioneer settlers had reached the Pacific Coast. A dispute with England over the boundary of Oregon Territory aroused the cry of "Fifty-four Forty or Fight!"—a demand that the territory be extended to the 54° 40′ parallel. The matter was settled peacefully, but the temper of the people was clear. Destiny was forming a great nation. Now President Polk saw the need to add to Texas the great southwestern territories and round out its unbroken sweep from the Atlantic to the Pacific. No one dreamed of the immense wealth of gold and other minerals, of oil, nor even of the countless products of the soil of this southwestern area, that in future years would enrich the whole mighty American Republic. But to acquire it was the firm objective of President Polk.

While determined to defend Texas by arms if necessary, the President tried diplomacy with the Mexican government. He sent a special envoy, John Slidell of Louisiana, with an offer to purchase all the territory west of Texas clear to California. The current *Presidente,* Mariano Paredes y Arrillaga, refused to receive Mr. Slidell, on the grounds that General Taylor and his troops had "invaded" Mexico by being in Texas. In a public statement, President Polk assured the American people:

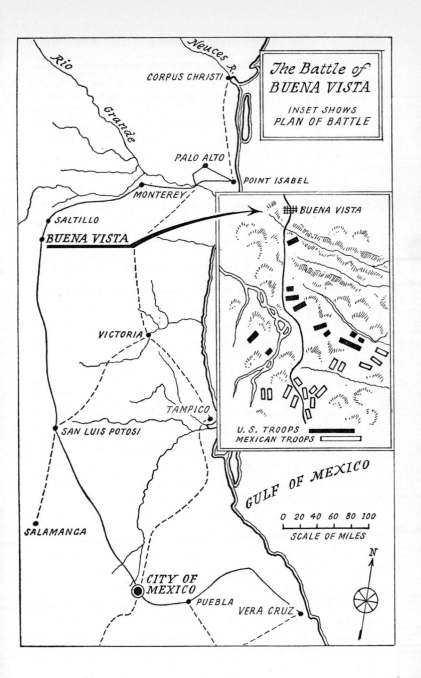

The Battle of
BUENA VISTA

INSET SHOWS
PLAN OF BATTLE

Rio Grande

Neuces R.

CORPUS CHRISTI

PALO ALTO

POINT ISABEL

MONTEREY

SALTILLO

BUENA VISTA

VICTORIA

TAMPICO

SAN LUIS POTOSI

SALAMANCA

BUENA VISTA

U. S. TROOPS
MEXICAN TROOPS

GULF OF MEXICO

0 20 40 60 80 100
SCALE OF MILES

N

CITY OF
MEXICO

PUEBLA

VERA CRUZ

It is a wise maxim of the Father of his Country that to be prepared for war is one of the most efficient means of preserving peace. . . . It is my settled purpose to pursue such a course of policy as may be best calculated to preserve, both with Great Britain and Mexico, an honorable peace, which nothing will so effectively promote as unanimity in our councils and a firm maintenance of all our just rights.

While this pronouncement was being pondered by the people all over the nation, General Taylor received an order from the War Department to march his force from Corpus Christi southward to the Rio Grande, and to be ready for hostilities. He and his officers had spent the seven months at their camp on the Nueces drilling the troops with stern discipline. The force had been augmented to about 2,800 men—about half the entire United States Army—and included the 3d, 4th, 5th, 7th, and 8th infantry regiments; the 1st, 2d, 3d, and 4th artillery battalions and the 2d regiment of dragoons. Taylor's order designated his force as the "Army of Occupation."

On March 8, 1846, the general led his army across the Nueces River into the disputed territory which constituted virtually an act of war. Taylor and his staff rode ahead with the dragoons, while in the rear were two hundred lumbering supply wagons. Over the 180 miles of sun-warmed coastal area of Texas, this first American Army of Occupation marched and camped and marched again. At Point Isabel, ten miles from the Rio Grande, the expeditionary force set up a supply depot; thence on to the northern bank of the river, about five miles from its mouth, opposite the town of Matamores. Here Taylor made camp, threw up fortifications and pointed his artillery meaningfully toward the town.

After several weeks of waiting and watching by the American forces, General Pedro de Ampudia arrived at Matamores with a large force, and sent an "order" to General Taylor to draw back to the Nueces River. Taylor countered with a blockade of the Rio Grande, hoping this might force the Mexican army to withdraw for lack of supplies. On April 23 Mexican cavalry units were seen crossing the Rio Grande about thirty miles upstream. Taylor sent a company of dragoons under Captain T. B. Thornton to observe their movements. The Mexicans ambushed the American cavalrymen, killing eleven and taking the others, several of whom were wounded, across the Rio Grande as prisoners. General Taylor's dispatch announcing this event reached President Polk on May 11. In a stirring message to Congress the President declared:

"Mexico has passed the boundaries of the United States, has invaded our territory and shed American blood upon the American soil. . . . War exists, by the act of Mexico herself."

The declaration of war, passed by Congress two days later, was but a ratification of Polk's words.

"Old Rough and Ready" in the Field

Now the eyes of the nation turned toward Texas and the general of the troops, this soldier with his rugged face, large nose, tousled gray hair and firm mouth. Of all the commanders who have honored the military services of the United States, Zachary Taylor was the most informal in dress. He rarely wore a uniform, being content with a campaign hat bearing the insignia of an officer. He assumed that all subordinates would understand his rank and his authority.

This Virginia-born soldier was the son of an officer in the Revolutionary War. Reared in the frontier state of Kentucky, Taylor was given his first military commission in 1808 by President Jefferson as lieutenant in the 7th Infantry. Throughout nearly four decades he had led the life of a regular army officer: in the Indian campaigns under General William Henry Harrison, through the War of 1812 in posts of the Northwest Territory, as major in the Black Hawk War, as colonel in the war against the Seminole Indians in 1837. He had gone from one garrison and one command to another, building solidly his reputation as a hard-headed, determined man, ready to take orders but more anxious to give them. His soldiers called him "Old Rough and Ready."

General Harrison, "Old Tippecanoe," was Taylor's hero. Both were Whigs by political conviction. When Harrison became President in 1841, he promoted Colonel Taylor to brigadier general and granted his request to be assigned to the Southwest. Taylor bought a big plantation near Baton Rouge, hoping to retire to rural life some day. Now a war was postponing that retirement, but Zachary Taylor did not mind. He was eager for action.

General Winfield Scott was the Army's senior officer and its only major general at the declaration of war. Polk had planned to place him in command of the operations against Mexico, but hearing of Scott's criticisms of the administration's "expansionist policies," the President left General Taylor in charge of that faraway expedition. Now the President, Secretary Marcy and their advisers mapped three distinct campaigns against Mexico: Taylor would invade from the Rio Grande. Brigadier General John E. Wool would head another army to occupy the central provinces of northern Mexico and aid Taylor in his invasion and occupation. A new "Army of the West," assembling at Fort Leavenworth on the Missouri River under Brigadier General Stephen W. Kearny, would march into New Mexico and on westward to California to seize all the southwestern region. Long before the declaration of war, President Polk had formed a plan to annex California. In June 1845 he had sent Commodore John Sloat with a fleet of gunboats around to the Pacific under instructions to occupy San Francisco if war should start.

After the successful ambush of Thornton's squadron, the Mexican forces under a new commander, General Mariano

Arista, moved across the Rio Grande with the objective of destroying the American supply base at Point Isabel and then attacking Taylor's army. Leaving two artillery batteries and several infantry companies under command of Major Jacob Brown to protect the camp and fort opposite Matamores, Taylor led the main body of his troops to Isabel by a forced march of eighteen hours. Arista seized this chance to attempt what he was sure would be a quick victory. He turned his 6,000 green-and-scarlet-uniformed troops to a direct assault upon Brown's sparse garrison. The American artillery opened up on the Mexican columns pointblank, while infantry riflemen took deadly aim. Arista hurriedly withdrew, rested his army for a few days and moved northward to meet Taylor's force.

In a report to the War Department written at Point Isabel on May 6, General Taylor said: "If the enemy oppose my march, in whatever force, I will fight him." When this dispatch was made public some weeks later, following the American leader's victories in the field, his words aroused a wave of patriotic fervor.

On May 7 the army moved toward the Rio Grande, and the next morning found the whole enemy force deployed along the roadway, near the village of Palo Alto. With that deliberate coolness which officers and men had learned was characteristic of this rugged frontier soldier, Taylor halted, sat sideways on his horse, surveyed the scene before him, and pondered.

"They will attack with cannon," he said. "We will answer them in the same way."

The general's surmise proved correct. Ten pieces of artillery opened the action of this first battle of the war. The Mexican cannon were at too great distance for much damage. In the 3d Infantry Regiment of the American army was a young West Pointer, Second Lieutenant Ulysses S. Grant. In his memoirs Grant described how ineffective was the Mexican fire:

As we got nearer, the cannon balls commenced going through the ranks. They hurt no one, however, during this advance, because they would strike the ground long before they reached our line, and ricochetted through the tall grass so slowly that the men would see them and open ranks and let them pass.

Taylor ordered forward his most effective guns, two which threw twelve-pound explosive shells and several eighteen-pound solid shot cannon. "Tell your men to take careful aim!" roared the general at his artillery captains, as the four-horse caissons rolled forward. The "careful aim" devastated the Mexican ranks. The American infantry advanced with its fire, and the Mexicans wavered. Arista's cavalry tried to turn the right of the American line, but troops of the 5th Infantry supported an artillery battery under Major Samuel Ringgold and turned back the attack—at the cost of the gallant major, struck down by an enemy bullet. By nightfall the Mexican army was in full retreat.

Arista fell back three miles to a strong position in a dry ravine called Rasaca de la Palma, determined to use his superior numbers to win a decisive engagement. Again the Americans, outnumbered two to one, moved resolutely forward, to find the Mexican force ready for battle, their cannon in place and the infantry behind breastworks of logs and brush. Again the Mexican artillery answered. Then General Taylor, with the true commander's sense of the value of vigorous attack, ordered his dragoons to charge the Mexican breastworks. He followed this with an infantry charge.

The flashing sabers and bristling bayonets of the Americans struck terror among the Mexicans. One by one their units broke and started a retreat toward the Rio Grande. Many plunged into the river and to their death. The Americans took scores of prisoners. In the two battles, the Mexican force lost about four hundred killed and twice that many wounded, while Taylor reported a total of fifty-three killed and eighty-three wounded. General Arista reformed his shattered regiments south of the Rio Grande, but his offensive was broken.

The American general's officers and men begged to pursue Arista and try a complete defeat of the enemy, but two factors held Taylor back: his cautious nature, and the shortage of wagons for his equipment, ammunition and supplies. Taylor had begged the quartermaster general in Washington for the wagons, but that officer explained later that he had no information "to enable me or the War Department to determine whether wagons could be used in Mexico." Of this situation Colonel R. Ernest Dupuy, historian of the United States Army, has succinctly written: "Already, it appears, the dead hand of bureaucracy lay heavy upon the War Department."

Great Spaces and Iron Men

News of these victories on the Rio Grande prompted thousands of volunteers to make their way across the long stretches of Texas or by water to Corpus Christi to enlist. General Taylor moved his headquarters and camp to the town of Camargo, on the San Juan River a few miles from its junction with the Rio Grande. He and his officers spent most of the summer and fall occupying towns and building forts upon the Rio Grande, drilling recruits and laying in stores and supplies, along with denouncing the Quartermaster Corps for being so tardy not only with wagons but with medicines and other essentials for the army. Fever and dysentery from the stifling heat and brackish water struck down hundreds of the troops. In one Tennessee regiment, typical of all the units, an average of six men were buried every day for weeks.

Meanwhile, General Kearny and his Army of the West, its principal unit a regiment of Missouri volunteer infantry under Colonel Alexander Doniphan, were moving southwestward over the trail toward Santa Fe in one of the most remarkable marches in military history. Day after day the troops plodded along. Through heat, dust and mud they marched, fighting thirst and fatigue through the summer days, adding to their hard rations the meat from herds of bison so numerous as to appear like dark shadows upon the great plains. With these troops were about five hundred young Mormon men, many with their families, equipped as soldiers and ready for their share of the fighting, in return for being conducted safely to the Great Southwest.

Senor José Armijo, governor of New Mexico, evacuated Santa Fe at the approach of the invading Americans, and on August 18 Kearny and his men marched grandly into this capital without firing a shot. The general issued manifestos to the people, announcing that New Mexico henceforth was to be a part of the United States.

Leaving Colonel Doniphan and his Missourians to hold and "pacify" New Mexico, General Kearny and the rest of his force pressed westward. They soon met the famous scout and Indian fighter, Kit Carson, conducting a party on the long trail to Washington, who brought the startling news that California was already occupied by American troops. At the declaration of war, Commodore John D. Sloat had landed his men at the village of Monterey, and his successor, Commodore Robert F. Stockton, with the help of the exploring engineer, John C. Frémont, had planted the American flag over towns all about California. Kearny and his force nevertheless moved on, reaching San Diego on January 29, 1847, worn and fatigued from the merciless march.

By early September, despite losses from sickness, the cautious general considered that he had an army ready for the invasion of Mexico. He still lacked wagons, but bought hundreds of mules and burros to carry the ammunition, tents and supplies. His drill sergeants had whipped the mass of volunteers from states all over the Union into well-disciplined companies and battalions. His command now mustered about

12,000 troops, of which 3,000 were regulars. Among his sea-
soned volunteers was the regiment of mounted Mississippi
Rifles, jauntily wearing red coats and white trousers, many
of them sons of the men who had fought with Jackson at New
Orleans, now commanded by General Taylor's son-in-law,
Colonel Jefferson Davis.

Taylor selected a combat force, balancing his regulars with
about the same number of the best of his volunteers, and led
the 6,000 hardy soldiers along the valley of the San Juan
toward his next objective, the city of Monterrey. This town of
10,000 inhabitants, lying at the base of the Sierra Madre
Mountains, was a key commercial center. Once in possession
of Monterrey, General Taylor could take Saltillo and push
on into the heart of northern Mexico. General Ampudia had
replaced the unsuccessful Arista, and knowing the importance
of Monterrey was waiting in the city with a strongly entrenched force. His position was ideal for defense. To the
north was a wide plain, where he posted a battery of artillery.
To the northwest were hills fortified with cannon; to the south
the San Juan and the lofty mountain range. Inside the town
was a strongly fortified citadel, with guns turned upon every
approach. General Ampudia and his 9,000 men felt secure.

Taylor cautiously advanced his troops to within sight of the
city. A cannon shot roared toward them, booming the Mexican
general's challenge. American scouts rode up with the ominous
news that Antonio Lopez de Santa Anna was back from exile,
had assumed his old role of El Presidente, and was advancing
from San Luis Potosí with a strong army to reinforce
Ampudia. Taylor dispatched Major Joseph Mansfield, chief
engineer officer, with a squadron to reconnoiter the region.
With this unit was Lieutenant George Gordon Meade, who,
like many of the young officers in this invading army, was
a graduate of West Point and destined to play a conspicuous
part in the Civil War. The engineers reported that the western

edge of Monterrey could be flanked and an advance made to seize the Saltillo road, thus cutting communications with Santa Anna's force. The commander promptly dispatched Brigadier General William J. Worth with 2,000 troops, who accomplished this dangerous mission against enemy units that made valiant and stubborn resistance.

The remainder of the three-day battle was a series of determined assaults, in which the bravery and leadership of General Worth was outstanding. Worth begged to lead his men against the nearest fortifications, high upon a hill called *Loma de Federación*. Taylor agreed, and made a diversion with a brigade at the east of the city. Again Ampudia's soldiers fought bravely. Worth's men advanced from one position to another and into the city, while other columns penetrated the eastern defenses. Final assault upon the citadel was made by Worth's troops, among them the Mississippi Rifles, moving under shelter from house to house by cutting great holes in the walls. Long after this battle Taylor was criticized by some of his officers and men for failure to coordinate the attacks, but none questioned his bravery. Throughout the fighting the general rode about on his gray horse, personally issuing orders, careless of his own safety, sickened at the loss of life and the suffering of the wounded.

Although the Mexican force still far outnumbered that of the invaders, General Ampudia called for an armistice. Lacking in heavy guns for an artillery assault to dislodge the defenders, realizing that a siege would mean death to many women and children, and anxious to avoid further bloodshed, Taylor granted the armistice. He generously allowed eight weeks suspension of fighting, the Mexican forces to surrender the city. Losses were heavy: for the Americans, 120 killed and 368 wounded; losses of the defenders of Monterrey were not accurately recorded, but apparently they ran higher than those of the Americans.

Here was another victory for Old Rough and Ready, and for his hardy officers and men! But President Polk refused to approve the eight-weeks' armistice. Concerned because of Taylor's increasing political prestige, Polk toyed with the idea of appointing Robert Patterson, a Pennsylvania militiaman and supporter whom the President had commissioned a major general from civilian life, to replace Taylor. Patterson had proved to be a capable leader with Taylor's force, but fearing adverse public reaction Polk decided that General Winfield Scott should take command in Mexico. With Scott's orders went agreement to a plan which Scott had persistently advanced: an invasion toward Mexico City through the coastal towns of Vera Cruz and Tampico.

"I Will Meet Santa Anna——!"

Antonio Lopez de Santa Anna was indeed back in the saddle of civil and military dictatorship in Mexico. Since his defeat by Sam Houston's Texans on the San Jacinto, he had led a checkered career, sometimes in exile and sometimes in restless retirement at his villa. He had lost a leg in battle against the French at Vera Cruz. Now the brash and crafty man who still called himself "the Napoleon of the West" was plotting to overthrow General Gomez Pedraza. He sent a messenger to President Polk in Washington, with the proposal that if the United States would help Santa Anna return to Mexico, the general would sign a treaty "to adjust the boundaries" between the two countries. Unfortunately, the President saw possibilities in the plan. His Secretary of the Navy wrote a note to Commodore David Conner, commanding the ships in the Gulf:

COMMODORE: If Santa Anna endeavors to enter the Mexican ports, you will allow him to pass freely.

Respectfully yours, GEORGE BANCROFT

On a summer night the Mexican general, in civilian clothes but wearing the air of a cocky emperor, bustled through the port at Vera Cruz. His partisans at Mexico City welcomed him and seized control of the government. Santa Anna repudiated all the promises made to the gullible *americanos*, recruited thousands of volunteers, joined forces with Ampudia and took the field to oppose General Taylor's victorious march.

"Death to the *gringos!*" was his battle cry.

General Scott decided to make a personal visit to the hero, who was now his subordinate officer in the field, and sent an order for Taylor to meet him at Camargo so that they might make plans for the expedition to capture Mexico City. The officer riding with the message was captured by Mexican scouts and murdered. Within hours Santa Anna was reading Scott's instructions to Taylor. The crafty Mexican leader decided to strike first at Taylor's army, and after annihilating that force to turn to the defense of his capital.

Finding that Taylor was not at Camargo, General Scott returned to Vera Cruz and issued an order that struck Taylor like a blow on the head. The conqueror of Palo Alto, of Resaca and Monterrey was directed to send 9,000 of his troops —most of his force, including the regulars—to Vera Cruz to come under Scott's command for the campaign against Mexico City. Taylor would be left with only enough troops to hold a defensive line. Scott was kind enough to express regret that the victorious divisions under Taylor had to be broken up, but, he said, military necessity made it imperative, and "any benefit that may result to me, personally, from the unequal division of troops, will lessen the pain of your consequent inactivity."

Sensing that this move was designed to induce him to retire from his command and perhaps from the military service, Old Rough and Ready would not give his political enemies that satisfaction. He concluded a lengthy letter of protest to General Scott with these words:

"But however much I may feel personally mortified and outraged by the course pursued, . . . I will carry out in good faith, while I remain in Mexico, the views of the government, though I may be sacrificed in the effort."

Taylor sadly dispatched Generals Patterson and Worth with their divisions to join Scott's army. He had advanced to Saltillo, 50 miles below Monterrey. General Wool, meantime, had penetrated with little opposition to Monclova, ancient capital of Coahuila. Taylor ordered Wool to bring his brigade to Saltillo. The combined force totaled about 4,700, of which only 453 were regulars: three batteries of artillery, commanded by Captains Braxton Bragg, Thomas W. Sherman and John M. Washington, and four companies of dragoons. All the rest were volunteers. But Wool's men were hardened by their long marches. There was still Colonel Jeff Davis' regiment of Mississippi Rifles; a regiment of Arkansas cavalry under Colonel Archibald Yell, former governor of his state; a regiment of Kentucky cavalry under Colonel Humphrey Marshall and another of Kentucky infantry under Colonel William McKee; two regiments of Indiana infantry under Brigadier General Joseph Lane; two regiments of Illinois infantry commanded by Colonels John J. Hardin and William H. Bissell, and two companies of Texas rifles—all with recruits from many states.

Opposing this force was Santa Anna with his army of 20,000 counting upon a swift campaign to defeat the *gringos* and liberate Monterrey. The Mexican chieftain's plan left Vera Cruz with a little garrison, but he counted on an ally worth many pieces of artillery to hold Scott and the invaders in check. Yellow fever had broken out in the city!

General Taylor faced the alternative of making a stand and risking his army, or withdrawing. He never hesitated. He called no council of war to debate his duty. He simply said:

"I will meet Santa Anna—and it will be on ground of my choosing!"

Taylor moved his force southward to Agua Nueva, on the road leading to San Luis Potosí. This ground he chose proved to be a mistake, for its open fields offered little chance for defensive action. General Wool pointed out to his commander the advantage of falling back eleven miles to a narrow pass—*La Angostura*—just below the large *hacienda* of Buena Vista, and Taylor reluctantly pulled back to that point. The pass was about three miles wide, with a stream at the west side of the road, beyond which were wide gullies deep enough to stop artillery and cavalry movements. On the east side the ground swelled gradually toward the mountain range, cut by several ravines which carried torrents of water in rainy seasons.

Santa Anna reached Agua Nueva, and finding the abandoned American camp he assumed that his enemy was in full retreat. Taylor rode back to Saltillo to inspect his small garrison there, as scouts had reported that a Mexican cavalry brigade under General Vincente Minon was approaching that town. Early next morning Old Rough and Ready was back at the pass, where General Wool had placed the units in readiness for battle. Every man standing by his weapons knew that more depended upon this engagement than holding a mountain pass. Defeat would wipe out the fruits of the previous victories and open the way for Santa Anna to invade Texas.

"To the Memory of George Washington!"

The morning sun of February 22, 1847, shines down brightly on the rocky mountainsides guarding *La Angostura*. With banners flying, his officers mounted on hardy ponies, and with his men in colorful uniforms, Santa Anna halts his columns, 20,000 strong, in distant sight of the American force. The sharp notes of bugles sound and the Mexican army moves slowly forward. The small American force waits grimly, the company officers and their sergeants making final inspections to see that all pieces and ammunition pouches are in order, that all mounts are properly saddled, that all cannon are loaded and the balls, powder and swabs in place for heavy action.

Taylor has given the password of the day, and now it is shouted by officers and men alike: "To the memory of George Washington!"

Eleven o'clock—and Santa Anna's forward squadron is within cannon shot. General Taylor, astride his steed Whitey back of the center of his columns, waits for the first shock of the attack. Instead of cannon or musket shot, there is a deathly stillness, as a Mexican officer breaks out with a white flag. Flanked by a soldier on either side, he gallops to the American front line. He is escorted to the general.

"What is your message?" gruffly asks Taylor.

"Our general, El Presidente," begins the officer, "wants the Americans to understand that they are surrounded by an overwhelming force, and can be saved from defeat only by surrender."

Flushing in anger, Taylor cuts the messenger off with a curt remark that nothing can be decided "except by our gunpowder."

The riders wheel and return to their general. At 3 o'clock in the afternoon, Mexican howitzers and cannon open with a bombardment. The shot and shell cause little damage, because of the long range and poor marksmanship. Taylor holds his fire, content to let the enemy chieftain waste his ammunition.

Again Santa Anna sends a flag of truce. This time his riders bring a message that astonishes and enrages the American commander: "Santa Anna wants to know what General Taylor is waiting for!" Taylor slides sideways upon his mount, glowers down at the messengers and growls:

"Tell Santa Anna I am only waiting for him to surrender!"

There is some light skirmishing on the flanks that extend to the slopes of the sheltering hills. Darkness descends, and the firing ceases. Still concerned about the store of provisions and ammunition at Saltillo, Taylor gallops there with the regiment of Mississippi Rifles and four Illinois cavalry companies, an artillery battery rolling along behind.

Whatever may be Santa Anna's memories of defeat in Texas, he is now the confident braggart. He gathers much of his force before a huge bonfire and harangues them with a bombastic speech, while cheers from his men echo in the ears of the American sentries. The troops of both armies sleep with their arms at their sides.

It is a sleepless night for General Taylor, for he decides that there will be no more need for Colonel Davis' rifles at the battle near Buena Vista and gallops back to the pass with them. Dawn is breaking and the fighting has already begun; Santa Anna has sent a regiment of light infantry up the mountain side to the American left, and General Wool has engaged them. By clear daybreak the Mexican commander orders his main attack. His forward column strikes squarely at the American center. Captain Washington's battery presses to the front and turns its fire point-blank upon the Mexicans. The column halts, and is soon in retreat, leaving a line of dead and wounded.

General Ampudia is in command of the attack on the left flank, held by an Indiana regiment. Here a majority of the Americans are raw recruits. They waver as the Mexican fire again roars upon them. Pressing his advantage, Ampudia orders forward his whole column. The Americans fall back, exposing the entire left flank. It is apparent that the Mexican commander plans to reach the road behind the American lines, and thus cut off retreat and liaison with the force at Saltillo. Taylor sees the danger and calls up Colonel Davis. "Check that column!" is the general's order.

Davis rushes his regiment, with part of the 2d Kentucky and two batteries of artillery under Captain Bragg, to stem the tide of Mexican infantry and mounted lancers. With conspicuous bravery the Southern colonel leads his troops, and as bravely the supporting infantry and handful of cannoneers stand to their task. The accurate aim of the Americans brings the Mexican line to a halt, then sends it in retreat to the foot of the mountain.

The American left flank is saved, but soon it sustains another attack, as Santa Anna sends forward a brigade of cavalry. Again Colonel Davis meets the charge, and his riflemen force the riders to retreat. A ball strikes the intrepid Mississippian in the foot, but he refuses to leave his regiment until forced to do so from loss of blood. As the colonel is helped to the rear he shouts to his men, "Stand fast!"

General Taylor calmly directs every movement of the engagement from a hill back of his troops, sweeping the field with his glass and issuing orders in short, terse words. At a moment when Bragg's battery is hard pressed, Taylor rides up and calls out, "A little more grape, Captain Bragg!"

The Mexican general tries repeatedly to gain the rear of the American army, and with each attempt the choice of the battleground, with its protecting mountains and the valley at the right, proves wise for the defenders of the pass. In open terrain Santa Anna's superior numbers could turn the flanks of Taylor's force and rake the columns at will.

As the battle reaches its height, Santa Anna assembles nearly 4,000 of his best lancers for a charge upon the American right-center. With bugles sounding and pennants waving, the riders approach in columns of regiments, every rider of the lead regiment mounted on a white pony. Taylor orders General Lane's Indiana volunteers and Lieutenant Kilburn's battery to strengthen the line at that point. At seventy yards, the eager Indiana infantrymen begin firing without orders. The Mexican regiments attempt to countermarch to get out of range, and thus they expose their flank to the withering fire of the American artillery. Kilburn's guns throw chain-shot into their ranks. The Mississippians add their raking fire. Again the Mexican bugles sound retreat.

On the right, the Arkansas and Kentucky cavalry regiments under Colonels Yell and Marshall are engaging a heavy force. With repeated charges the Mexicans break through the stubborn defense, placing the whole American flank in a critical position. Again Taylor uses his artillery with telling effect against the outmoded methods of open attacks by columns, as shell and round shot stop the advance. The American musketmen close up, cutting off several thousand Mexicans who have gained the rear. At the head of his column, Colonel Yell falls mortally wounded.

At this point Santa Anna resorts to a despicable ruse. He sends forward another flag of truce. Taylor orders all firing to cease and dispatches General Wool to confer with the Mexican general. No sooner have the officers met than a trumpet sounds, and the trapped Mexican regiments dash through and rejoin their main force. Having accomplished his purpose, Santa Anna haughtily informs General Wool that he only desires to learn "what General Taylor intends to do." In speechless anger Taylor hears Wool's report.

Now the desperate Mexican leader organizes his last great assault. He sends 12,000 of his best troops bearing down upon the right flank, held by Illinois and Kentucky infantry. The Americans fall back, some of the troops retreating in panic to a ravine. Taylor realizes that the most critical moment of the battle has arrived, and again places his main dependence upon artillery. Captain Bragg again leads the guns to position and directs their fire. Canister rains into the Mexican ranks. Unable to force their troops to face those deadly batteries, Mexican officers see their columns retreat in disorder. The American dragoons, cavalry and infantry combine to turn the retreat into a rout. Not even "the Napoleon of the West," riding among his units with flashing sword, can rally the fleeing men.

Meanwhile General Minon and his cavalry have slipped through a narrow mountain pass and gained the Buena Vista road. As they approach the small American garrison at Saltillo, they are met with such withering artillery and rifle fire that they fall back in disorder. With splendid courage, Lieutenant William Shover sallies out with two field guns, and although unescorted his leather-legged gunners chase the enemy riders for three miles until they disappear behind the hills—a feat to crown all the splendid exploits of the artillery during the entire decisive battle!

Midafternoon, and a heavy rain begins to fall, soaking the soldiers who gather up their wounded comrades. Through the dismal night the general and his troops prepare to renew the struggle. The light of morning discloses that Santa Anna has withdrawn his army. With tears of relief, General Wool embraces Old Rough and Ready Taylor.

To the Halls of Montezuma

Whatever Santa Anna's intentions may have been as the day ended, heavy losses of his troops—591 killed, 1,049 seriously wounded and 1,854 prisoners or missing—caused him to abandon any further attacks and retreat to Agua Nueva. He left a field strewn with the dead and wounded. The Americans buried their fallen foemen and ministered to the wounded. Taylor's report listed the cost of the victory to his army: 267 killed, 456 wounded and 23 missing; among the 69 officers who gave their lives leading their troops were Colonels Yell, Hardin and McKee.

Santa Anna's army endured terrible hardships on the march back to San Luis Potosí. More than a thousand died of thirst and disease, while twice that number deserted their leader. The Mexican commander moved his crippled army to Cerro Gordo and entrenched.

General Scott and his forces led a well-executed attack upon Vera Cruz, using landing boats under cover of navy gunboats to seize the beach and attack the city—the first such amphibious operation in United States history. With outstanding gallantry, Lieutenant U. S. Grant, with Worth's division, and a Virginia officer of engineers, Captain Robert E. Lee, took part in this operation.

General Scott penetrated 260 miles into the interior of Mexico, with a force about half that which opposed his march. His generalship and the bravery of his troops won every battle fought. They took Cerro Gordo, Contreras, Churubusco, and Molino del Rey, stormed the fortress of Chapultepec and marched triumphantly into the halls of the Montezumas in Mexico City.

Hotheads urged the seizure and annexation of all Mexico, but President Polk called for calmer action. The United States paid 15 million dollars for the great southwestern territory and California, and by the treaty of Guadalupe Hidalgo set the boundaries between the United States and Mexico.

General Taylor's victory near Buena Vista won for him the nomination for President over his nearest rival General Scott—and the election. It won for the United States Army, and especially for the Artillery Corps, prestige to add to that gained at New Orleans and at San Jacinto. Two of Captain Braxton Bragg's fieldpieces, captured by the enemy and retaken in the battle, were given places of honor at West Point, with the inscription:

"Lost Without Dishonor—Recovered With Glory."

The boundaries set by the treaty with Mexico have been changed only once, by the peaceful Gadsden Purchase, never by military aggression from either side. While friendship between the two countries was marred briefly in 1916 by the actions of the extremist leader Pancho Villa, a lasting peace is now shared by the United States and her Latin good neighbor south of the Rio Grande.

CHAPTER TEN

Grant Besieges Vicksburg

On a warm morning in August 1861, under a clump of trees in the little town of Ironton, Missouri, a colonel in the United States Army and his staff engaged in a brief ceremony. The colonel walked from a house that had served for some days as his headquarters, his long blue coat flapping about his legs, a black felt hat with its officer's cord pulled down on his head, his rust-colored beard twitching as he rolled the end of a cigar in his mouth. He faced the group of officers standing under the trees. His adjutant, a major, stepped forward.

"Colonel Grant," the major began, "I take pleasure in reading you this order from the War Department."

The order promoted Ulysses S. Grant to brigadier general. He would continue in his command and in his operations against the Confederacy in southeast Missouri and along the Mississippi River. The adjutant handed Grant the order, with two silver stars—one for each of the new brigadier general's shoulders—while the officers cheered.

"Thank you, gentlemen," said Grant, and turned back toward the house. And thus began the hard, rocky journey of General U. S. Grant toward ultimate command of all the Union forces, and victory over the armies of the Confederate states in the most tragic civil war in history.

Hostilities had begun when a Confederate unit commanded by Brigadier General P. G. T. Beauregard fired on and captured Fort Sumter, in the harbor of Charleston, South Caro-

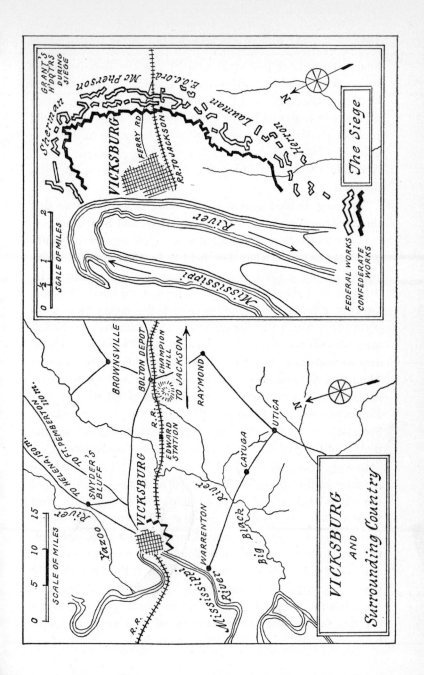

The Siege

SCALE OF MILES
0 ½ 1 2

FEDERAL WORKS
CONFEDERATE WORKS

GRANT'S H'DQTRS DURING SIEGE
Sherman
McPherson
E.O.C. Ord.
Lauman
Herron
VICKSBURG
FERRY RD.
R.R. TO JACKSON
Mississippi River
N

VICKSBURG AND Surrounding Country

SCALE OF MILES
0 5 10 15

TO HELENA 150 MI.
FT. PEMBERTON 110 MI.
Yazoo River
SNYDER'S BLUFF
VICKSBURG
BROWNSVILLE
BOLTON DEPOT
CHAMPION HILL
TO JACKSON
EDWARD STATION
R.R.
RAYMOND
WARRENTON
Big Black River
CAYUGA
UTICA
Mississippi River
R.R.
N

lina, on April 12 of that year. Actually, for four decades events had moved steadily toward armed conflict, as rival political leaders in the North and the South struggled to increase their numbers in Congress by the addition of new states that would prohibit slavery on the one hand or be favorable to it on the other. In 1858 a former member of Congress from Illinois, Abraham Lincoln, debating with Senator Stephen A. Douglas declared:

"A house divided against itself cannot stand. I believe that this government cannot endure half slave and half free."

Lincoln's election as President was a challenge to the southern states to assert what they held to be their right of sovereignty and leave the Union. South Carolina took the lead. By the first of February 1861, Mississippi, Louisiana, Alabama, Georgia, Florida and Tennessee also had seceded. It was apparent that North Carolina, Virginia and Arkansas would follow, with Texas, Kentucky, Missouri and Maryland inclined also to withdraw. Delegates from the seceding states met at Montgomery, Alabama, and formed the Confederate States of America. They elected Jefferson Davis of Mississippi their President, and on February 18, 1861, this former colonel, Secretary of War and United States Senator stood on the portico of the Alabama State House and was sworn into office.

Lincoln earnestly believed it was his duty to prevent the breakup of the Union, and he hoped to do so peacefully, but the shells that roared from Confederate cannon into Fort Sumter ended the political debates and oratory. The South had opened its appeal to arms. Lincoln called for 75,000 volunteers "to put down the rebellion." They were to serve for only ninety days, which many Northern enthusiasts thought would be sufficient to bring the South to her knees. The President must have thought otherwise, and set up plans for carrying on the war for as many months—or years—as might be necessary.

All during the harried hours of April and May the President saw his call for troops being answered. He placed aging General Winfield Scott, hero of the final campaign in the war with Mexico, in command at Washington. Scott remembered the good services of Captain—now Colonel—Robert E. Lee, in that war and during the twelve peacetime years since, and convinced Lincoln that Lee would be a good man to head the Union army in the field. At his home in Arlington across the Potomac from Washington, Lee considered the offer for several troubled days and gave his answer:

"I cannot draw my sword against Virginia!"

Lee resigned his commission in the United States Army and offered his services to President Davis, who gladly appointed him general of the Virginia troops. The Confederate capital had been moved to Richmond, and there Lee found enthusiastic reports of recruiting all over the South, of officers and even civilians forming companies, battalions and regiments, of young blades eager to test their metal against the insolent abolitionists of the North. President Davis had at hand a wealth of personnel for regimental, division and corps commanders, since the Southern states had furnished the majority of the officers for the war with Mexico. He was backed by the warm-blooded Southerners' love for a crusade, and most of them considered this cause worthy indeed.

The people of the Northern states generally, while not eager for war, were with Lincoln in hoping to preserve the Union and to settle for all time the question of the extension of slavery. In the New England states recruiting was hearty; in the states from New York westward it was satisfactory. Even in the "delta" region of southern Illinois, popular Democratic Congressman John A. Logan resigned his office to go into the Union army. Sentiment in the border states of Missouri and Kentucky was sharply divided.

From the start it was apparent that there would be two

principal theaters of the war: In the East, along the seaboard states from Maryland to Georgia; and in the West, throughout the states of the Mississippi Valley. When the pages of the long conflict were closed, each section had produced a truly decisive battle. In the West it was the victory of General Grant and his land and naval forces in the siege and capture of Vicksburg. In the East, the defeat of General Lee and his Confederate army in their mighty invasion thrust across Maryland and into Pennsylvania, at Gettysburg.

Captain Grant Back in Uniform

Grant had proved a cool and gallant junior officer with Taylor and Scott in Mexico. Serving at various army posts until 1854, he had resigned his commission under a cloud, accused of excessive drinking. He had lived on a farm near St. Louis for six years, then moved to Galena, Illinois, to clerk in his brother's leather store. The ex-captain hoped his military training would fit him for some place in the Union army, and wrote to the adjutant general in Washington, volunteering his service. His letter was found, unanswered, in a file of the War Department ten years later, when he was President of the United States. It was Governor Richard Yates of Illinois who gave Grant his chance, asking him to muster in several regiments of volunteers. Grant did the job in soldierly fashion. Yates appointed him a colonel and assigned him to command an unruly regiment. Grant firmly disciplined his troops, and led them on expeditions into Missouri for several weeks, chasing Confederate units who were too much on the move to wait for battle.

Meantime, in the East, people were impatient to get on with the war and to end it quickly. Congressmen echoed the popular clamor and demanded that Lincoln promptly subdue the "rebels." To do the subduing, Brigadier General Irvin McDowell was ordered to move a Union army into Virginia.

On July 21, 1861, at the creek called Bull Run, near Manassas Junction, he met the Confederate forces under Major General Joseph E. Johnston, with General Beauregard, conqueror of Fort Sumter, second in command. Soldiers of both sides fought with reckless bravery, but the Union forces were not yet well organized and the Southern troops sent them reeling, then running, back toward Washington.

This was no sham battle: Bull Run began a real war, a war of fighting and bloodshed. Both North and South learned at Bull Run that the struggle could be long and exhausting.

In the West, General Ben McCullough, commanding about 6,000 Confederate troops, moved from Arkansas into southwestern Missouri, and was joined by General Sterling Price, leading 5,000 Missouri home guards. Brigadier General Nathaniel Lyon, in command of Union forces at St. Louis, marched with 5,200 troops to meet this superior Confederate army. On the banks of Wilson Creek near Springfield their battle took place. It was one of the most sanguinary engagements of the entire war for the number of troops taking part, with 556 killed and more than 2,000 wounded.

General Lyon lost his life and General Price was wounded. Every officer above the rank of major on the Union side was killed or wounded, and the Confederates suffered comparable casualties, as the officers on both sides led their units into the fighting. Troops of a Louisiana regiment, dressed in their gray uniforms, were mistaken for the men of an Iowa regiment also wearing gray and were able to cut to pieces a portion of the Union line. The tragic battle ended with the withdrawal of the Union forces. The engagement at Wilson Creek prompted a major change in tactics for both the Union and the Confederate armies: officers of rank above captain were expected to direct their troops while remaining behind the combat line. And after that battle, blue uniforms became standard for all Union troops, and gray for the Confederates.

Lincoln chose Major General George B. McClellan, a vigorous—often impetuous—officer to the important command in Washington, while John C. Frémont, the glamorous explorer of the Far West, Republican candidate for President in 1856 and now major general, was given charge of the Department of the West with headquarters at St. Louis.

Early in September a Confederate division under Major General Leonidas Polk seized Columbus and Hickman on the Kentucky banks of the Mississippi River. Frémont planned to drive Price and his army back into Arkansas, and to prevent Polk sending reinforcements to Price he ordered the new brigadier general, U. S. Grant, who had set up his headquarters at Cairo, Illinois, "to make a demonstration on both sides of the [Mississippi] River."

To make a military demonstration somewhere was what Grant eagerly desired to do, so he moved quickly and occupied Paducah, Kentucky, lying strategically on the Ohio River at the mouth of the Tennessee. During November his growing forces were engaged in frequent skirmishes with the Confederates, his sharpest battle being at Belmont, Missouri, opposite Columbus, Kentucky, where the Confederates were routed and then rallied to regain their field and camp. From this the general's troops learned a valuable lesson—not to take a victory for granted until finally won.

President Davis appointed Major General Albert Sidney Johnston to command in the West, and that able and experienced officer set up his positions of defense from the Mississippi to Bowling Green, Kentucky, with his center at the two former United States Army posts now controlled by the Confederates, Fort Henry on the Tennessee and Fort Donelson on the Cumberland. Now Grant had in mind a major plan of campaign: to capture the two river forts, thus cutting the Confederate command in two, and then to move down the Mississippi to Vicksburg, striking a fatal blow at resistance in the whole western area. He appealed to the new commander of the Department of the West, Major General H. W. Halleck who had replaced Frémont, to let him move into this campaign.

General Halleck was a capable lawyer, intensely proud and ambitious for fame, intolerant of the opinions of others and incapable of the decisive leadership that marks a true general. For weeks he kept Grant waiting for a reply. Finally Grant went to St. Louis to beg his commander personally to let him attack Forts Henry and Donelson. Halleck dismissed him contemptuously. The winter wore on, while Grant, like a watchdog chained to his kennel headquarters in Cairo, pulled at the collar of his inactivity.

General Grant never relaxed his stern discipline, drilling his troops and husbanding his ammunition and supplies for the day of action. He stood for no graft in the contracts to supply his army with food, uniforms and equipment. He canceled many contracts for goods he considered priced too high; some were sales made by Mr. Leonard Swett, a prominent Illinois lawyer who had placed Lincoln's name in nomination for President at the Republican convention of 1860. Not only that; Grant ordered Swett to leave the headquarters and threatened to shoot him if he came back. Swett stormed into Washington and complained to Lincoln himself. The President had been following Grant's progress with keen appreciation both for the general's military skill and his rugged honesty.

"Maybe you'd better stay out of Cairo," Lincoln solemnly advised his friend. "If General Grant threatened to shoot you, he's just the man to go ahead and do it!"

"An Unconditional and Immediate Surrender"

In Washington, General McClellan was giving most of his time and attention to plans for campaigns into Virginia, leaving the war in the West to Halleck and Brigadier General Don

C. Buell, commander of the Department of the Ohio, at Louisville. Halleck doubtless decided that some activity in his department was needed. On February 1, 1862, he finally cut the leash holding Grant in check and that mastiff bounded to his task of capturing the river forts.

Grant followed the rule of all successful commanders, to use whatever means are at hand to accomplish the best offense or defense. He asked the Navy to carry a big share of the campaign. Commodore Andrew Foote gladly cooperated, steaming from Cairo with four of his new ironclad gunboats. Grant advanced with about 15,000 men in two divisions led by his friend from Illinois, Brigadier General John McClernand, and his old schoolmate at West Point, Brigadier General Charles F. Smith. Striking quickly on the morning of February 6 with a bombardment by the gunboats and an hour's sharp investment by his troops, Grant saw the Confederate flag over Fort Henry come down in surrender. Despite the efforts of his force to prevent it, most of the Confederate garrison escaped and made for Fort Donelson, twelve miles to the east.

Grant wired the news of this victory to Halleck, and added: "I shall take and destroy Fort Donelson on the eighth, and return to Fort Henry."

No doubt the hard-hitting general with his navy comrades would have done just that, except for violent rainstorms that flooded the roadways between the forts. With the greatest difficulty the columns marched along and the artillery caissons slithered and sloshed through mud. By the night of the twelfth, Grant's army was surrounding Donelson. For two more days, in freezing weather, the Union troops, augmented by divisions under Brigadier Generals William T. Sherman and Lew Wallace, invested the fort. By the morning of February 15, Grant had 25,000 troops in action.

Inside were 21,000 Confederate troops, including those

that had escaped from Henry, under Brigadier Generals Gideon J. Pillow, Simon B. Buckner and John B. Floyd, the latter the weak and irresolute Secretary of War in the cabinet of President James Buchanan. Commodore Foote, joined by Captain Henry Walke with his gunboat *Carondelet,* arrived below the fort. Grant hoped that the boats could come into action before the troops attacked, but a heavy Confederate force moved from the fort and sent McClernand's division, at the right of the line, in retreat. The way was open for the whole Confederate force to escape.

Grant rallied his troops, sent Smith's division on a counter-attack, and the Confederates drew back to the fort. Their guns opened upon the Union vessels on the river, inflicting heavy damage. All day the sharp fighting continued.

That night within the fort there occurred a remarkable council among the three Confederate generals, in which the fearful Pillow and the cowardly Floyd turned the command over to Buckner for surrender, and escaped by boat to Nashville, while the cavalry regiment under Colonel Nathan Bedford Forrest also escaped by fording the river. At daylight Grant was reading a note from Buckner, asking for terms of surrender. In the Union commander's terse reply were these words:

"No terms except an unconditional and immediate surrender can be accepted. I propose to move immediately upon your works."

Buckner surrendered his entire army, with its arms, ammunition and supplies, along with the troops, many of whom Grant paroled at once on promises they would not return to "secessionist armies." The capture of Henry and Donelson cost Grant's forces 446 killed and 1,775 wounded, and the Confederates lost 236 killed and 1,018 wounded.

The important victory, breaking the Confederate defense line in the West, brought joy to the North and gloom to the

South. Grant and his two subordinate brigadiers were promoted to major generals. There was no joy in the heart of General Halleck. He sent telegrams of congratulation to Commodore Foote, and even to the governor of Kansas for supplying some of the troops, but never a word of commendation to Grant. General Buell was at Nashville, and Grant made the trip up the Cumberland to confer with him on plans to join their forces to meet the Army of General Johnston, assembling at Corinth, Mississippi. On the pretext that Grant had left his command without permission, Halleck ordered him to turn over his army to General Smith, and remain, virtually under arrest, at Fort Henry. Halleck wired the War Department, asking to be appointed commander of all the forces in the West—"In return," he said, "for Forts Henry and Donelson"!

It was a dark day for the victor of Paducah and the river forts, who was learning the bitter lesson that in any organization, civil or military, there can be a General Halleck eager for recognition and power, willing to sacrifice associates and friends to get it. Halleck got his promotion in command, and with his ego thus inflated he restored Grant to active duty and wrote him:

"I wish you, as soon as your new army is in the field, to assume immediate command, and lead it to new victories."

From President Davis in Richmond had come critical inquiries as to why his armies were making no great progress to halt the Union invasion, and General Johnston was answering by concentrating a force of 40,000 troops at Corinth, including Brigadier General Braxton Bragg's division from its station at Pensacola, Florida. Grant advanced his army to Pittsburg Landing, about twenty miles from Corinth, to await Buell before attacking the Confederate force.

But Johnston did not wait. On Sunday morning, April 6,

near a small church called Shiloh, he attacked with sudden fury. The Union troops fought desperately, but were driven back to the river. Grant seemed unable to form any plan for effective defense or counterattack. Tragedy rode the crest of the Confederate victory, for General Johnston was mortally wounded—an irreparable loss to the Confederacy. General Buell reached the scene of battle as the day closed. Monday morning saw the Union forces rallying and counterattacking. Beauregard, succeeding Johnston in command, contested every attack with generalship of the highest order. But Grant had resumed the decisive spirit he so lacked the day before and with Buell's reinforcement gained the lost ground. The majority of soldiers on both sides had never been in battle, but they fought with splendid courage. More than 3,500 brave soldiers of the Blue and the Gray gave their lives at Shiloh and about 16,000 others were wounded.

Thus the plan of the Confederate offensive in the West was broken. But Halleck, still longing for personal glory in the field, came down and assumed command of the Union army. Grant felt keenly the embarrassment of being set aside, and asked to be transferred to another command. General Sherman, whose division had borne the brunt of the attack at Shiloh, begged him to remain.

"Something will turn up for you," was Sherman's remark. Grant stayed, and after a few weeks of ineffective leadership, Halleck was promoted to command in Washington. In October, Grant was again restored to his army, becoming the ranking officer of the Union forces in the West. His plan for a campaign to gain the whole Mississippi Valley was now badly delayed, but Union victories at Corinth, at Island Number Ten and other points on the Mississippi completed the setting for his blue-clad troops to clear the "Father of Waters" of Confederate control.

The Union Needs a Victory

Disappointed in their hope that the rebellion could be put down quickly, the people of the Northern states were growing restless and critical of the administration. Despite admiration for Mr. Lincoln, his supporters lost strength in the election of November, 1862. In the East, a succession of Union commanders had not been able to match General Lee's brilliant military tactics. Confederate resistance was much more stubborn, and Southern bravery much more real, than Northern partisans had anticipated.

General Grant was anxious for a decisive victory, and believed that the capture of Vicksburg, most important rail and shipping center between Memphis and New Orleans, would "break the back of the Confederacy" in the West. Fortunately for the Union, President Lincoln, and General Halleck in his Washington headquarters, agreed. The campaign proved long and difficult, filled with discouraging failures. But as the struggle progressed it brought out not only this general's grim determination to win, but also those other qualities that stamped Grant as a great military leader: initiative, resourcefulness, the ability to make firm decisions and the will to act upon them without delay.

The United States Navy, true to its tradition of bold action, had already accomplished a mission necessary to Grant's plan, when in April 1862 Admiral David G. Farragut stormed gallantly up the Mississippi with his gunboats, past the blazing guns of Forts Jackson and St. Philip, and captured New Orleans. In his command was a capable lieutenant, George Dewey (destined to win the gratitude of his country in a decisive battle of his own). Now New Orleans was occupied by a Federal force under Major General Nathaniel P. Banks, former member of Congress and Speaker of the House. Only the 150 miles of winding, twisting river between Port Hudson and Vicksburg remained in Confederate hands.

Vicksburg was ideally located for defense, standing on high ground overlooking a great loop in the river. Batteries lined its high banks and gun emplacements guarded all other approaches to the city. Commanding the Confederate troops in Mississippi and responsible for Vicksburg's defense was Major General John C. Pemberton, a lieutenant in the same regiment with Grant in the Mexican War, a Northern man who became a Southern sympathizer.

First—the attempt from the river. Grant now commanded a formidable army of 50,000 troops. He ordered his close friend and able subordinate, General Sherman, with 20,000 troops, joined by 12,000 more from Union forces in Arkansas, to go down the river and land at Chickasaw Bluffs on the Yazoo River north of Vicksburg. Grant would move with his main force through Mississippi to Jackson, east of the city. Pemberton could not meet both armies at once.

Barely had the Union forces started, when on December 20 a hard-riding cavalry regiment under Brigadier General Earl Van Dorn swooped down on Grant's base of supplies at Holly Springs, Mississippi, and captured 1,500 troops along with the supplies. This held back Grant's advance, while Pemberton withdrew into Vicksburg. When Sherman's troops reached the Yazoo the Confederate artillery was posted and ready. Commodore David D. Porter brought his gunboats to Sherman's aid and threw shells at the Confederate batteries, but the Union infantry, trying to storm the muddy bluffs, was repulsed with heavy loss.

The capture of Holly Springs gave Grant some anxious moments. His troops could get no more supplies over the long line from Cairo to Memphis to Mississippi. But the general turned this setback to good account. He ordered his officers and men to begin taking food and provender from stores and farms nearest at hand, and thus his army learned that it could "live off the country"—a fact that was to have an important influence on the campaigns ahead and on all Grant's future military operations.

Second—the attempts "by dredge and shovel." It was obvious that no Union troops could be carried around the narrow peninsula made by the loop of the river opposite Vicksburg, through direct and enfilading fire from defending batteries. So Grant adopted a plan to widen an old canal which would bypass the loop and allow transports and gunboats to go by Vicksburg out of cannon range. For four rainy, cold, dreary weeks in February and March the cutting and dredging went on, by soldiers and 1,200 hired Negro laborers. The river, swollen from rains, swept away the dams protecting the works and the attempt failed dismally. Another scheme, to cut a canal from the river to Lake Providence, seventy-five miles north of the city, was started, and abandoned as impractical.

Grant stamped about in his muddy boots, consulting his maps and talking to his engineers about another plan: to get his transports from Moon Lake, 155 miles north of Vicksburg, into the Mississippi, so that his troops might attack the city by striking east of the Yazoo batteries. Again the work was started, and again Confederate batteries halted the project. Still another plan was tried: to assault the Yazoo defenses from both sides by widening the tributary bayous. Porter guided his transports loaded with supplies and his defending gunboats up the narrow waterways, while Sherman led the infantry of his corps along the banks, cutting, digging, dragging through endless mud. Jonathan Adams, a private in that big pick-and-shovel detail, wrote in his diary: "We have been in water and mud so long, it is a common joke amongst us soldiers that we are all growing tails like beavers." Confederate sharpshooters in trees and bushes picked off the bluecoats at all hours of the day. Grant ordered the expedition back. His officers asked: "What next, General?"

In another daring exploit, Admiral Farragut led his squadron past the batteries of Port Hudson in his flagship *Hartford* and blocked the mouth of the Red River, bottling up several Confederate ships loaded with food and supplies for the defenders of Vicksburg.

Now it was April. Grant had not taken Vicksburg, but word had spread all over the North that he was trying. That was something. And President Lincoln sent a man from Washington, Charles A. Dana, Assistant Secretary of War, to observe personally this commander who did not hesitate to discard tradition and who kept doggedly at his task.

Third—to encircle Vicksburg. Now Grant proposed his most daring plan: to get below Vicksburg and advance against the city in an encircling movement from the south. Sherman protested that it would be fatal to be cut off from their supplies. Grant replied that they were living on the country, and would keep on doing so.

In three weeks time, forty miles of "corduroy" road—logs placed upon the muddy ground and spiked together—were laid, from Milliken's Bend on the Louisiana side to a point twenty-one miles below Vicksburg. At midnight on April 16 Commodore Porter ran five gunboats and three transport barges, each of the latter towing a flatboat of coal for use of the navy vessels, past the blazing Confederate batteries of Vicksburg. All his boats were hit several times, and one transport was sunk. Five nights later, six more transports and four gunboats ran the perilous gauntlet, with loss of only one barge.

Grant now had seven transports to ferry his troops across the Mississippi and nine gunboats to protect them. Over the log road in a long night march, McClernand's corps and a part of the corps of General James B. McPherson tramped and stumbled. Sherman was ordered to stay on the Yazoo, make a big show of attacking the city, then some night later to follow his comrades over the corduroy. General Pemberton knew that a crossing would be tried, but would not divide his force to prevent it for fear of Sherman's attack. By the morning light of April 30, the astonished Confederate scouts saw that about 20,000 of Grant's army had crossed over during the night, with equipment and artillery, and were camping under shelter of Porter's gunboats riding at cable on the river.

Grant immediately dispatched troops to seize Grand Gulf, ten miles up the river, and to capture Port Gibson, eight miles to the south. Overcoming sharp resistance, the Union forces held these points, controlling all the river south of Vicksburg. The rest of McPherson's corps and Sherman's corps were ferried over, and by May 6 all units of Grant's army stretched their blue-coated columns in camps below their general's tent at Grand Gulf.

Headquarters: In the Saddle

President Davis dispatched General Joseph E. Johnston to take command in the West, imploring him to gather an army at Jackson and unite with Pemberton to crush the invading force under the Illinois general. The governor of Mississippi issued a proclamation for troops, and thousands of volunteers enlisted.

Grant was now in hostile territory, opposed by two Confederate armies totaling about 43,000 men, but he decided to strike boldly while his opponents were still divided. He set his army at once on the march—not toward Vicksburg, but eastward—away from the Mississippi and his line of communication and supplies, straight toward Jackson and the Confederate force. As Grant mounted his horse on that morning of May 7, he handed a dispatch to his adjutant, Colonel J. A.

Rawlins, to be carried by rider to Memphis and telegraphed to the War Department:

"I shall communicate with Grand Gulf no more. . . . You may not hear from me again for several days." Years later in his memoirs the general was to say with fine candor:

"I knew well that Halleck's caution would lead him to disapprove of the course, but it was the only one that gave any chance of success. The time it would take to communicate with Washington and get a reply would be so great that I could not be interfered with until it was demonstrated whether my plan was practicable."

McPherson's corps moved on the right, with a division commanded by former Congressman John A. Logan proudly leading the advance. Sherman and McClernand took roads farther north, nearer the Big Black River. All units remained in supporting distance. On May 12 Logan came upon a Confederate division posted near Raymond, sixteen miles from Jackson. The battle was sharp and hard, but the raw Mississippi troops were no match for the seasoned Union forces. The Confederates retreated to Jackson.

General Johnston arrived the next day. Grant ordered McPherson's corps to the attack, and Sherman's corps to move with all speed to support it. Torrential rains fell that night and during the next morning. Water and mud delayed the weary Union troops, but by noon both McPherson and Sherman confronted the city. An artillery barrage and an infantry charge forced the defenders out of Jackson. Grant rode in, and slept that night in the bed General Johnston had occupied the night before.

News reached the Union commander that Johnston had ordered Pemberton to advance from Vicksburg and attack from the rear. Obviously, Johnston himself, who had moved northward, would strike from his position. Here was the moment of supreme risk for Grant's invading columns. To be caught in that cross fire could bring disaster. By morning the tired, dirt-grimed Union troops had about-faced and were on the march again.

Pemberton's army, fresh and eager for the kill, had moved out twenty miles to Champion Hill. Here, under cover of a wood commanding all the approaches from the east, the Confederate general wisely selected his field of battle. McClernand's corps, stepping in its tracks of a few days before, was now in the lead, with McPherson moving up from the roadway to the south. To Sherman had been assigned the work of destroying factories, bridges, railroads and all other items of military value in Jackson, and the general was doing his task in the thorough manner for which later in this tragic war he became so noted.

The battle began at 9 o'clock on May 16, following a day and night of exhausting march for the Federal troops. Pemberton's men hurled their fire from the hillside upon the center of McClernand's line. The Union soldiers, though seasoned and hardened by their campaigns, seemed outfought for a time and ready to retreat. But Logan's division turned Pemberton's left flank, and Grant staked the rest of the battle on a grand charge. Cold steel won the day, and the Confederates fell back.

Pemberton retreated to the Big Black River, determined to make another stand against Grant's relentless drive. Behind a bayou he posted his infantry and cavalry, backed by eighteen batteries of artillery. When Union artillery failed to drive the defenders out of their works, repeated charges by McClernand's infantry proved effective. Pemberton fell back into Vicksburg, with McClernand's victors closely pursuing and McPherson's corps in support. Sherman, meanwhile, crossed the Big Black to strike toward the Yazoo River and cut off any possible move Pemberton might make to join Johnston.

Now Grant closed his trap of three army corps tightly about

Vicksburg. McClernand swung to the left while McPherson moved to the center. Sherman held the right, and from the very Chickasaw Bluffs which this general had attempted unsuccessfully to storm weeks before, he pointed his guns toward the Confederate entrenchments outside the city. Admiral Porter's gunboats patrolled the river above and below the range of those Confederate batteries on the Vicksburg bluffs, vigilant to prevent escape or communication by water.

In all American history, seldom were the qualities of a general in the field better displayed than by U. S. Grant in the six weeks campaigning after landing his troops on the east bank of the Mississippi. He had fought and won six distinct battles and numerous skirmishes, marched his troops 180 miles, maintained them on the country, captured 6,000 prisoners, 88 pieces of artillery and numerous military stores, at a cost of 695 killed and 3,750 wounded and missing. His opponent's losses were about 2,000 killed and twice that number wounded. For two weeks his headquarters had been in the saddle, day after day, with his troops. Now he was surrounding Vicksburg.

On the day General Pemberton fell back into Vicksburg he addressed his troops:

"You have heard that I am incompetent, and a traitor, and that it is my intention to sell Vicksburg. Follow me, and you will see the cost at which I will sell Vicksburg. When the last pound of beef, bacon and flour, the last grain of corn, the last cow and hog and horse shall have perished in the trenches, still we shall not surrender!"

The Siege Begins

It is the morning of May 20, and General Grant assembles the commanders of his corps, divisions and brigades, with their staffs, for a council of battle. He announces his plan to take Vicksburg by storming the defenders' works. The men will be given only two days' rest. The attack will begin at 8 o'clock with an artillery barrage, and at 10 o'clock the whole infantry line will move forward in a charge. The general pulls out an enormous watch.

"Each officer will set his watch with mine," he says—the first recorded instance of synchronization of military timepieces.

The morning of May 22 dawns warm and clear. Precisely at 8 o'clock all the artillery of that grim line circling Vicksburg booms in unison. For two hours the bombardment roars. Pemberton's guns answer but are inadequate to silence more than a handful of the Union batteries concentrating their fire upon parapets and emplacements. The Confederate general makes ready for the infantry attack he knows will follow the artillery assault. Many of the defending breastworks are torn up, but the men of the Gray crouch under their shelters and wait. At 10 o'clock there is silence. The Union general's order has been passed from colonels to majors and captains to the soldiers, and now it is heard by all the Union infantry:

"Charge their line! Charge—with the bayonet!"

Now begins a fearful demonstration of a courageous attack and an equally courageous resistance. The men in blue swarm over the hills across the uneven terrain, through thickets, in and out of great holes which the explosions of their shells have torn, up toward the Confederate lines. The fire of Vicksburg's defenders rains full upon them, and man after man in those advancing ranks goes down. Approaching the line of forts and entrenchments, the Federal troops rush into the deep ditches bristling with stakes that form the hurriedly constructed outer protection. Here the exhausted soldiers halt and struggle, crouching against the earthen walls to avoid that withering fire from over the parapets. At numerous points the attackers gain the crest of forts and battery stations by ladders, but are driven back. Many units retreat under that deadly fire.

Night comes on at last, and those who have stayed close by the embankments for safety are withdrawn. The assault, made at the price of about seven hundred casualties, has failed.

In his council with his generals and staff officers that night, U. S. Grant is grim and brusque. After a few preliminary words, he rumbles:

"We will invest Vicksburg. Let the siege go on until the enemy troops surrender!"

First task of the Union forces is to move closer to that defending ring of entrenchments and build another ring for the forward besiegers. Here again the Union general scorns tradition. Every graduate of West Point has been taught some fundamentals of military engineering. Very well, says Grant, they can use that knowledge now, as he calls all West Pointers to direct the work of mining and sapping. The sound of picks and shovels and other lowly tools is heard the length of those encircling miles, as all hands fall to digging, grading, tunneling, piling logs and stones, and mixing mortar. Foreign military observers, resplendent in their uniforms and trappings, are amazed. Here is a general who forces officers to direct labor!

Trenches are fortified with sandbags, topped with logs, the bags spaced above the ground so that rifles can be fired between them, yet permitting men to appear behind them without being seen by the defenders. Highest points in the uneven terrain are selected for the artillery batteries. Grant has only six thirty-two-pound siege guns, but again the Navy comes to the rescue, as Porter moves up from the river a battery of large-caliber long-range guns. The field artillery pieces are spaced among them. Still there are no trench mortars, greatly needed to toss explosive shells at slow speed into the opposing trenches. Walnut and hickory logs are bored out, bound with iron bands and set up for use.

There are eight roads leading into Vicksburg. Grant posts detachments upon each to guard against surprise attacks. He sends Major General F. P. Blair, former member of Congress and Secretary of War, now ably commanding a division, to clear out a unit of Confederates posted between the Yazoo and Big Black. Steadily the Union reinforcements arrive, from Missouri, from Memphis, from Tennessee. Every day they are added to strengthen the smoking ring of the siege or to augment the force being formed under Sherman to move against Johnston if that Confederate commander should attempt a rescue.

May passes, and the long days of early June bring Pemberton no promise of relief. On June 7 a force of Negro troops, which Grant has mustered into service and posted at Milliken's Bend, is attacked by three regiments under Major General Richard Taylor, who has marched his force from Arkansas. The Negro soldiers prove they can use their firearms effectively, and with the aid of a division from McClernand's corps they repulse the attack.

Grant decides to try to open a breach in the Confederate works by mining Fort Hill, one of Pemberton's strongest entrenchments. For three weeks the work of digging the tunnel goes on. Anxiously the Confederate troops watch or attempt to halt the work with artillery fire. So close moves the tunnel to the walls of the fort that the Union soldiers converse with and banter the "Johnny Rebs." At night the soldiers of the opposing forces, at many points of the lines, meet and swap commodities—usually Northern food for Southern tobacco.

On June 25 the tunnel is completed. The long powder train is lit, zig-zagging its snaky way beneath the defenders of Fort Hill. The explosion sends men, rifles, guns, planks—all the material of the shattered fort, into the air, leaving a dirty, smoking crater. Into this hell-hole the 32d Illinois Regiment of Logan's division storms, to be met by a withering Confederate fire. For four hours the battle for the crater rages. The remnants of the 32d give way to other Illinois units. Survivors are to refer to it ever after as "Logan's slaughter pen." Finally the Confederates hold it. The attempt to break through has failed.

And Hunger Wins

Assaults upon Pemberton's line day after day move the Union position steadily closer. Relentlessly the Union sharpshooters pick off their quarry when heads and bodies show above the parapets. Confederate ammunition is about gone. Unexploded shells from Union cannon are carefully gathered up for the powder in them. Now Grant's gunners elevate their navy siege pieces to blast at objects in the city proper, and the people take to cellars and dugouts, shaken in morale and weakened by terror.

Steadily the noose of hunger tightens about the civilians and their line of weary defenders. By the last week in June all the meat and flour have been eaten. The soldiers are making bread out of ground peas. Horses, mules and dogs are turned into food by troops or the inhabitants. And still Pemberton stubbornly holds out. He declares that he will starve with his men.

Pemberton's "Johnnies" learn from conversations with their antagonists that they may not have to starve after all. "When you all going to take Vicksburg, Yank?" an emaciated Southerner calls out. "Fourth of July is the day when we celebrate!" comes the answer.

On July 3 the Confederate general hoists a white flag. His principal aide, Brigadier General John S. Bowen, comes blindfolded with a letter to Grant, proposing the appointment of commissioners to arrange for surrender. Grant answers:

". . . Men who have shown so much endurance and courage

as those now in Vicksburg will always challenge the respect of an adversary, and, I can assure you, will be treated with all the respect due them as prisoners of war."

Grant orders a truce. General Pemberton appears on the works at a point designated, opposite McPherson's center, just at the left of the ruins of Fort Hill, flanked by General Bowen and Colonel Milton Montgomery. A group of staff officers follow. Grant steps leisurely forward, followed by General McPherson, General Smith and officers of the staff.

As if on signal, hundreds of heads and shoulders appear above the breastworks on both sides. The battle is over. For the first time the men can look in safety upon that waste of terrain over which so many messengers of death have sailed. The faces of the Confederates are gaunt and haggard. Not a man among them, from general to orderlies, has eaten a decent meal for three weeks. In silence the soldiers watch these two commanders, former comrades of the 3d Infantry Regiment, approach.

Colonel Montgomery steps forward. "General Grant, I present General Pemberton!"

The generals shake hands. Pemberton says: "General Grant, you will recall that I was at Monterrey and Buena Vista." A few more pleasantries. Then—"I meet you in order to arrange for the capitulation of Vicksburg and its garrison. What terms do you propose?"

"Unconditional surrender!" Grant's answer cracks like a whip.

"Never, so long as I have a man left!" Pemberton retorts.

Grant replies that never has his army been in better condition to continue the siege. The heat of these remarks spends itself, and as if by some mutual impulse Grant and Pemberton walk away from the other officers and sit down beneath a tree scarred and torn by the impact of bullets. There Grant blows great puffs of smoke from his cigar, while Pemberton pulls at blades of grass and chews them as they talk. The victorious Union general agrees to submit his terms in writing.

Those terms provide that paroles shall be made out and signed by the officers and men, and that the Confederates can march out of their lines, the officers taking with them their regimental clothing, and one horse each. There are grim smiles at the latter stipulation.

"Kindly remind your general," comments Pemberton to Grant's messenger, "that our horses have all been eaten!"

"To Major-General Grant: You Were Right——"

With the siege ended, Union officers and men fell to the task of supplying food for the 29,400 hungry prisoners, about 4,000 of whom were wounded, and the civilians of Vicksburg. About eight hundred Confederate soldiers had given their lives in the battle, while the Union troops had lost 545, and 3,688 were wounded.

Grant dispatched General Sherman with his corps to disperse the army under General Johnston, and after sharp resistance at Jackson the Confederate force retreated eastward. Port Hudson was no longer tenable and on July 9 surrendered to General Nathaniel P. Banks its 6,000 troops with all arms and supplies.

"Vicksburg broke the back of the rebellion," said Union veterans, in their stories of the campaign during the rest of their lives. It did more than that: it made possible General Grant's leadership for all the Union cause. Called to command at Chattanooga he won another victory, and in March 1864 was given the Army of the Potomac, matching his generalship with his worthy Virginia foeman, General Lee, until the surrender at Appomattox Court House.

Among the plaudits of a rejoicing North after Vicksburg

was a letter, the words of which indicated the greatness of the writer:

WASHINGTON, July 13, 1863

To MAJOR GENERAL GRANT:

I do not remember that you and I ever met personally. I write now as a grateful acknowledgment for almost inestimable service you have done the country. I wish to say further . . . that I thought you should go down the river and join General Banks; and when you turned northward, east of the Big Black, I feared it was a mistake. I now wish to make a personal acknowledgment that you were right, and I was wrong.

Yours very truly,
A. LINCOLN

CHAPTER ELEVEN

Lee Meets Defeat at Gettysburg

On June 3, 1863, a Union balloonist, riding at anchor near Falmouth, Virginia, on the bank of the Rappahannock River across from Fredericksburg, urgently called through his megaphone to his comrades below:

"Pull me down! Pull me down!"

When he stepped from his balloon basket, spyglass still in hand, he waved toward the Confederate lines which he had been watching for days from his aerial perch.

"They are marching!" he said. "The Johnny Rebs are heading North!"

They were indeed. Everything had been put in readiness the day before. Wagons were loaded, horses given double rations, cannon limbered, and all the equipment of an army for a long trek stacked and ready to go. Among all the troops of the Army of Northern Virginia the word had been passed:

"We're going North! We're going to take Pennsylvania, then capture Philadelphia and Baltimore—and end the war!"

Now in the early light of a glorious spring day the order "Forward—march!" resounded. Company officers whacked their sergeants across the shoulders in comradely greeting, men threw their tattered hats into the air and the "rebel yell" broke from thousands of throats. Fifes and drums caught up the strain of "Dixie" as artillery and camp wagons rolled. Orderlies dashed here and there relaying commands. The steady tramp of marching feet began.

Union cavalry scouts came dashing back to their lines, and to the headquarters of their commander, General Joseph Hooker, to confirm the news: The Confederates were heading toward Culpeper Court House.

Well might the Confederate officers and men have felt confident of victory. For weeks they had planned this "big invasion" of the North. Around their campfires they had boasted how they would soon show the "damyankees" how to fight. They had supreme confidence in their leader, this neatly uniformed general with graying hair and beard, blue eyes and expressive voice, Robert E. Lee. The battle-tested men from all communities of the South followed their commander with intense loyalty and with the faith of those who believed that their cause was just.

Since the spring of 1862 most of their battles had been victories for the South. They had met the Army of the Potomac under General George B. McClellan in the Virginia peninsula, and in severe fighting at Fair Oaks and the "Seven Days' Battle" had forced the Federals to withdraw. At the second Battle of Bull Run, led by Generals James "War Horse" Longstreet and Thomas J. "Stonewall" Jackson, they had again defeated the best of the Northern forces. On a mid-September day they had crossed the Potomac and marched to the rolling hills of Sharpsburg near the Antietam River in Maryland. Only the most critical Southerners blamed Lee for failing to win that bloody battle of Antietam, while much more blame was heaped upon General McClellan by the government in Washington for his failure to attack Lee's weary troops again next day.

Back in Virginia, Lee rested his veterans and recruited more men during the quiet autumn. President Lincoln and his Secretary of War, Edwin M. Stanton, settled upon General Ambrose E. Burnside to lead the next attempt to defeat Lee's forces, surround Richmond and strike at the beating heart of

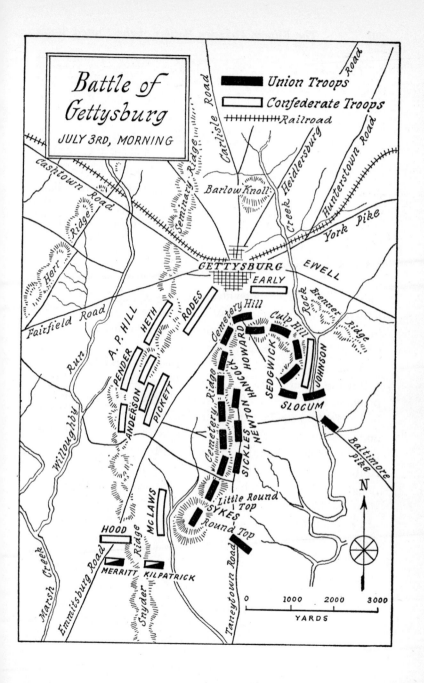

Battle of
Gettysburg
JULY 3RD, MORNING

Union Troops
Confederate Troops
Railroad

Carlisle Road
Cashtown Road
Herr Ridge
Fairfield Road
Willoughby Run
Marsh Creek
Emmitsburg Road
Snyder Ridge
Seminary Ridge
Barlow Knoll
GETTYSBURG
EARLY
A. P. HILL
PENDER
HETH
RODES
ANDERSON
PICKETT
Cemetery Hill
Cemetery Ridge
NEWTON HOWARD
HANCOCK
SICKLES
Culp Hill
SEDGWICK
JOHNSON
SLOCUM
Little Round Top
SYKES
Round Top
McLAWS
HOOD
MERRITT
KILPATRICK
Tarneytown Road
Baltimore Pike
Rock Creek
Brenner Ridge
EWELL
Heidlersburg Road
Hunterstown Road
York Pike

N

0   1000   2000   3000
YARDS

the Confederacy. In December Lee met Burnside's vigorous thrust at Fredericksburg, midway between Washington and the Confederate capital, repulsing the invader's frontal attacks with heavy loss.

Again there was a pause in the struggle in the East, while Grant was moving doggedly southward along the Mississippi in the West. General Hooker was selected to replace Burnside, and he marched his refreshed force toward Chancellorsville, Virginia. On the rolls of his invading Army of the Potomac were about 132,000 men, twice the number of the Confederate strength. General Lee delayed the Federals by a series of defensive moves as brilliant as any in the entire war. On May 2 he sent Stonewall Jackson to flank Hooker's right wing at Chancellorsville, and the Union troops withdrew in defeat. But this victory cost the Confederacy a heavy price, for Jackson fell, mortally wounded by one of his own soldiers who mistook him for a Union officer.

"I have lost my right arm!" mourned General Lee.

But the general still had many able and experienced commanders in his Army of Northern Virginia. He and his staff had organized its 75,000 officers and men into three infantry and one cavalry corps, and named as their leaders his four best lieutenant generals: James Longstreet, R. S. Ewell and Ambrose P. Hill for the infantry, and J. E. B. Stuart to command the cavalry. Each infantry corps contained three divisions, led by as able generals as West Point had produced. The artillery of 293 guns, commanded by an expert strategist, General William N. Pendleton, was divided into three regiments, each with its four battalions assigned to an infantry corps. Most of Lee's subordinate officers were sons of plantation owners or Southern business leaders, their families known and respected, neighbors to the men they commanded. To the soldiers of the Confederate ranks, that march to the North in late June 1863 was the promise of final triumph for Dixie.

President Jefferson Davis and his Cabinet, harassed by mounting problems of civil administration, left to Lee and his generals the decision whether to carry the war into Northern territory. The Confederate commander rejected a proposal of General Longstreet to divide the army and send one corps to help sweep the Federals from Tennessee, thus forcing Grant to stop his steady pounding on Vicksburg. Lee feared that to divide his force meant forfeiting his one great chance for an offensive campaign against the North. He understood the hazards of leaving his home grounds, but pointed out that foodstuffs and clothing were plentiful in the North, to be had for the taking in exchange for Confederate notes.

As the divisions under Ewell and Longstreet took up the march from Fredericksburg, Hill with his corps delayed to watch the Union army and to cover the march. Hooker was eager to attack the remaining Confederate force. He felt that with his greater numbers he could crush Hill's corps and sweep down upon Richmond. He telegraphed the War Department:

. . . THE HEAD OF HIS COLUMN WILL BE HEADED TOWARD THE POTOMAC, WHILE THE REAR WILL REST ON FREDERICKSBURG. AFTER GIVING THE SUBJECT MY BEST REFLECTION I AM OF THE OPINION THAT IT IS MY DUTY TO PITCH INTO THE REAR.

But neither President Lincoln nor his commanding general, Henry W. Halleck, approved the plan of pitching into Lee's rear.

"Lee's army, not Richmond, is your true objective," Lincoln personally wired the general.

Fate—and Roads—Lead to Gettysburg

On June 6, Robert E. Lee—satisfied that Hooker would not attack in force—mounted his white charger, Traveller, and with his aides and a cavalry guard rode forward to join the leading regiments of his army. Hooker ordered every unit of his army to be ready to march. There was no choice as to his duty now. His task was to move parallel with Lee's forces, keeping between the Confederates and Washington, making a stand when the time and place appeared right.

Union engineers threw their pontoon bridges across the Rappahannock. Two regiments of Vermont and New Jersey infantry were the first to dash over. The cavalry under General Alfred Pleasanton followed. Hooker ordered Pleasanton to "contact" the Confederate cavalry and thus gain vital information about the whole campaign. The contact with Stuart's riders brought on an all-day, severely fought engagement at Brandy Station, in which the Union loss in killed and captured totaled more than a thousand, while the Confederates lost about six hundred. For the first time in the war, Union cavalrymen met Confederate upon fairly equal terms—and held their own.

Now all three Confederate corps were moving up the Shenandoah Valley, as swiftly as men could march and horses could draw the cannon and wagon trains: Ewell's II Corps in the lead; Longstreet's I Corps following and the units of Hill's III Corps catching up; while two divisions of Stuart's cavalry alertly guarded the Blue Ridge Mountain passes that led from the east. The forward brigades captured Winchester, Virginia. Crossing the Potomac at Shepherdstown, Virginia, and Williamsport, Maryland, the whole Confederate army converged upon Hagerstown, Maryland, and pressed on northward up the Cumberland Valley. On June 25 Ewell's corps reached Chambersburg, Pennsylvania, followed closely by the corps of Hill and Longstreet, and on the night of June 27 all the infantry and artillery divisions of the Army of Northern Virginia camped on Yankee soil.

General Lee ordered Ewell to move eastward with the objective of capturing Harrisburg, the state's capital, and York near the Susquehanna River, thus to control the rail and water ways to Baltimore and Washington. With no opposition except from small bands of Pennsylvania militia, Ewell led two of his divisions, under Generals R. E. Rodes and Edward Johnson, along the Harrisburg road as far as Carlisle, while the remaining division under General Jubal A. Early took the road toward York. As Early's four brigades—Brigadier General J. B. Gordon and his Georgians in the lead—tramped and rumbled along, the officers and men paused at the town of Gettysburg to refresh themselves and their mounts and to beat the dust out of their hair and beards, not knowing that there they would soon be locked in deadly combat. On they marched and rolled to York.

Meanwhile, General Stuart, Lee's "cavalry eyes" and the Confederate chieftain's constant source of information on Union troop movements, stung by his failure to win a victory over the Federal cavalry at Brandy Station, decided on a campaign of his own. He led his remaining four divisions eastward, crossed the Potomac and pushed northward to Rockville, Maryland, barely fifteen miles from Washington. There he captured a big Union wagon train, loaded with supplies, on its way to Frederick. Slowed by this loot, keeping his raiders between the Union forces and Washington, Stuart continued across Maryland into Pennsylvania and to the Susquehanna, expecting to rejoin the main Army of Northern Virginia for the victorious march upon Philadelphia or Baltimore. On June 28 his horsemen burned the bridge at Sykesville, and the next morning they tore up a section of the railroad tracks leading to Baltimore. Finding that Early had left York, the cavalry leader headed toward Carlisle, unaware that all Lee's forces were converging on Gettysburg. The ill-starred raid had taken Stuart away from his commanding general at a time when his hard-riding squadrons were desperately needed for reconnaissance.

On June 25, General Hooker, to keep his army parallel with the advancing Confederates, crossed the Potomac at Edward's Ferry and led his advance corps to Frederick, Maryland. At Harper's Ferry and nearby Maryland Heights 10,000 Union soldiers were garrisoned. Hooker felt that these troops should join his command as he prepared to confront Lee, and he wired General Halleck to that effect. That gentleman, fuming pompously in his armchair in Washington, decided that the officer in the field was wrong, and refused to let Hooker have the garrisons. This action, crowding closely upon other disagreements with Halleck, prompted Hooker on June 27 to ask to be relieved of his command. Halleck had anticipated the request and had agreed with Lincoln and Secretary Stanton upon a successor.

At 2 o'clock on Sunday morning, June 28, at the beginning of the most fateful week in this tragic Civil War, Lieutenant Colonel James A. Hardie, of the War Department staff, appeared at the Union camp outside Frederick. Officers and soldiers of the guard escorted him to the tent of General George Gordon Meade, a Pennsylvanian commanding the V Corps.

"The general is sleeping, sir," protested a sentry.

"You will wake him up at once," Colonel Hardie barked crisply. "Orders direct from Washington." The sleepy general partially donned his uniform and was handed a dispatch. Astonished, he studied it intently.

"Major General George G. Meade will assume immediate command of the Army of the Potomac."

Meade turned to Colonel Hardie and suggested that General John F. Reynolds, commanding I Corps, should be named for the place. "The appointment has already been made, sir!" Hardie said.

General Meade was a tall man, with sparse, dark hair, thin face and a spade beard. His eyes had the look of a calm, unhurried person, but he often became nervous and irritable. Graduating from West Point with the class of 1835, George Meade was trained as an engineer officer. He had led his division bravely at Fredericksburg and at Chancellorsville. Now he found himself unexpectedly thrust into the leadership of the army. Next morning General Hooker wished Meade well and bade him goodby.

Scarcely had Lee's first units left Fredericksburg when President Lincoln issued a call for 100,000 additional troops. Hundreds of recruits trudged southward to join the forces in Maryland, a majority from Pennsylvania, the state facing imminent invasion. The Army of the Potomac which Meade had suddenly inherited now mustered about 92,000 officers and men, of which 88,289 were effectives, in seven infantry and one cavalry corps. Each infantry corps contained about 12,000 troops, generally with three divisions, of from two to four brigades—each of these major units about half the size of those in the Confederate force. Corps and divisions were commanded by major generals, with seniority the strict rule in succession. General Reynolds of I Corps was Meade's close friend and fellow Pennsylvanian. The others in order were: II, Winfield Scott Hancock; III, Daniel S. Sickles; V, Meade's corps, of which George Sykes assumed command; VI, John Sedgwick; XI, Oliver O. Howard; and XII, Henry W. Slocum. In General Pleasanton's cavalry corps were about 7,800 well-seasoned officers and men. Chief of artillery was Brigadier General Henry J. Hunt, with one brigade of his gunners, wearing red-striped trousers, attached to each corps.

Troops from every state except those in the Confederacy marched with that army to their rendezvous with destiny. From Frederick for miles southward, under the starry sky of that June night, those troops were sleeping from the fatigue of forced marches. In Lee's army were troops from every state in the Confederacy, and they, too, were sleeping from a similar fatigue. On both sides, the great majority of officers above the rank of lieutenant colonel were graduates of West Point. Some officers under Lee had been classmates of Meade. Many were comrades in arms in the war with Mexico. The same regulations governed drill and army routine for both sides. The commands issued by officers and noncoms to the men in blue were the same as those given to the men from Dixie. Soon they would be in a life-and-death struggle. Soon the Army of the Potomac would set up the rock of Union resistance against which the high tide of Confederate strength would surge and beat in vain.

It was past 10 o'clock on the night of June 28, when Major John W. Fairfax of Longstreet's staff brought General Lee his first news that the Union army had crossed the Potomac and was scattered through Maryland with its center at Frederick—and with a new commander. The Confederate chieftain realized at once that the campaign to capture Harrisburg and possibly Baltimore must be abandoned, and his invading army quickly concentrated. Lee advanced with Longstreet's corps to Chambersburg, then eastward to Cashtown, a small village eight miles west of Gettysburg, leaving one of Longstreet's divisions, commanded by General George E. Pickett, to guard the trains and supplies in the rear. Orders were sent to Ewell to call his divisions back at once and assemble near the Cashtown rendezvous.

Neither Lee nor Meade chose the quiet little town in southern Pennsylvania as the scene for a decisive battle. Neither general was ready for a full attack or a complete defense, and neither commander was on the field when the battle opened. Fate set the time and place. Fate—and several roads radiating from Gettysburg like spokes of a wheel from its hub, which brought together the opposing armies.

Meade's first plan was to form a defensive line across the Maryland-Pennsylvania border, and he prepared to assemble all his corps for that purpose. But ranging in the van of the Union forces was General Reynolds, capable and daring and the senior officer next to Meade, commanding the left wing of the Army of the Potomac—composed of the I, III and XI Corps. Reynolds had no order to bring on a battle while the army's units were scattered among the towns and along the roads south and west of Gettysburg, but that impetuous Pennsylvanian confided to his second in command, General Abner Doubleday, that it was necessary "to attack the enemy at once to prevent him plundering the whole state."

On June 29 Reynolds reached Marsh Creek, just six miles south of the assembling Confederate force at Cashtown. Early next morning he sent forward the cavalry division accompanying his corps, commanded by Brigadier General John Buford, with orders to occupy Gettysburg. Buford's riders came upon the advance Confederate regiments: North Carolina troops in General Hill's corps, marching toward Gettysburg to lay in supplies, particularly shoes for some of their comrades whose feet were entirely bare. With a true cavalry officer's understanding of his responsibility, Buford posted his units to guard the approaches to the town. He stationed his strongest force, dismounted and armed with carbines, with supporting artillery, on Seminary Ridge—so named because of the Lutheran Seminary located upon its crest near the Chambersburg pike, three-fourths of a mile west of town.

Informed of the contact with the Union cavalry, General Hill made his own fateful decision to march his whole corps to Gettysburg, and sent word to General Ewell, moving with his corps from Carlisle to Cashtown, to make Gettysburg his objective.

Thus the stage was set for the greatest single battle between men of the same nation, speaking the same tongue, and—until the unhappy resort to arms—owing allegiance to the same flag and nurtured in its common traditions of liberty. Thus began this tremendous drama of unparalleled heroism and sacrifice that was Gettysburg.

First Day to the Confederates

It is 5 o'clock on the morning of July 1, 1863, and in the early light the leading regiments of a division of Hill's corps, commanded by General Henry Heth, are moving along the road to Gettysburg. In the van is a brigade of Mississippians, followed by units made up of twelve regiments from North Carolina, three each from Virginia and Tennessee and one from Alabama. Officers and men are in fine spirits, tramping along with their standards of Stars and Bars waving in the hot breeze, under this order from General Hill: "Occupy Gettysburg!"

Riding far out along that Chambersburg pike, a Union corporal in a New York regiment spies the advancing Confederate column and gallops back toward his comrades standing guard west of Gettysburg. He fires his piece to give the alarm, and the sound echoes across the countryside. General Buford orders all his force to make a stand at a wooded ridge half a mile beyond Seminary Ridge. There the men dismount and deploy with their carbines to meet the Confederate tide.

"Stand fast for battle!" is the order.

At 8 o'clock the Confederate column swings over a ridge a mile distant from the Union forces. The bluecoats quickly move forward a fieldpiece and its thunderous BOOM! sends its greeting toward the Mississippians. Buford, still in Gettysburg, greets a lieutenant colonel from General James S. Wadsworth's staff, of Reynolds' I Corps, who had ridden ahead to purchase supplies. The cavalry commander advises the officer to return at once to his unit.

"Why—what's the matter, general?" the officer asks, just as that first cannon's roar echoes against the houses of Gettysburg.

"*That's* the matter!" shouts Buford, as he mounts his horse and gallops away to join his troops.

As the Confederate regiments press forward, they deploy to engage the Union guardians of the road and the town beyond, their fieldpieces answering those of their opponents. Between the skirmish lines is a small stream, Willoughby's Run, from both banks of which the rattle of musketry begins.

Meantime, General Reynolds had led his I Corps to the edge of Gettysburg. Hearing the firing, he and his staff gallop to the seminary, his leading brigades following at double-quick. Reynolds and Buford mount the cupola of the seminary building and survey the scene about them. They see to the west the cavalry, holding at bay the gathering Confederate columns. To the east they view the town, and at its southern edge Cemetery Hill, the community's burial place. A broken ridge extends southward for about three miles, where Little Round Top hill rises and just beyond a still higher hill, Round Top. From Cemetery Hill, like the curve of a giant fishhook, the eminence curves eastward to Culp's Hill and back south again. Between those rocky uplands and Seminary Ridge the glasses of the two officers reveal farms and rural homes, the fields bisected by the road from Emmitsburg, from which units of Reynolds' I Corps now swarm toward the seminary.

The two generals agree that their combined force must hold the Confederates in check until Meade can assemble all his army for the battle. Again astride his horse, Reynolds rides along the edge of the wooded tract, posting the troops of his I Corps as they hurry into the skirmish lines. As the Pennsylvanian glances back toward his advancing units, he suddenly falls from his horse, killed instantly as his head is pierced by a bullet from a Confederate sharpshooter.

Here is a severe loss to the Union forces at a critical moment. General Doubleday assumes command. Confederate infantry charges, repeated at intervals for two hours, cost both sides dearly, but tell most heavily on the line of defending Union soldiers. Doubleday sees the forces on his right steadily pushed back by a brigade of Alabamans of General R. H. Anderson's division, one Union brigade withdrawing to the very outskirts of the town. Confederates range down the grade of an unfinished railway paralleling the Chambersburg road, and into a cut through a ridge; troops of a Union brigade rush up to pour musket fire into the cut, and hundreds of the Confederates surrender.

Skirmishers at the left of Doubleday's line, where Willoughby's Run meets a wooded copse, are heavily engaged by Tennessee and Alabama troops under Brigadier General J. J. Archer. The 1st Brigade of General Wadsworth's division, made up of men from Wisconsin, Michigan and Indiana, veterans of the Virginia campaigns, wearing black hats and proudly calling themselves "the Iron Brigade," sweep through the wood, cut off Archer's brigade and capture half its troops —including General Archer.

General Lee and his staff, anxiously hurrying to the scene of battle that began without his orders, finds the roar of cannon and the staccato of musket fire dying away. Unable to overpower the Union line, General Heth rests his men, waiting the arrival of Ewell's corps from Carlisle.

At 11 o'clock General Howard and his staff, riding ahead of his XI Corps, arrive at the battle scene. Since Oliver O. Howard is Doubleday's senior, he takes command of the field. A quick survey of the topography and the odds against the Union line convinces Howard that the battle to the west of Gettysburg will be only preliminary, and that if the Federal troops are forced back, Cemetery Hill and the rocky uplands south of it must be their defensive line.

"God helping us," Howard says to his staff as he points toward the cemetery, "we will hold that hill until Meade and the rest of the army come!"

As the three infantry divisions and the artillery of the XI Corps arrive, Howard places most of his batteries on Cemetery Hill and prepares to prolong the infantry line facing Heth's Confederates beyond Seminary Ridge. But at 2 o'clock Ewell's leading brigade of Georgians move from the Carlisle road into the fields north of Gettysburg. Howard directs General Carl Schurz, German-born St. Louisan, to deploy his brigades north of the town, almost at right angles to I Corps, to meet the new gray tide.

From Hill's forward battle line General Lee sees the blue-coated forces maneuvering into their new positions. He hears a shout from Heth's troops as they recognize their reinforcements as the division of General Rodes, hero of Stonewall Jackson's offensive at Chancellorsville. These soldiers have marched since before dawn, but without pausing for breath and before making complete contact with the flank of Hill's corps they deploy and heavily assault the Union right. The battle surges in furious artillery firing and close-order infantry charges. Observing that Rodes's brigades are meeting stiff resistance, General Heth rides up to Lee and suggests to his chieftain that he attack on his front. Lee answers:

"No, I am not prepared to bring on a general engagement today. Longstreet is not up!"

But almost at that moment, General Early's division arrives from its long march from York, and its four brigades from Louisiana, Georgia, Virginia and North Carolina strike Schurz's right flank. Now General Lee issues the orders that carry his legions to victory on that first sanguinary day at Gettysburg: Heth's whole division forward to the attack! A reserve division to flank Doubleday's left, while Ewell and Early are engaging the Union right!

With a "rebel yell" resounding over Willoughby's Run, Heth's southern soldiers sweep forward—forward over the stream, forward to the seminary where Doubleday's survivors fight stubbornly until overcome. Rodes's brigades rally and with Early's brigades threaten to envelop Schurz's corps. Outnumbered and assailed on three sides, the Union line gives way. Battalion and company officers struggle to prevent complete rout of their units, while back through the town that has cringed all day at the roar of battle, back to the hills and ridges the bluecoats retreat, flanked and pressed by shouting, firing infantrymen of the Confederate army. About 5,000 Union prisoners are soon being disarmed and herded to the rear.

General Lee rides beyond the seminary and stands gazing at the retreating Federal units. Sensing that the fortunate turn might yield further gains, the Virginian suggests to Hill that the disorganized foe be dislodged from those uplands. But Hill, ill of fever, protests that his men are weary and need to be reassembled. Ewell hesitates to attack, sending word to his commander that the whole Army of the Potomac might soon come up. Longstreet arrives, and after surveying the scene urges Lee to abandon further attacks and move quickly to flank Meade's army and gain a position between the Federal force and Washington.

There is no Stonewall Jackson—or even Jeb Stuart—to press forward while victory is within grasp. Still, numerous subordinate commanders beg to move before night falls, to take Cemetery Hill and nearby Culp's Hill and thus hold the most advantageous positions for the battle next day. Brigadier General Gordon, at the head of his hard-fighting Georgians, leads the pursuit of the XI Corps to the very foot of Cemetery Hill until ordered by Ewell to halt. In his memoirs, written after years of distinguished public service, Gordon relates:

Neither General Early nor General Ewell could possibly have been fully cognizant of the situation at the time I was ordered to halt. The whole of that portion of the Union army in my front was in confusion and flight. . . . As far down the lines as my eye could reach the Union troops were in retreat. Those at a distance were still resisting, but giving ground, and it was only necessary for me to press forward in order to insure the same results which invariably follow such flank movements. In less than half an hour my troops would have swept up and over those hills. . . .

Where Brave Men Give Their Lives

By midafternoon of that fateful July 1, General Meade realizes that the place for the battle has already been selected, and sends orderlies galloping to remaining units of his army with word to come by forced marches to Gettysburg.

At 3:30, as sounds of battle die away, General Hancock arrives with orders from Meade to assume command of the field. This general of the II Corps, beloved by all his fellow Pennsylvanians and respected by all in the Army of the Potomac, is greeted with cheers. With characteristic vigor he regroups the survivors of the I and XI Corps and the cavalry upon the giant fishhook of the Union position, spreading them out behind rocks and trees so that Confederate spyglasses might not disclose the weakness of the units. At 5 o'clock General Sickles' III Corps marches in from Emmitsburg, and soon afterward General Slocum's XII Corps from Two Taverns.

Before dusk, from the cupola of the town's almshouse, General Lee surveys the preparations of his assembling foemen and calls a council of his generals. The gray-bearded commander and every officer present, all schooled and experienced in battle tactics, understand the advantage the Union forces hold in their high terrain, behind which orders can be quickly carried and concealed maneuvers promptly made, while their own line of devoted Southern soldiers now extends in a great arc of more than three miles from the town west and southward along Seminary Ridge. Still Lee councils an attack at the earliest possible moment next morning, to strike both ends of the Union line—Ewell's corps on the left, to seize Culp's Hill; Longstreet's corps on the right, to turn that flank; when both flanks are thus demoralized, Hill's corps will attack the center. Again Longstreet advises that the army withdraw from the battle and move southward into Maryland.

"No!" Lee responds, pointing toward the Union positions. "The enemy is there—and there I mean to attack him." He orders Longstreet to bring up his remaining units quickly, and to attack with the divisions of Generals J. B. Hood and Lafayette McLaws.

One hour after midnight Meade arrives, haggard from anxiety and loss of sleep. By the light of a full moon he reorganizes the positions, as hour by hour the Union regiments and brigades tramp wearily in.

The soldiers from Dixie in Ewell's corps are up from their brief rest in the fields around Gettysburg at 3 o'clock. They drink their coffee and eat their bacon and hardtack. At 4 o'clock they stand in ranks with rifles ready. But no bugles sound "Forward!" Their brigades must wait for Longstreet to begin the attack. The sun comes up in sultry silence, except for the noises so familiar to the troops on both sides: the pounding of hoofs as staff officers dash here and there, the marching of infantry units to their positions, the clank of picks and shovels building artillery lunettes, the lumbering of cannon and caissons to their stations.

Every moment strengthens the Union defensive line. At 7 o'clock Hancock's II Corps comes in and is placed on Cemetery Hill, with the I Corps withdrawn for reserve. Two divisions of the V Corps arrive and are held behind the ridge in reserve. General Hunt and his artillery officers station their formidable batteries all along the line.

At 8 o'clock a rider brings General Lee a message from his willful lieutenant, Longstreet, stating that a brigade of McLaws' division and Pickett's division are yet to reach the field, and requesting that the attack wait until these troops come in. Lee firmly orders the corps commander to begin the attack as soon as possible, striking the Federal line at the Emmitsburg road.

Between the lines, near the center, from the home and buildings of the Bliss farm, Confederate sharpshooters keep up a dangerous fire upon all blue uniforms in sight. New Jersey and Delaware troops volunteer to rush the nest. The Dixie marksmen are captured, and shouts go up along the Union line as the buildings are fired.

Noon comes, and the early hours of the hot afternoon still bring no attack. But War Horse Longstreet's troops are all in, except Pickett's divisions, and the brown-bearded lieutenant general is massing his troops in a wooded tract at the right of the Confederate line. Meade's chief of engineers, General Warren, suspecting that the forest shelters the rendezvous, orders a lone cannon shell fired into it. The flash of bayonets of startled soldiers confirms Warren's guess, and also makes clear that the Confederate line could envelop Little Round Top and enfilade the Union line. More dangerous still, Sickles has advanced his 1st Division, principally Michigan, New York and Pennsylvania infantry and Maine and Rhode Island artillery, to the Emmitsburg road, its center at a peach orchard on the Ward farm, thus forming an exposed apex.

At 3 o'clock Colonel E. P. Alexander, Longstreet's artillery chief, directs the first volleys into that shining target of Sickles' advanced position. At 3:30, in steady order, the four brigades of Hood's division, followed by the four brigades under McLaws, move across the open fields toward the Emmitsburg road. The brigades halt and form into triple lines of fronts by regiments.

"Forward—charge!" rings the command.

With a yell that resounds over the rolling countryside, the Confederate soldiers come on the run. The Union artillery opens, its screaming shells tearing gaps into the thundering ranks. But the ranks close up. The attack falls with fury as

Brigadier General William Barksdale's four Mississippi regiments strike Sickles' exposed angle. The impact of the assault
drives the Union line back. Wave after wave of Confederate
battalions roll into the peach orchard. Six batteries accom-
pany the infantry, and fire at point-blank range at the Union
artillery. So many artillery horses are killed or disabled that
nearly all the guns which are not captured by the Confederates are drawn back by hand.

Every foot of ground about the buildings of the Ward farm
is fiercely contested. In the yard of the farmhouse Captain
Edward P. Bigelow, commanding a battery of the 9th Massachusetts, stands with his four guns. He is ordered to hold
his position to slow the Confederate advance while a new
artillery line is formed. His gunners continue to fire into the
charging Mississippians and Georgians, who come to the very
muzzles of his guns. Then, badly wounded, Bigelow helps pull
the smoking cannon to safety. His battery loses his two lieutenants, six of the seven noncoms, ten of the fifteen privates,
and eighteen of the twenty-four horses.

Meanwhile, at the extreme right of the Confederate line,
the four Alabama regiments under Brigadier General E. M.
Law advance toward the slope of Little Round Top. General
Warren and his aide, Colonel Washington Roebling, come
upon Brigadier General Strong Vincent, of the V Corps, moving to support Sickles in the rocky depression at the foot of
this hill, and explain the need of beating the Confederates to
the top. General Vincent shouts, "I'll take the responsibility!"
and wheels his men to the left. His four regiments, from as
many states, with their artillery battalion, hurry up the slope,
followed by the four regiments commanded by Brigadier General S. H. Weed. As the Confederates push up the other side
they are halted by withering fire. The Union troops hold the
summit—but Vincent falls mortally wounded.

General Meade hurries to the rear of Sickles' hard-pressed

troops and begins calling up reinforcements from other parts of his line. The left flank of this corps, at the base of Little Round Top, extends to a rocky ridge studded with huge boulders, called forever after "the Devil's Den." Here for three hours the gallant men in gray and blue fight it out with volleys from their muskets and the cold steel of their bayonets. A New York battery is planted there, and New York infantrymen bear the brunt of the attack made by troops proudly named "Hood's Texas Rangers."

Early in the engagement, General Hood is wounded, and Law takes command of the division. The Rangers capture and hold the den, but are repulsed in every charge they make up Little Round Top. The single Arkansas regiment in Lee's army valorously supports the attack. The intermingled heaps of the wounded and the dead form breastworks, and a small stream east of the den, Plum's Run, is reddened with the blood of the brave. General Sickles falls, one leg shot away, and his command passes to General David B. Birney.

To the east of the peach orchard is a wheat field, with grain ready to be cut. Here Brigadier General J. B. Kershaw's South Carolina infantrymen swing to the attack, and here the Union soldiers make a stubborn defense as regiments from Connecticut, Michigan and Pennsylvania meet the repeated charges. Some of the stone fences lining the fields are taken and lost as many as ten times. Deeds of bravery are commonplace on both sides. Brigadier General S. Wiley Crawford, commanding the 2d Division of Sykes's corps, draws up his troops in columns of companies. He gallops to the head, seizes the standard of the leading regiment, flashes his sword and orders "Forward!" With a shout the division hurls itself, behind its gallant leader, into the melee of the wheatfield. The Union line steadies, but retreats under renewed attacks.

Near the wheat field is the Rogers farmhouse. During the late afternoon's struggle, the Union soldiers are astonished to see the kitchen door open and buxom Josephine Rogers appear, heedless of the minnie balls flying thick and fast, her apron filled with freshly baked gingerbread. Loyal to the Union cause, she explains that she has remained in the house to prepare refreshments for its fighting men!

General Lee Reaches for Victory

Intent upon the battle on his right flank, and sensing that victory there might result in Union retreat all along the line, Lee holds up the attacks of his two other corps until late afternoon. Then he orders General Hill to send a division forward by brigades, those on the right to lead and the others to follow in echelon. He hopes that this assault will extend all the way around to Culp's Hill. Four brigades of General G. T. Anderson's division move forward—C. M. Wilcox's Alabama "Yellow Hammers" in the lead, followed by E. A. Perry's brigade of Florida regiments, A. R. Wright's Georgians and Canot Posey's Mississippians.

Braving the fire from cannon and musket volleys as they move up the slope, Wilcox's brigade charges the right of Sickles' corps, meeting Brigadier General Andrew A. Humphreys' division of New Hampshire, New Jersey, New York and Pennsylvania troops. Almost at the same moment, the Georgians reach Hancock's infantry positions and with frantic courage seize a line of the breastworks. The Union line is cut. Confederate cannonballs demolish the porch of Meade's headquarters. But shouts rise from the Federal troops as Meade sends in newly arrived regiments of General Sedgwick's corps. The Union line counterattacks, and the Confederate brigades, reduced by half their numbers, retreat sorrowfully down the slope. The echelon attack has failed.

Still General Lee reaches for victory. He orders two brigades of General Early's division, waiting through the long day in the town, to move out for another attack upon Cemetery Hill.

Brigadier General H. S. Hays's five regiments of "Louisiana Tigers" and Colonel J. E. Avery's three North Carolina regiments, moving in close-order waves, charge with reckless bravery. The Tigers are enfiladed on the way up by Maine batteries, while the rest of Hancock's cannon turn on the North Carolinians, but both brigades sweep over the first line of Union breastworks. They look in vain for the support promised them by General Rodes's brigade of 5,000 men, which might help them to hold the hill until Confederate artillery can enfilade the troops of Howard and Hancock and bring on a general retreat of the Federal forces.

At that critical moment in the terrible struggle at Gettysburg, Hancock brings up a brigade of Ohio, Indiana and West Virginia troops under Colonel Samuel S. Carroll, and the Tigers and their Carolina comrades are repulsed with heavy loss.

Dusk begins to draw its merciful curtain over the carnage, as one more Confederate assault brings partial victory to the gray hosts. On the extreme Union right, General Slocum's corps has been drawn upon all afternoon for troops to reinforce the hardpressed line on the ridge. Those who remain have spent the anxious hours piling up huge stones for breastworks. Now Ewell's artillery opens upon them with canister and shells, followed by an infantry charge of General Edward Johnson's division. This is Stonewall Jackson's old command, composed principally of Virginians. The regiments under Brigadier General George H. Steuart lead the assault, overcome the resistance of the depleted Union ranks, and hold one line of the breastworks at the summit throughout the night.

As though guided by a fate determined to defeat the Southern cause, General Jeb Stuart has brought his cavalry corps all the way to Carlisle before he learns of the battle at Gettysburg. Late on that second day he leads his riders, so exhausted that many are asleep on their weary, foam-flecked mounts, to within hearing of the sounds of battle on Culp's Hill. Forming for a charge, Stuart's advance units are suddenly attacked by Union cavalry under Brigadier General David M. Gregg. Stuart is forced to withdraw and camp for the night.

On both sides in the gathering darkness, stretcher-bearers work doggedly, bringing in the wounded to hospital tents hurriedly improvised and lit by wax candles.

At Spangler's spring, gushing its clear, cold water from the base of Culp's Hill, there is a gentlemen's armistice as hundreds of weary soldiers from both sides, some almost crazed from the thirst of heat and exertion, gather to drink, to fill canteens, buckets, and casks. Several men of the Maryland regiment in Steuart's brigade find themselves face to face with Maryland Union infantrymen, some their neighbors and friends. One Confederate soldier greets a brother in the blue-uniformed ranks. In the sultry shadows, the boys from the Free State sing in unison the refrain, "Maryland, My Maryland!"

Both Lee and Meade call councils of their corps and division generals, their battle leaders with uniforms encrusted with sweat and dust. Whether wearing the gray or the blue, their faces are anxious and taut. The Confederate commanders can count some gains from the terrific sacrifices of their uncoordinated assaults: Longstreet holds Devil's Den and the base of Little Round Top; Johnson holds Culp's Hill almost to the Baltimore road; the Union center has been pierced, only to be lost again through lack of support; and Stuart is close by to throw into the scales of the next day's battle the weight of his experience and daring. The Southern chieftain knows full well that his hard-fighting army has not yet won the battle, but counsels that victory can still be gained by extending the line on Culp's Hill to seize the Baltimore road and cut this line of Union communication and retreat, with a grand assault also on the Union center.

For Meade the situation is grave. The Union commander raises the question with his generals whether the Army of the Potomac should give up the ground and retire toward Washington. Captain Ulric Dahlgren, a Federal scout, is ushered into the council room. He has captured a Confederate rider with a message from President Jefferson Davis to General Lee, indicating that the Army of Northern Virginia cannot be reinforced. Meade calls for a vote on the question of retreating, and when all his generals vote to continue the battle, Meade declares:

"Gentlemen, we will stand and fight it out here at Gettysburg!"

It is agreed that an attack to regain Culp's Hill must be the first action. There is only a brief rest, in their tents or under the hot, moonlit sky, for the officers whose orders soon will send again into mortal combat thousands of soldiers from communities all over the North and the South.

At 4 o'clock on that historic third of July, as the first streaks of red show in the sky, General Slocum orders the artillery fire to begin against the Confederates on Culp's Hill; at the same time General Ewell sends reinforcements to hold the breastworks and resume the offensive. In the tracks they made the evening before, the Gray and the Blue mingle again in a death grapple that lasts for four hours. Daylight finds attacks and counterattacks sweeping over the hill and into the fields below. By the rocky breastworks, the heaps of wounded and slain grow higher. Still the Union defenders hold, while Confederate support fails to arrive. At 11 o'clock, bugles call the Southern survivors back to their positions on Rock Creek east of town.

Informed that Federal artillery and infantry are entrenched on Little Round Top, Lee realizes that his flank is dominated and abandons his plan for another attack upon the Union left. But his plan for a grand assault upon the center, at the ridge south of Cemetery Hill, still stands. Pickett's division, which had arrived late the evening before, will form one of the attacking columns, and Heth's division the other. Wounded the day before, Heth has turned over his command to General Johnston J. Pettigrew.

In the early morning light, Lee stands with Longstreet on Seminary Ridge. The brown-bearded lieutenant general hesitates to endorse Lee's plan, pointing out that it would be costly in lives.

"It is now our only hope for victory," says Lee. Pointing to a clump of trees that fronts Hancock's line, the Confederate chieftain orders:

"Let the center of the attack fall there!"

The Tragic Charge

Lee next counsels with his artillery officers, ordering them to prepare for the infantry charge by a tremendous cannonade. At 9 o'clock General Pendleton begins the work of assembling the guns from Hill's and Longstreet's corps. Colonel Alexander masses seventy-five cannon east of the Emmitsburg road, while Colonel R. Lindsey Walker, commanding the artillery of Hill's corps, ranges sixty-three cannon on Seminary Ridge to the northward. These guns, roaring in concert, are to blast a hole in the Federal line through which the brigades under Pickett and Pettigrew will charge on their way to victory.

Watching these movements through their glasses, Union officers marvel at the audacity of the plan. Will the Confederates move in the open across those fields? To be prepared, General Hunt brings up eighty cannon to the Union front, massed principally on Hancock's salient. It is noon before the Confederate columns move out of their sheltering woods and breastworks and advance to the rear of their cannon. The firing on Culp's Hill has ceased, and General Lee understands the awful meaning of that silence: there can be no support, no cross-fire on the ridge, from his troops at the left of his line. Now everything depends upon the valor of the officers and men about to make the charge on the center.

At exactly 1 o'clock, two "Napoleon" guns of a New Orleans battery send their round shot shrieking toward the Union line. That is the signal for the 136 other artillerymen, holding the lanyards of their pieces, to "let go!" The roar shakes the countryside. Meade signals for his guns to answer, and the greatest artillery duel ever fought up to that hour begins. Shell and round shot of various sizes whiz and shriek through the air from both directions. The lighted fuses attached to the shells cut great ribbons of red and yellow through the blue smoke.

Union infantrymen crouch behind stone and wooden breast-works, taking the barrage bravely. General Hunt rushes up batteries on the gallop as his guns are demolished by the Confederate fire. Screaming shells fall upon the house Meade uses as headquarters, and the commanding general hurriedly retires to the headquarters of General Slocum, removed from danger and also from close direction of the battle. General Hancock with three staff officers gallantly rides from one end of his corps to the other, shouting words of encouragement and calling upon his men to stand firm.

Shortly before 3 o'clock Colonel Alexander sends a note to General Pickett:

"General—if you are coming at all, you must come at once."

Now under the smoke and haze hanging over the space between the two great armies a sudden silence descends. The ears of the soldiers throb from the noise that has beat upon them. The battered lines of the Union corps are being re-formed while the wounded are being hurried to the rear. The last moment for Confederate victory has come. For General Longstreet, whose heart has never believed a victory at Gettysburg possible, the moment is one of intense anguish.

General Pickett rides up to his corps chief, his uniform immaculate, his long auburn hair falling to his shoulders—every inch a soldier and a Virginia gentleman. With gloved hand he salutes as he asks:

"General, shall I advance?"

Longstreet makes no reply. His eyes, gazing vacantly at Pickett, are moist. Pickett salutes again:

"Sir, I shall order my division forward!" he says.

Over the battle-strewn fields the flower of the Army of Northern Virginia begins its steady march, the flags of forty-seven regiments fluttering in the sultry air, the long three-deep ranks of gray-uniformed troops extending half a mile. The afternoon sun glints from the sabres of five hundred officers and from the bayonets of 14,500 men, as the Confederate divisions begin the charge that writes the final chapter of the story of Gettysburg, and becomes one of the most famous episodes in military history.

Pickett's three brigades of Virginians are on the right, flanked by Pettigrew's division of four brigades of troops from Alabama, Tennessee, North Carolina, Mississippi and Virginia; while in support of Pettigrew march two brigades of North Carolinians under General Isaac Trimble, many of the men wearing bandages for wounds from the first day's battle. Veterans of many battles are these. Courageously they march to meet the most seasoned troops left to the Army of the Potomac. Across the intervening 1,400 yards they come, driving back the Union skirmishers at the Emmitsburg road, on toward the ridge. For a few moments they pause. Then from scores of bugles and from the throats of hundreds of officers and noncoms there sounds the order:

"Forward—charge!"

The leading regiments rush forward. Union cannon open directly into their ranks, while muskets blaze upon them the messages of death. Heedless of the hundreds who fall, the gray-coated lines thunder up the slope. Wave after wave of the front-line Virginians reach the stone fences and barricades of the ridge. For a time they take possession of Hancock's forward positions.

Three regiments of Vermont Green Mountain Boys make a brave charge from their breastworks against Trimble's flank. The 8th Ohio and the 125th New York Regiments also make valiant assaults upon the attacking divisions, but cannot stop the tide. Charge upon charge of shouting Confederates push the wavering Union line back. At the apex of the breastworks, held by Pennsylvania troops under Brigadier General Alexander S. Webb, and remembered in all accounts as "the angle," the fiercest fighting of the day takes place. Here Pettigrew's Tennessee regiments plant their colors, and to their left a Georgia brigade drives back the Pennsylvania defenders. Ohio troops rush up to avert a rout.

Leading Pickett's 3d Brigade is Brigadier General Lewis A. Armistead, who served with Hancock when they were lieutenants in the 6th Infantry during the Mexican War. Armistead places his hat on the point of his sword and calls:

"Boys, we must use the cold steel. Who will go with me?"

With a shout, the men of his brigade leap forward. They reach the artillery line and capture several cannon. Watching in profound anxiety, Lee sees through his glass the Confederate Battle Flag, with the blue flag of his beloved Virginia, waving upon that battle-churned crest. About one hundred North Carolina soldiers have thrust several yards beyond this line, reaching "the high-water mark" of the Confederate invasion.

But Hancock draws reinforcements for Webb's brigade and soon a fresh storm of artillery and musket fire breaks upon the attackers. General Armistead falls, mortally wounded. His men reel back. Wilcox awaits the order to advance with his brigade, to be followed by other units of Longstreet's and Hill's corps.

"Any further sacrifice would be needless!" Longstreet comments, grim-faced, to his staff.

At this moment, General Hancock falls from his mount into the arms of staff officers, painfully wounded in the groin. He is carried to an ambulance, where his wound is found to be caused by a ten-penny nail. "Then the Rebs are running short of ammunition!" the Pennsylvanian exclaims. "Send in all the V and VI Corps!"

Now the Confederate retreat begins. One of Hancock's officers, Major Jesse B. Young, wrote of it:

Flanked on the right and on the left, lines of skirmishers going out to gather them in, their cause lost, their hopes blighted, their generals dead or dying, their flags captured, hundreds fling themselves to the ground to escape the tempest of fire that sweeps the field, or turn to the rear in the despairing hope of making escape across the plain over which they had come so proudly an hour before. Thus, in unspeakable disaster, the charge of Pickett and Pettigrew came to an end, and the great charge took its place in the pages of history, an enduring picture of courage, of unavailing heroism, of surpassing martial splendor.

General Lee is aware of the awful meaning of that disordered retreat. When Pickett rides up to report the failure of his charge, the Virginian sadly tells him, "It is all my fault!"

General Meade reaches the front line and surveys the fields strewn with the dead and the wounded, but risks no counterassault to rout the retreating Confederates. The Union commander is content with his defensive victory.

Unaware that the infantry attack has failed, General Stuart launches a cavalry battle beyond Culp's Hill. Brigadier General Gregg's Union squadrons are ready, and for an hour the riders clash in close-order charges and furious fighting

with sabers and pistols. Brigadier General George A. Custer
and his Michigan horsemen vigorously support the Union defense and counterattacks. At 6 o'clock Stuart suspends the battle, closing this epilogue to a battle already ended.

"The Brave Men, Living and Dead——"

So fell the curtain on this sanguinary conflict. Through the
deepening darkness, the one-horse carts used as ambulances
were guided by flickering lanterns over the reeking fields, as
stretcher-bearers of the Gray and the Blue gathered up their
wounded and their dead. Gettysburg was turned into a vast
hospital. Churches and homes were filled with the most seriously wounded, while volunteer nurses, men and women of
the town and countryside, helped the overworked surgeons
at the merciful task of binding up wounds and amputating
shattered limbs. After three days of intense heat, the rains
came on that night of Friday, July 3, with cooling winds.

Casualties on both sides were appalling. General Lee's official report listed 2,592 killed, 12,709 wounded and 5,150
missing. Losses by the Union army were given in General
Meade's report at 3,155 killed, 14,529 wounded and 5,365
missing. There were 12,220 Confederates captured. More
than 6,000 of these were wounded, and 2,810 died of their
wounds. In the last great assault, two of Pickett's three
brigade commanders were killed, and the other seriously
wounded. Almost every field officer in the division was either
killed or wounded, and among those who gave their lives were
eight of the ablest colonels of the entire Army of Northern
Virginia. The 26th North Carolina Regiment lost five hundred of its eight hundred men in the first day's fighting, and
on the morning of July 4 had only eighty present for duty. So
ran the roster of many units.

Such was the cost of the battle: Won by the fortunate position of the Union army on the great defensive fishhook, and

by the dogged determination of the generals of corps and divisions rather than by the skill of its temporary commander-in-chief; lost by the Southern warriors through the absence of Lee's "cavalry eyes" at the beginning, through the failure to coordinate their assaults with proper support, and through General Lee's overconfidence in his officers and men—his hope that they might accomplish what proved to be the impossible.

Late on the rainy Saturday afternoon, Lee began his retreat. Whether Meade used too great caution in not flanking his opponent and cutting off the retreat, with the possibility of ending the war then and there, was bitterly debated in the North. But certain it was that Lee's army had not been routed; he could still defend.

Back across the Potomac—back to Virginia—came Robert E. Lee and the survivors of his army. The general offered to resign his command, but President Davis firmly refused. For nearly two years more, against tremendous odds in manpower and resources, Lee led the cause of the Confederacy—the cause lost at Vicksburg and Gettysburg.

Today, amidst the calm beauty of Gettysburg's environs, are to be found the greatest number of monuments and markers of any battlefield in the world. They were raised for the most part by veterans of the Blue and the Gray, who returned to view in friendship the field where they had fought in that mighty engagement of July 1863.

Defeat for the Confederate forces saved the Union. The man who was determined that the Union must be saved, Abraham Lincoln, stood on the battlefield hallowed by "the brave men, living and dead," in November of that bleak year, and sounded this challenge for the people of the nation that had yet to bind up its wounds:

"It is for us, the living, rather, to be dedicated here to the unfinished work which they who fought here have thus far so nobly advanced. . . ."

CHAPTER TWELVE

Dewey Conquers the Spanish Fleet

On the island of Cuba during 1895, resistance of the people against the rule of Spain flared into open rebellion and war. Resistance was nothing new for the Cubans. Since the 1860's there had been revolutions and civil conflict on the island, but now the sentiment for independence from Spain was riding a high tide.

"Cuba libre!" was whispered from man to man. *"Cuba libre!"* was shouted when no Spanish uniforms were in sight.

Early in 1898 President William McKinley, reflecting the overwhelming sentiment of the American people for Cuban independence, formally requested the government of Her Majesty Queen Christina of Spain, regent for her son Alphonso XIII who was heir to the throne, to suggest a date when the civil war in Cuba might be brought to an end. No satisfactory answer was given.

As a token of friendship for the Cubans, and of readiness on the part of the United States to oppose Spanish tyranny on the territory of this close neighbor, the battleship *Maine* was dispatched from Key West, Florida. On January 24, 1898, she dropped anchor and rested in the pleasant waters of Havana Harbor.

The sky on the night of February 15 was somewhat overcast, and the lights on the deck of the *Maine* seemed from the shore to gleam with shadings of pink and orange. Captain C. D. Sigsbee was writing in his cabin. Some of the crew were on shore leave.

There was a rumbling, roaring BOOM! Then a louder, fearful, ripping crash. Flames shot up through the deck of the *Maine*. For several seconds, glowing sparks settled upon the stricken ship and the murky water. Then darkness and silence.

The Spanish warship *Vizcaya* was anchored near by. Near also was the Ward Line steamer *City of Washington*. Boats were lowered from these ships and rushed to the *Maine*. Survivors, many of them wounded by the blast, were picked up. By the next morning's light, Havana citizens crowding the waterfront saw the battered forward deck and the masts and turrets of the sunken man-of-war sticking above the waves. The American flag still fluttered over the wreck. Two hundred and fifty-eight officers and men of the battleship had lost their lives. Eight more wounded later died.

Feeling ran high throughout the United States. While many still hoped to avoid war, sentiment was overwhelming for an accounting with Spain, and for complete independence of her last possessions in the Western Hemisphere.

Revolutions against Spanish rule in South and Central America had stripped the once proud and powerful empire of most of her territory in the New World during the lusty, roaring years of settlement and expansion in the first half of the nineteenth century. Now only Cuba, largest island in the Caribbean Sea, and Puerto Rico, sizable island to the southeast, remained under Spanish rule.

Internal dissension, corrupt administration, heavy taxation and general unrest on the part of the inhabitants had marked the preceeding century of Cuban history. Active rebellion was headed by such popular leaders as Máximo Gómez, Antonio Macco, José Marti and Calixto Garcia.

Spanish authorities answered by attempts at still tighter control. When war broke again in 1895, the Spanish govern-

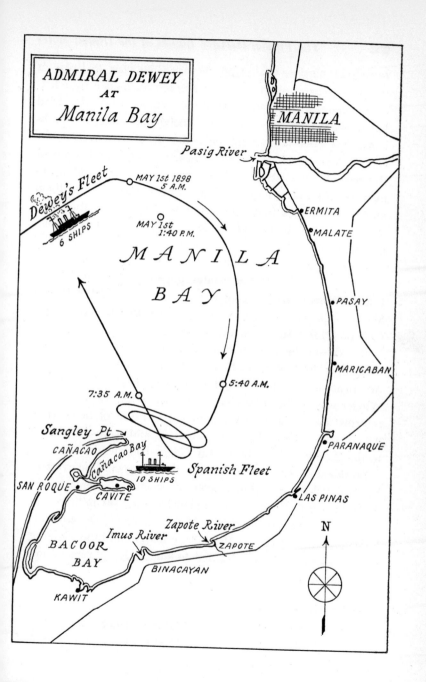

ADMIRAL DEWEY
AT
Manila Bay

MANILA

Pasig River

Dewey's Fleet

MAY 1st 1898
5 A.M.

MAY 1st
1:40 P.M.

6 SHIPS

ERMITA

MALATE

M A N I L A

B A Y

PASAY

5:40 A.M.

MARICABAN

7:35 A.M.

PARANAQUE

Sangley Pt

CAÑACAO

Cañacao Bay

Spanish Fleet

10 SHIPS

LAS PINAS

SAN ROQUE

CAVITE

Zapote River

Imus River

ZAPOTE

BACOOR
BAY

BINACAYAN

N

KAWIT

ment sent General Valeriano Weyler y Nicolau to Cuba as governor-general, with orders to enforce obedience by whatever means he deemed best. Stern and cruel, Weyler tried harsh military measures to solve social and economic problems. Not content to fight only the armed *insurrectos,* he carried his expeditions against the homes and plantations of the people. He destroyed crops, drove the peons and workmen into the towns, and then herded many thousands of them and their families into concentration camps. Starvation and misery took their toll of at least 200,000 helpless Cuban people.

American citizens became aroused at such wanton cruelty and injustice. The United States government formally protested. General Weyler contemptuously reminded the United States of General William T. Sherman's march to the sea and General Philip H. Sheridan's campaigns in the Shenandoah Valley during the American Civil War.

Leaders in the Spanish War Ministry understood what American intervention would mean, and hoped to avoid it. Weyler was replaced by General Blanco, who instituted some reforms, including an act granting a measure of home rule. American relief supplies were admitted and were distributed to the starving and ill by Consul-General Fitzhugh Lee.

President McKinley was hopeful that war could be averted, but realized the importance of preparations for an emergency. At his request Congress unanimously voted 50 million dollars for national defense. The War and Navy Departments hummed with activity. Battleships, cruisers and other fighting and auxiliary craft were hurried to shipyards for repairs and conditioning.

"Remember the Maine!*"*

Responsibility for sinking the *Maine* was not immediately determined, but popular feeling placed the blame on Spanish

authorities. Sensing this feeling, one of the President's subordinates did not share his opinion that war could be avoided.
He was Theodore Roosevelt, Assistant Secretary of the Navy,
who in his brief time in office had electrified that branch of the
service by his vigorous support of preparedness in ships and
men, training and supplies. Roosevelt had as his close adviser
Captain Alfred T. Mahan, a recognized authority on naval
tactics. On February 25 Roosevelt sent a cablegram to Commodore George Dewey, commanding the United States fleet
in Asiatic waters:

DEWEY, HONG KONG:

ORDER THE SQUADRON EXCEPT THE MONOCACY TO HONG KONG.
KEEP FULL OF COAL. IN THE EVENT OF DECLARATION OF WAR
SPAIN, YOUR DUTY WILL BE TO SEE THAT SPANISH SQUADRON DOES
NOT LEAVE ASIATIC COAST, AND THEN OFFENSIVE OPERATIONS IN
PHILIPPINE ISLANDS. . . .

ROOSEVELT

Commodore Dewey lost no time in complying. He dispatched a cable to United States Consul O. F. Williams at
Manila, asking him to obtain secretly all possible information
on fortifications, submarine mines, and the general defenses
about the city and harbor. He also requested that Mr. Williams keep close watch on the Spanish fleet, based at this capital city of the islands.

Dewey called in from their various stations the ships of
his fleet. The *Boston* and the *Concord* were in Japanese ports,
and they arrived within a few days. The cruiser *Raleigh* made
a fast run all the way from the Mediterranean. The *Monocacy*,
an antiquated destroyer, was laid up at Shanghai and her officers and crew were ordered to Hong Kong for duty on other
ships.

The commodore gave detailed attention to overhauling the
vessels, intensive drill for the men of his ships and matters of

supply. On March 11 Dewey cabled that ammunition and coal should be sent from San Francisco. He received the reply that the *Baltimore* was en route from Honolulu with ammunition, and that he should purchase coal from the British authorities. He promptly ordered a steamer full of the fuel. When the coal arrived in the steamship *Nanshan*, the enterprising Yankee commander bought the vessel as well, to use as a collier. He also purchased the steamer *Zafiro* as a supply ship. He did not arm the *Nanshan* and the *Zafiro*, since he wanted them free to purchase supplies at neutral ports if war began.

On April 19, in his quarters on the flagship *Olympia*, Commodore Dewey entered in his journal that the work of painting the ships of his fleet in "war colors"—which changed their gleaming white to a neutral gray—was completed.

The day before, Congress had voted a resolution demanding the withdrawal of Spain from Cuba. During the following week, the fleet that had assembled at Key West steamed toward Cuba with orders to blockade Havana and other ports. On April 24 the Spanish government declared war; on the following day Congress declared that war had existed since April 21.

The conflict between the once mightiest empire on earth and the future greatest republic of the world reached its climax in a battle in which Commodore George Dewey and his fleet won a victory that ushered in the era of modern naval warfare and established the United States firmly as a world power.

President McKinley called for 125,000 volunteers to augment the small force of the regular army, and they began converging on camps in Georgia and Florida to be drilled and equipped for the Cuban campaign. As trains filled with recruits pulled into stations along the way, patriotic citizens were on hand to pour hot coffee and to shout:

"Remember the *Maine!*"

In Congress, a witty and popular Confederate veteran, "Private" John Allen from Mississippi, proposed that members of Congress join the army in a body and go to Cuba to fight, declaring:

"I do not want any commission. I want to show Old Glory that I can do just as good fighting *under* her as I did when I fought *against* her as a private soldier!"

Within minutes after the declaration of war, Secretary of the Navy John D. Long dispatched this message to Dewey:

WAR HAS COMMENCED BETWEEN THE UNITED STATES AND SPAIN. PROCEED AT ONCE TO PHILIPPINE ISLANDS. COMMENCE OPERATIONS AT ONCE PARTICULARLY AGAINST SPANISH FLEET. YOU MUST CAPTURE VESSELS OR DESTROY. USE UTMOST ENDEAVORS.

For George Dewey, this cable was the crowning point of half a century of service for his country. Since his graduation from the Naval Academy in 1858, this calm, determined man had trained and prepared for such a moment when his fighting ships would face the enemy in battle action. Early in the Civil War he was assigned to Admiral David Farragut's command, and the influence of that master of naval fighting had made its lasting imprint upon him. Like all the young officers of the United States Navy at the time, he thrilled to the story of Farragut's conquest of Mobile Bay, when that sea dog issued his famous order: "Damn the torpedoes! Full speed ahead!"

As executive officer of the old steam sloop *Mississippi,* George Dewey served with Farragut during the stirring campaign against the Confederate forts below New Orleans in April, 1862. He was on the *Mississippi* at the Battle of Port Hudson when the guns from the river squadron assaulted the Confederate stronghold. His coolness under fire, when the *Mississippi* ran aground and was abandoned after being set on fire by the fort's batteries, won high praise from his captain, H. H. Bell, whose official report included the words:

"I have much pleasure in mentioning the efficient service rendered by Executive Officer George Dewey, who kept the vessel in her station during the engagement, a task exceedingly difficult from the darkness, and thick smoke that enveloped us from the fire of our own vessels, and the burning gunboats."

Assigned to the *Agawan,* Dewey sailed with the Union fleet engaged in blockade missions in the Atlantic. Promoted to lieutenant commander as the war closed, Dewey became a close student of battle strategy. He carefully studied the plan of attack upon Forts Walker and Beauregard at Hilton's Head in November, 1861, executed by Admiral S. F. Du Pont, whereby the vessels filed in line and fired at the Confederate batteries while in motion. He recognized that the steam-powered man-of-war opened a new chapter in naval tactics. He became convinced that accurate fire from a moving vessel was the secret of offensive seapower in the future.

By the slow promotions of peacetime naval routine, Dewey moved up to commodore, and for ten years was on duty as chief of the Bureau of Naval Equipment in Washington. Staff officers in the Department of the Navy, presuming that he would want to retire in 1897, planned to appoint an officer his junior in rank to command the Asiatic fleet. Prompted by a strange premonition, Commodore Dewey begged to be given sea duty and assigned to the Pacific.

Now his great opportunity had come. His task was to destroy the naval and shore defenses of Spain's most important possession in the Pacific area, the Philippine Islands. This archipelago of more than 7,000 islands, large and small, comprising 114,500 square miles, lay five hundred miles from the coast of China at the nearest point. Discovered by Ferdinand Magellan in 1421 and named for King Philip II, the islands became a string of pearls in the jewelbox of Spanish exploration and conquest, and now stood as the last bastion of Spanish power in the Orient.

The British government had frowned on American intervention in the "Cuban matter." On receiving the news of war, the governor of the British Port of Hong Kong requested the American naval squadron to leave the neutral harbor and waters within forty-eight hours. The international settlement at Hong Kong seethed with rumors and opinions as to what would happen to the luckless Americans now challenging the might of Spain. All seemed agreed that the Spanish fleet at Manila would be more than a match for Commodore Dewey's cruisers. Besides, the fortifications around Manila were impregnable.

In the forty-eight-hour interlude, Dewey and his staff found time to attend a dinner given by the British regimental officers, and heard the toastmaster's farewell words:

"A fine set of fellows, these Americans, but unhappily we shall never see them again!"

The Fleet Heads for Battle

Anxious as Dewey was to be on his mission, he hoped for the arrival of Consul Williams from Manila, for he knew that this official would bring with him valuable information about the defenses of the capital and the condition and strength of the Spanish fleet. Accordingly, the commodore moved his ships to Mirs Bay, thirty miles from Hong Kong on the Chinese coast. Williams arrived on the morning of April 27.

Now the ammunition was distributed and all hands put through their drills at station. All ships were given a final inspection by the commodore and his staff. The battle fleet headed into the Pacific with flags flying and the band on the deck of the *Olympia* playing "Hail, Columbia!"

Nine vessels made up the file of naval craft steaming resolutely toward the Philippine Islands. Following the 6,000-ton flagship *Olympia* were the other cruisers of from 3,000 to 4,500 tons: *Baltimore, Raleigh* and *Boston;* the 1,710-ton cruiser *Concord;* the 1,300-ton *Hugh McCullough,* a revenue cutter carrying four guns; and the 892-ton gunboat *Petrel;* while the *Nanshan* and the *Zafiro* brought up the rear. Speed had to be held to that of the slowest vessel, the collier, or about eight knots. The weather was calm and the tropical sky was clear as the fleet began the voyage to attack the Spanish fleet under Admiral Montojo that guarded Manila. Dewey knew that about half the Spanish colonial fleet was in the Atlantic, based at Cape Verde Islands, commanded by Admiral Pascual Cervera. Now he studied the reports brought by Consul Williams, which indicated that the American attackers would be outnumbered by the Spanish ships of this Asiatic fleet, in addition to having to run the gauntlet of shore batteries for miles before the harbor could be entered. Concerning torpedoes and mines, Williams had obtained no accurate information, but a cable from the American consul-general at Singapore on April 26 warned Dewey that the channel leading into Manila Bay had been mined.

The commodore was not alarmed. He calmly discussed with his staff the likelihood that the electric mines would deteriorate so rapidly in the tropical waters that they would be ineffective. Furthermore, the commander had faith in the marksmanship of his gunners. For this very battle they had been drilled, day after day, for months. The junior officers had wondered why the "Old Man" was so insistent upon the crews being able to smash targets with the ships under full steam. Now they would know.

Officers and sailors all knew the tremendous importance of a victory. A mere attack and withdrawal would not be enough. The squadron was 7,000 miles from home base, with neutral ports closed to them. But no one doubted the wisdom or questioned the leadership of the stocky, white-haired, gray-mustached man in the cabin of the *Olympia*.

The flagship's captain, C. V. Gridley, older than Dewey and ill, had begged his commodore since the rendezvous at Hong Kong to be allowed to command in battle. He was the senior captain. It would break his heart to be left out of action. Dewey assured him: "Captain, you have your ship!" Another veteran captain, Frank Wildes, was the *Boston*'s master. Just before the departure from Hong Kong, Commander B. P. Lambertson arrived by mail steamer from the United States, under orders to replace Wildes. The captain protested almost tearfully. Dewey, with an eye both to fairness and morale, settled nicely the matter by leaving Wildes to command the *Boston* and making Lambertson his chief of staff. It was a most fortunate move, for Lambertson proved to be a capable and daring executive.

Manila Bay has a wide, semicircular shore, in the center of which is the city of Manila; at the southern end is a small peninsula extending into the bay for some five miles, and here the strong fort of Cavite was situated. In the passage lie several islands, Corregidor and Caballo being the largest and dividing the entrance into two channels, Boca Grande and Boca Chica. Studying their detailed maps, the commodore and his staff were unable to understand why the Spanish squadron had not moved from Manila Bay to Subig Bay, about twenty-nine miles north of Corregidor. Here was the strongest possible defensive position, either to prevent entrance or to cut off retreat from Manila Bay. Later the Americans learned that Admiral Montojo wanted to fortify this position, but with typical procrastination had waited until war was declared, and then made a nervous attempt to plant batteries and lay mines. Without stronger defenses, Montojo found the position untenable. And, as Dewey recounted years later in his memoirs:

So on the morning of the 29th the Spanish squadron steamed back to Cavite. The attitude of the commanding officers must have been the attitude of the personnel. Any force in such a state of mind is already half beaten. The morale of his squadron, as revealed by Montojo's report after the battle, bore out my reasoning before the war had begun, that everywhere the Spaniards would stand upon the defensive. This must mean defeat in the end, and the more aggressive and prompt our action the smaller would be our losses and the sooner peace would come.

As he approached the Philippines, Dewey sent ahead the *Boston* and *Concord* to reconnoiter Subig Bay, and later dispatched the *Baltimore* to support them if the enemy should be found. The three cruisers were waiting when the rest of the squadron drew up.

The commodore called his commanders to the flagship. He informed them that the squadron would enter Manila Bay that night. He gave no written orders. Quite informally, Dewey told the captains to follow the lead of the flagship. The Spanish fleet was their objective, he said. They were to fire on the fleet at the first shot from the *Olympia*. And, the commodore grimly reminded them:

"You will waste no ammunition, gentlemen. Remember— we are thousands of miles from home!"

The officers were rowed back to their vessels, and the engines began turning again. Night came on and the squadron moved quietly toward Corregidor and the entrance to the bay, all lights extinguished except for the faint glow of the pilot lamps.

"You May Fire When You Are Ready—"

It is four bells, two hours before midnight on the evening of April 30, and the first flash of a Spanish signal light shines through the darkness. All hands are ordered to their stations. Gunners and crewmen take the places made familiar by repeated drills and battle practices, eager and ready for action.

The small island of El Fraile is known to be the first forti-fied land. Four of the ships glide by, half a mile distant, when a Spanish battery opens with a shot that passes between the *Raleigh* and the *Petrel*. Several of the American ships answer. Two more shots from the battery, and then it is silent. All lights on Corregidor and Caballo Islands are extinguished. Apparently the Spaniards reason that without the usual guid-ing lights, inexperienced pilots cannot steer the channel. Dewey has provided for that. At the *Olympia's* wheel stand men who know the Boca Grande entrance like a book.

Greatly to the Americans' surprise, no torpedo boats can be sighted dashing away with news of the fleet's arrival, and no guns open from Corregidor or Caballo. In order to reach the harbor at daybreak, Dewey greatly reduces the speed.

It is midnight, and the crews are ordered to sleep at their guns and other posts. Eight bells, 4 o'clock, with the red glow of the first of May in the eastern sky, and they are wakened again. Coffee is served all hands, and all stand again to battle stations.

The precise timing of the squadron's speed by its com-mander brings the vessels into the bay at 5 o'clock, just at the break of dawn. The *McCullough, Nanshan,* and *Zafiro* stand toward the shore, to be out of battle range. Into the northern end of the bay, four miles above the city, the American war-ships steam. Three batteries near the harbor open fire. Their shots pass far overhead.

Fifteen minutes later, clear daylight breaks. Around the great curve of Manila Bay the six ships continue, with speed stepped up to eight knots, the *Olympia* leading the *Baltimore, Raleigh, Petrel, Concord* and *Boston* in that order. The Span-ish fleet is sighted, ranged in crescent-shaped battle line in front of Fort Cavite. Nearest is Montojo's flagship *Reina Cris-tina*. Next in line are the *Castilla, Don Juan, Don Antonio de Ulloa, Isla de Luzon, Isla de Cuba* and *Marques del Duero*.

Beyond Cavite Point are two smaller gunboats. Far out into the harbor are at least a score of small torpedo craft. Hurried calculations show that although there are seven Spanish ships in battle line, the fifty-three heavy guns and the fifty-six lighter guns of the American squadron outweigh the total of thirty-one heavy and forty-four lighter guns carried by the opposing ships. As Dewey has surmised, accuracy of fire will decide the battle—that, and a fact the American commodore cannot yet know: his smooth-running battleships have far better equipment than the old Spanish vessels, and his officers and men are far superior in discipline and training than the enemy crews.

The commodore stands on the bridge of his ship and surveys the enemy fleet through his glass. Calmly he signals the vessels to close up to intervals of two hundred yards. At 5:15 the guns from the Spanish ships open up with a tremendous roar, followed at once by the batteries from Cavite. It is an anxious moment for the American officers and crews—until they realize how erratic is this firing. Most of the shots are passing far overhead.

Guns are kept on the targets, that fiery line of Spanish ships near Fort Cavite, the American crews turning the huge pieces as their throbbing vessels move in a great curve to the right. At two and one-half miles, the American fleet is sweeping toward the harbor, with the Spanish squadron on the starboard quarter and the city of Manila to port. Dewey lowers his glass, turns to Captain Gridley and quietly says:

"You may fire when ready, Gridley!"

The veteran officer hurries to the conning tower to give the command. In an instant, an eight-inch gun of the forward turret of the *Olympia* booms out. At the signal, all the starboard guns of the squadron begin blazing away. Shots from the very first salvo bury themselves in the hulls and decks of the Spanish ships.

Several mines in the harbor explode, but none near enough to damage an American ship. When the fleet comes to within one and a half miles of Cavite, the *Olympia* leads sharply to the right, followed by the rest of the squadron. Then the port guns roar, hurling their shells into each of the seven targets and also into Fort Cavite and the batteries of Sangley Point, the nearest shore.

With intense relief, the American officers and men find that few enemy shots are damaging their ships. It becomes apparent that the guns on the fort and shore have been placed to fire at long range, on the assumption that no attackers could get inside the bay, while the baffled gunners on Montojo's ships simply have no skill at hitting moving targets. Two miles of running while the port guns fire, and Dewey leads his fighting craft in a complete turn. The navigator at his side, Lieutenant Calkins, announces that there is deeper water than the charts show, so while the starboard guns thunder again, the course is taken closer to Cavite.

Three great ellipses are thus made by the attacking American vessels, making six 2-mile runs past the Spanish squadron, only 2,000 yards distant at the nearest point. On each run, the devastation caused by the deadly fire of the American naval gunners becomes more apparent.

A Spanish torpedo launch makes a desperate attempt to reach the *Olympia*. The American light guns send her down bow first. Another launch puts out, but again Dewey's gunners prove their skill. The craft is badly damaged and runs to beach to prevent sinking.

The *Don Juan* sallies out of line and steams toward the *Olympia* head-on. Admiral Montojo himself is no coward, for he brings his flagship to the support of the *Don Juan*. Both ships are met by the concentrated fire of every forward gun on the *Olympia* and the *Baltimore*. One eight-inch shell smashes the *Reina Cristina*'s steering gear. Another explodes in the forecastle and kills or wounds all the members of the crews of four rapid-fire pieces. The mizzen mast falls, bringing down the admiral's flag. Another shell blows up an ammunition room. Still another makes a complete shambles of the sick bay.

The *Reina Cristina* limps back toward the battle line. Although the Americans do not know it, the flagship is sinking, and at 7 o'clock Admiral Montojo abandons her, carrying his flag to the battered *Isla de Cuba*. The *Castilla* next makes a sortie, but is met by the broadside fire of three of the attackers in unison. All but one of her guns are disabled, and smoke begins pouring from her cabins.

At 7:35 o'clock the commodore decides to withdraw the squadron, to redistribute ammunition if necessary, and to take stock of battle injuries to men and vessels. He signals "Cease Firing!" and leads to a distance of 4,000 yards away from Cavite. Next he signals an order that is to be repeated in appreciation of his human qualities by unnumbered thousands of his grateful countrymen:

"Let all hands have breakfast."

Again the captains and their staffs assemble on board the *Olympia*. Each is surprised that no American ship has suffered great damage. The *Olympia's* hull has been pierced a few times and the rigging is cut in several places. The *Baltimore* has been hit five times, one projectile wounding two officers and six men. The other ships are scarcely marked; and not an American has been killed.

Smoke almost completely obscures the Spanish squadron, when shortly after 11 o'clock the *Olympia*, her four fellow warships and the little *Petrel* come in to finish the task. Only the small *Don Antonio de Ulloa*, and the shore batteries, remain to oppose the squadron. Dozens of shells rain on the *Ulloa*, and she goes down with colors flying.

The gallant captain of the *Reina Cristina*, Don Luis Cadarso, meets his death while rescuing men from his burning vessel. The flagship slowly sinks to the bottom. All the other ships of the line that have not been sunk are now burning fiercely. Dewey sends the *Petrel* into shallow water to destroy the transport *Mindanoa* and several small gunboats. The battery at Sangley Point is finally silenced.

At 12:40 o'clock from the deck of a launch, the Spanish admiral raises the white flag of surrender. The victorious American squadron anchors in the harbor.

A World Power Is Born

The smashing triumph on the sea electrified all America. Congress voted the thanks of the people to George Dewey and to his officers and men, for their decisive victory. Most important result of the disaster to Admiral Montojo's fleet in Manila Bay was its disheartening effect upon the Spanish land and naval forces in the Caribbean. There remained two campaigns in that area, one on land and one at sea, before the war ended. Both were successfully executed by American arms.

The land expedition brought to Cuba the regulars of the United States Army and such recruits as the 1st Volunteer Cavalry, known as the "Rough Riders," headed by Colonel Leonard Wood, with the former Assistant Secretary of the Navy, Lieutenant Colonel Theodore Roosevelt, second in command. The American force of 16,000 men was commanded by Major General William R. Shafter, with subordinate commanders Major General Joseph Wheeler, a veteran of the Confederate Army, and Brigadier Generals H. W. Lawton and J. J. Kent. By gallant assaults upon El Caney and San Juan Hill, the way was opened for the capture of Santiago. On the morning of July 3 the Spanish commander, General Arsenio Linares, surrendered the city.

Admiral Cervera's fleet was cooped up in Santiago Harbor.

Watching the harbor's entrance, like hunting dogs around a quarry at bay, Admiral William Sampson's battleships, cruisers and auxiliaries rested vigilantly at anchor, guns and ammunition ready. Lieutenant Richmond Pearson Hobson made a daring attempt to close the harbor entrance. Manning an old collier, the *Merrimac*, Hobson and his brave crew ran into the narrows, lit the fuses of explosives, and swam for their lives. The *Merrimac* blew up and sank, but not before it had drifted lengthwise, so that the harbor was not effectively blocked.

On the morning of July 3, with Santiago beseiged by the American troops, Admiral Cervera steamed his fleet out of the harbor. In an exciting day of pursuit and fighting, the American fleet led by Admiral Winfield Scott Schley, won another victory, with all Cervera's ships sunk or disabled. Admiral Sampson received the surrender of the surviving officers. Santiago surrendered to the American troops on July 17.

Preparations for the conquest of Puerto Rico went forward under General Nelson A. Miles, but were cut short by an armistice, August 12. In December a peace commission met in Paris, headed by W. R. Day for the United States and Montero Rios for Spain. To Señor Rios fell the painful duty of signing away the colonial possessions of his Queen and country. "*Cuba libre*" became a reality. Puerto Rico, the Philippine Islands and Guam were ceded to the United States, in return for the payment of 10 million dollars.

Commodore Dewey returned to a hero's welcome in the United States. He was promoted to rear admiral, and later was made the third full admiral of the United States Navy, adding his name to that of his hero, Farragut, and to Admiral David Porter's.

The victories at Manila and in Cuban waters established the navy as the able defender of a nation grown to the stature of a world power. When, in 1906, President Theodore Roosevelt sent the principal ships of the fleet to Japan and on around the world, the prestige of the navy—and of the United States—was further enhanced.

From the time of the War with Spain, the United States moved slowly but surely toward the responsibilities of international leadership. More prophetically than he knew, Admiral George Dewey, resuming his peacetime duties in the Department of the Navy, told his countrymen:

"The United States now must help shape the destiny of the East."

CHAPTER THIRTEEN

The Americans Turn the Tide

On June 28, 1914, a large black automobile, carrying His Imperial Highness Archduke Francis Ferdinand of Austria and his wife through the streets of Sarajevo, capital city of the province of Bosnia and now a part of Yugoslavia, came to a halt at an intersection. A man sprang toward the car, whipped out a pistol and fired pointblank at the royal visitors, mortally wounding both. The fatal shots were fired by Gavrilo Princip, a Serbian fanatic who opposed Austrian rule.

The tragic incident threw Europe into turmoil. Tension fastened upon all the embassies and feverish activity began in all the offices of military staffs. What would the government of Austria-Hungary require by way of atonement for the assassinations? The answer soon came. It was a harsh ultimatum, demanding among other things, that Serbia punish whole groups of people known or supposed to be unfriendly to Austrian sovereignty. The Serbian government agreed to many of the demands, but the fuse of war was lighted. The Imperial German Government of Kaiser Wilhelm II backed Austria-Hungary's ultimatum, thus fanning the sizzling powder train into dangerous flame.

No apologies or restitutions could now avert the explosion. On July 28 Austria-Hungary declared war on Serbia. This Slavic kingdom appealed to Russia, which responded with a general mobilization. On July 29 the Kaiser called a council of war at his palace in Potsdam.

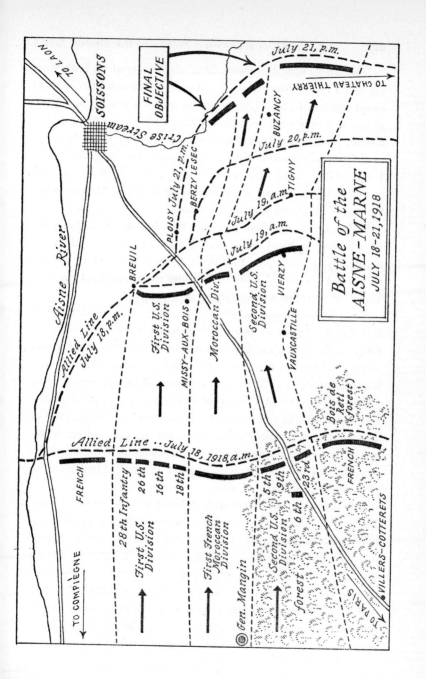

Battle of the
AISNE-MARNE
JULY 18-21, 1918

"*Der Tag!*" rang the toasts. War was declared on both Russia and France. Since the long-standing German plan of conquest against France contemplated an invasion through Belgium, war was declared against this kingdom as a matter of course, on August 3. Within hours the mighty hosts of gray-clad German divisions were rolling across the Belgian border. England had pledged to defend the neutrality of Belgium, and at midnight on August 4 the government of His Majesty King George V declared war on Germany.

So began World War I, a war that left in its tragic wake the greatest political and social changes in Europe and America of any period up to that time. It drew the curtain forever on the era of wars of mere armies and navies, and set the new stage for wars by whole nations and peoples.

The powder magazine of Old World tensions and rivalries that caught fire at so many points had been for a generation filling with the explosive substances of which wars were made. There had been a century of comparative peace after the defeat of Napoleon at Waterloo, ushering in the industrial revolution, lifting the standards of living in Europe and in the Americas, and to some extent all over the world. In 1899 at The Hague, the spokesmen for many nations solemnly resolved that international differences should be settled by peaceful means. As the new century dawned, idealists were even hoping to "outlaw" war.

But the forces of international intrigue were busy as ever. The war of 1870–1871, in which Prussia defeated France and took back the provinces of Alsace and Lorraine, left its legacy of bitterness. Nationalistic ambitions and entangling alliances shaped the foreign policies of all governments on the continent. Britain held to her ancient role of maintaining a balance of power. While the forces of world peace were hopefully planning, while education, science, industry and labor were opening wider the doors of a marvelously productive

age, no substitute for war was found. The European drill
fields echoed to the commands of officers who knew that the
eagle of Might still perched over the banner of Right.

Strongest of all the military forces was that of Germany,
with a standing army of more than half a million and a tremendous reserve of 3½ million men, trained and hardened by
universal military service. The reserve contained hundreds of
thousands of junior officers and noncommissioned officers for
every branch of the Kaiser's war machine. More than eighty
divisions were quickly mobilized as the war began, ready for
the two great campaigns, one to the westward against France
and the other eastward against Russia.

Germany's blueprint for victory had been worked out by
that master strategist, Count Alfred von Schlieffen, chief of
staff of the German army from 1899 to 1906. Every German
officer of the Kaiser's goose-stepping legions was steeped in
the tactics and the importance of the "Schlieffen Plan." It
called for a swift invasion of Belgium and France in order to
knock them quickly out of the war, then to deal with slower-
mobilizing Russia. Specifically, Schlieffen had insisted that
the northern, or right, wing of the forces invading to the West
must be kept strong, to swing in a great encircling movement
upon Paris. The Kaiser was confident that such a war of fast
action would bring speedy victory, and in a statement to his
armies on August 4 he declared:

"You will be fighting for your Fatherland. . . . You will be
back in your homes by the time the leaves fall!"

During the first two weeks of the war, trains carried the
German troops across the Rhine in endless streams. As the
Kaiser's divisions tramped and rolled from Aachen and other
border cities of western Germany, they met the rugged resistance of the hurriedly mobilized Belgians. At the fortified
city of Liège the Germans sprang the first terrifying surprise of the war: in the wake of their infantry and light

artillery there rumbled the heaviest cannon in existence, huge siege guns never yet tried in combat. These howitzers blasted down the ring of forts guarding Liège, and the German columns resumed their relentless march.

Directing the invasion as chief of staff was Count Helmuth von Moltke, a disciple of Schlieffen but lacking his teacher's imagination and daring. Commanding the forces in the capture of Liège was General Erich von Ludendorff, destined to become marshal of the German armies on the western front as the war stretched out to months and then into years. The German timetable called for the capture of Paris in five weeks. But an aging French general, Joseph Joffre, hero of French colonial campaigns and now commanding his country's beleaguered forces, quickly mobilized his army and led a force to meet the German advance at the eastern frontier. This move drew the main body of the German divisions in Belgium southward, weakening the right wing of the invading armies—the very action Schlieffen had warned against. Meanwhile "the first hundred thousand" British troops had rushed across the channel, in keeping with a treaty to defend the neutrality of Belgium.

By September 1 the Germans were at the picturesque Marne River, with advanced units in Meaux, just thirty kilometers (eighteen miles) from Paris. President Raymond Poincaré and his ministers fled to Bordeaux. General Joseph Simon Gallieni, directing the defenses of the capital, commandeered all the taxis and trucks of Paris, filled them with soldiers and sent them scurrying toward the Marne. On September 6 the moment of victory seemed at hand for the Germans, who had advanced 312 miles in thirty-two days, in combat all the way. On that day General Joffre issued this terse order to the French and British forces:

"Any troops that can no longer advance will at all costs hold the ground they have won, and allow themselves to be slain where they stand rather than give way."

During three days and nights of furious fighting on the Marne, thousands on both sides were slain where they stood. The great invasion was halted. The weary Germans began their retreat to the Aisne River. Paris, and France—for the time being—were saved.

The Stalemated War

For weeks following the battle of the Marne, German commanders on one hand, and British and French on the other, tried to outflank their opponents as their lines extended steadily westward in what has been called "the race to the sea." General Erich von Falkenhayn finally captured Antwerp in Belgium. General Sir John French with his British force tried unsuccessfully to break the German line at Ypres. Now the leaves were falling, and the war, far from being over, began what proved to be four years of exhausting stalemate as the armies dug into trenches with a "no man's land" between.

In the east, the Austrians vainly attempted to crush Serbia. Russian forces invaded East Prussia, and were making headway when an elderly German general, Paul von Hindenburg, was called from retirement, with General Ludendorff as his chief of staff. At Tannenberg, in a decisive battle, Hindenburg dealt the Russians a staggering defeat, driving them from East Prussia with a quarter of a million casualties.

For the years 1915, 1916 and 1917 the story of the great war can be written in the word "STALEMATE." It was the stalemate of the muddy, dismal trenches, with barbed wire in front, extending from the Vosges Mountains northwestward by Nancy, Verdun, Rheims, Laôn, Amiens and through Belgium to the channel. It was a war of limited offensives and defensives, of ground gained only to be lost again. Hundreds of thousands of lives were sacrificed in this war of dug-in armies and barbed-wire protected trenches.

1915. This year saw the unsuccessful naval campaign of Great Britain and France in the Dardenelles, to open communication with Russia from the Mediterranean. The first Canadian troops took positions in Flanders and northern France.

In April at Ypres, on a front about four miles wide, the Canadian and French troops were mystified to see a yellow-green fog billowing from the German lines. Slowly it drifted across no man's land. It carried with it smarting and suffocating death—gas! From that day forward, the gas mask was standard equipment of all the troops as the deadly fumes became a standard weapon.

On the eastern front, the Germans occupied Poland and found a new ally when Bulgaria entered the war. Italy came into the war on the Allied side. The German submarine became a terror to British shipping. The United States was maintaining an anxious neutrality, but people were shocked when on May 7 a German U-boat sank the British liner *Lusitania* with the loss of 1,198 lives, 124 of them Americans.

A great American industrialist, Henry Ford, chartered a ship, *Oscar II*, and sailed for Europe with the hope that he might end the fighting and "get the boys out of the trenches by Christmas."

1916. A tremendous German offensive under Crown Prince Wilhelm struck at Verdun, starting on February 21 with a terrific bombardment of the forts guarding the city. On a great curved line of German artillery fronting Verdun on three sides, the shells of massive siege guns roared. Every French unit that could be spared was thrown into the deadly cauldron of Verdun's defense. For four months the siege raged. The area became a blackened, churned-up region of debris and bones. At the height of the assault the defending General Henri Pétain wrote in his ledger:

Ils ne passeront pas! ("They shall not pass!")

They did not pass, and the city was never taken. On July 1 the British General Sir Douglas Haig began an offensive on the Somme River. The British brought into the war another new weapon—the great lumbering steel tanks. Rumania joined the war on the Allied side.

With incredible stupidity, German agents stirred up the government and people of Mexico against the United States, using a wild military leader, Pancho Villa, as the cat's-paw to make raids across the Rio Grande. President Woodrow Wilson dispatched a firm, capable brigadier general, John J. Pershing, with a small force to corral Villa. Pershing would have accomplished his mission but for being called back with his troops just at the moment of success.

In November 1916, a majority of the American people, grateful for their government's policy of neutrality, voted to keep President Wilson in office for a second term—on the slogan "He kept us out of war!" The President made a significant but unsuccessful attempt to end the war by negotiation, when on December 18 he asked the belligerent powers to state their peace terms.

1917. On the evening of January 31 in Berlin, Alfred Zimmermann, German foreign minister, handed a note to United States Ambassador James Gerard announcing that at midnight German submarines would begin unrestricted warfare in British and French waters and in much of the Mediterranean. "Unrestricted warfare" included the neutrals!

March brought a tremendous blow to the Allied cause: the collapse of Russia, surrender of its armed forces, a revolution that deposed the Czar, and late in the year, a separate peace with Germany. To assure more trouble for Russian internal affairs, German authorities put two Russian revolutionaries, Nikolai Lenin and Leon Trotsky, living in exile in Switzerland, into a railroad train and sent these disciples of

Karl Marx to Moscow. It was a train ride destined to be the most tragic for free peoples and governments in all history.

Through the gloom of the stalemated war and the loss of the Russian armies, one great light shone for the Allies: as the submarine attacks intensified, and the prospect loomed that Imperial Germany might dominate all Europe, sentiment in the United States grew for intervention. On April 2, 1917, President Wilson went before Congress and in a stirring message declared:

"The world must be made safe for democracy. . . . It is a fearful thing to lead this great peaceful people into war; but the right is more precious than peace. . . ."

So Congress declared war. It was to be war to end all wars, since it would make the world "safe for democracy." Under the spell of such idealistic slogans, the American people rallied to the great crusade.

A universal draft act was passed and conscriptions of young men for the army began. Secretary of War Newton D. Baker announced a plan of military organization which greatly expanded the regular army, called the National Guard units of the states into federal service and created new divisions from the drafted personnel. Scores of army camps were built, the Navy was enlarged, and several aviation fields were laid out to train pilots and mechanics for the small biplane "flying machines." Army and National Guard officers received fast promotions, while new officers began pouring out of the ninety-day training schools.

An American Expeditionary Force was planned, with John J. Pershing, now major general, its commander-in-chief. Son of a Union veteran of the Civil War living on a farm in central Missouri, Pershing was graduated from West Point as a second lieutenant of cavalry in 1886. In an army of only 20,000 men, young Pershing spent several years "pacifying" hostile Indians in the Southwest. He taught military tactics at the

University of Nebraska and West Point, and went to Cuba with his regiment in the war with Spain. In Cuba his commander unofficially cited him in these words: "Pershing is the coolest man under fire I ever saw."

At forty, Pershing was filling a desk job in Washington, still a first lieutenant and with little prospect for action or advancement. But action and a captaincy came in the Philippines, and in 1906 President Theodore Roosevelt, in one of the most unusual promotions in American military history, named Pershing brigadier general, jumping him over the heads of 862 senior officers. Now General Pershing was ready to bring all his experience, his determination and his high sense of duty, to the task of organizing and leading the American Expeditionary Force.

"The Yanks Are Coming!"

Allied commanders were begging for American troops to fill up their own depleted units. Secretary Baker promised the replacements. The first unit of the A.E.F. to set foot on foreign soil was a hurriedly recruited company of 150 medical corpsmen, who sailed on May 5, 1917, landed in Liverpool on May 18 and one week later were at Rouen, France. Pershing and his staff landed at Boulogne on June 13. Soon the 1st Division came, followed by the 2nd in August, the 26th "Yankee" Division from the New England states in September, and the 42d "Rainbow" Division of National Guard units from many states in November, and in December, the 41st, a replacement division. By March 1918 three more divisions were in training in or near the battle line: the 32d, 3d and 5th. Here was tangible evidence that "the Yanks" were coming in numbers enough to turn the tide of the war.

In soldierly fashion at his headquarters in Chaumont, France, General Pershing was solving the vast problems of organizing and supplying his growing A.E.F. He obtained permission of the War Department to promote officers and assign them to commands. He reorganized the Medical Corps, the hospitals and the postal service. He lifted the Chaplain's Corps to a position of recognized responsibility. He placed upon that vigorous young flyer, Colonel William Mitchell, the task of coordinating the Aviation Section for observation, directing artillery fire and combat. And most important, the commander-in-chief established an adequate Service of Supply, with Brigadier General Charles G. Dawes as his chief purchasing agent.

Die Amerikaner! German officers carefully cultivated the belief among their troops that the Americans were too soft to fight and too inexperienced in war to be effective. Besides, they had come too late to snatch victory from the Kaiser's armies, for a great new "peace offensive" was being planned by Marshal Ludendorff and his staff. The campaign would restore the "war of movement," cut off the British from the channel ports, capture Paris and end the war.

In mid-March the Seventeenth and Eighteenth Armies of Crown Prince Wilhelm and Prince Rupprecht, comprising sixty divisions, were massed with the Somme River as their center. Their line confronted both the British and the French, who had no more than thirty divisions in that sector. The German artillery was ranged so densely that from twenty to thirty batteries stood to each yard, the cannon almost hub to hub. Allied generals knew that an attack was planned, but their intelligence failed dismally to locate the sector or the extent until too late. At 4 o'clock on the morning of March 21 the hot-throated guns of the German armies sang in unison the most murderous battle chorus ever heard to that time. The roar of artillery broke from Arras to Noyon, on a front nearly sixty-five miles long. The fearful barrage was followed by waves of infantry and machine gunners.

The battered French and British units fell back. By the

smoke-filled light of sixteen fearful days the advance of the Germans continued. A gap of six miles was opened in the Allied line. Had the German command seized the advantage to fall upon the flanks of the retreating Allies, the routes to the channel and to Paris would have opened. Hurriedly the Allied generals established a unified command, with General Ferdinand Foch as commander-in-chief. To this grim, slender French officer, soon to be made a *Maréchal de France*, Pershing sent this message: "Infantry, artillery, aviation—all we have is yours to do with it as you please."

On April 9 the Germans with re-formed lines and rested troops opened a second attack, farther north on a front of twelve miles between La Bassée and Armentières. The British again gave way, fighting every inch of their retreat. For twenty days the offensive raged; then the armies of both sides sank down from exhaustion. On May 27 Ludendorff launched his next tremendous assault, this time against the French defending Rheims. The French fought furiously, but fell back along the *Chemin de Dames*. The Germans captured Soissons and moved relentlessly southward to Château-Thierry and the Marne.

Now Ludendorff paused to gain strength for what he hoped would be his drive for victory. His "peace offensives" had cost about 400,000 Germans killed, wounded or missing. The British had suffered some 300,000 casualties, the French about 200,000. The morale of the Allies was at its lowest point. French soldiers, straggling from the front in dejection, often called out to the Americans, "You have come too late!" Still Ludendorff was to write plaintively in his memoirs:

"Even after this second great defeat in one year, the Entente was not ready for peace."

More than faith in the brave *poilus* of France and their British and Belgian comrades sustained the hopes of Entente (Allied) leaders during those dark days. They knew that the

Americans were arriving in ever-increasing numbers. During April and May the 77th Division—first of the drafted "National Army" units, from New York City—the 4th Division of regulars, and the 28th "Keystone" Division of the Pennsylvania National Guard had come. Other divisions were promised at the rate of 300,000 troops a month.

Furthermore, on the day after the German offensive of May 27 began, the 1st Division, under command of General Robert L. Bullard, won for the American forces their initial success of the war, in their surprising capture of the town of Cantigny, north of Montdidier. On a front of two miles the American artillery blasted away at the German frontline trenches with French 75-millimeter guns; then the 28th Regiment, led by Colonel Hansen Edward Ely, moved forward, backed by all other units of the division, and the town was taken. Like hardy veterans the men of the 1st Division withstood repeated counterattacks, one of which was thwarted by the quick action of Major Theodore Roosevelt, Jr., in bringing his battalion of the 26th Infantry to strengthen the line.

Here was visible evidence that "raw American troops" could be trusted with offensive action. The victory, small in size, loomed large in its morale effect upon all the Allied forces. It was followed by General Foch notifying Pershing that he was calling the 2d and 3d American Divisions into the fighting line on the Marne.

The 3d Division, under General Joseph T. Dickman, relieved French units from Château-Thierry eastward, holding that town and the south bank of the river. On the night of June 6, the Yanks of this division in a gallant action stormed and captured "Hill 204" west of Château-Thierry. The 2d Division, General Omar Bundy, began a vigorous offensive to capture the *Bois de Belleau* (Belleau Wood), a dense, heavily fortified forest, crossed with an intricate pattern of German machine-gun and infantry emplacements. The 9th and 23d Infantry Regiments, under Brigadier General Edward Lewis, overcame stubborn resistance and captured Vaux. The two regiments of marines, led by Brigadier General James Harbord, behind a heavy artillery barrage fought their way through the town of Bouresches and into the forest. Not until June 25 was Belleau Wood cleared of the enemy. Next day the 2d Division was relieved by New England's 26th Division. The Yanks captured 1,680 prisoners, but at the fearful cost of about 10,000 casualties.

No chapter in the history of the United States Marine Corps was more gallantly written than that by Harbord's brigade at *Bois de Belleau*. The French proudly changed the name to *Bois de la Brigade de Marine*. Of the 1st Division at Cantigny, the 2d at Belleau and Vaux, the 3d at Château-Thierry, General Pershing wrote: "Their achievements gave an indication of what trained American troops would do." What they did, one month later, was to turn irrevocably the tide of the struggle on the western front.

Americans to the Battle Front!

On Sunday, June 23, aging but vigorous French Premier Georges Clemenceau came to Pershing's headquarters at Chaumont for a grand strategy conference with the Allied military commanders, Marshal Sir Douglas Haig for Britain, Generals Foch and Pétain for France and General Pershing for the United States, all with staffs of advisers. It was known that, despite huge losses from the spring offensives, the Germans still had 3½ million men on their front. The Americans had in France about 873,000 officers and men. Newest arrivals were the 29th and the 37th National Guard Divisions, and the 83d and 90th National Army Divisions, the latter made up of Negro troops, all with typically high American spirit and eagerness to win the war.

"We must win in 1919," Clemenceau told the commanders

at Chaumont. "We shall require 3 million Americans. Let us have forty-six divisions by October, eighty by next January and a hundred by July 1919!"

Pershing agreed to place this big order before the United States government. Foch then urged that one American regiment be assigned to each French division. That request Pershing flatly refused. When pressed by Clemenceau, the American general struck the table with his fist and declared that he had no authority or desire to dissipate American fighting strength—to say nothing of morale—simply as replacements for other troops. He was determined to form and lead an American army.

Most urgent of all, Pershing insisted, was an offensive against the salient of the Marne, now that the German assaults had carried them into a great bulge southward from Soissons to Château-Thierry and northeastward around Rheims. Foch, Pétain and Haig agreed to this. The generals mapped the attack for the "hinge" of the salient south of Soissons, with the Soissons–Château-Thierry road as the first target and a rolling back of the entire bulge as a hoped-for objective.

On July 10 Foch notified Pershing that he intended to use the American 1st and 2d Divisions, already tested in front-line battles, to lead the attack, fighting as a corps under General Charles Mangin, commander of the French Tenth Army and ablest of the French "attacking generals." Pershing had just formed these two divisions into an army corps, giving its command to General Bullard and promoting able General Charles P. Summerall to command the "Fighting First," while General Harbord, hero of Belleau Wood, was promoted to lead the 2d. The 1st was ready to entrain for a rest area, and the 2d had been for only five days at rest, when on Saturday, July 12, the order came for both divisions to move at once, by transportation which the French would supply, to the *Bois de Retz* (Forest of Retz) near Soissons.

On the morning of July 14, a young aviator, Quentin Roosevelt, youngest son of the former President, took off in his plane to make observations over the Marne salient. He was shot down near the town of Charméry. Learning his identity, his foemen respectfully buried his remains, placing his broken propeller to mark the grave.

Meantime, Ludendorff had completed plans for his own Great offensive, a massive attack by General Oskar von Hutier's army to flatten the Rheims salient and open the way through Château-Thierry to Paris. Into that sector of the Champagne country the German staff compressed a hundred thousand troops with a tremendous concentration of artillery. Opposite were two French armies, the one nearest Rheims commanded by the popular one-armed General Henri Gouraud, with the American Rainbow Division, and on the Marne the divisions under General Jean Degoutte, with his American units. On July 14 Paris was celebrating Bastille Day, as the moments ticked off to the midnight hour when the German guns would roar.

The Kaiser himself had graciously consented to be present to witness the start of this victory march, and at thirty minutes before midnight he was in Hutier's headquarters receiving the handshakes and bows of his generals. But the Allies did not wait for midnight. At 11:50 the darkness was shattered by the thunder of big French guns, their shells zooming squarely into the German front line. Promptly at midnight the German guns answered, and for three hours the tremendous blasts echoed from Rheims to the Marne and were heard in Paris itself.

At 3 o'clock the barrage lifted and the German infantry and machine gunners swarmed forward in great waves. French artillery brought down the attackers in rows, but the German survivors pressed on in the darkness. At dawn the Kaiser saw through his field glass the carnage of the fighting. Losses were appalling on both sides, but the French and Rainbow Yanks under Gouraud held firm.

On General Degoutte's sector the attacking infantry, after a heavy artillery barrage, moved forward to the river bank near Mezy. Here the Germans were stopped by the American 3d Division, and here the 38th Regiment of that division wrote a glorious page in the history of the A.E.F. Anticipating the attack, Colonel U. G. Alexander prepared a series of rifle pits on a hill overlooking the junction of the Marne with small Surmelin River, manned by a battalion under Major Guy I. Rowe. Although exposed at front and both sides, the battalion poured deadly fire all day upon the Germans attempting to cross the Marne. Near evening Major Rowe sent his colonel this dispatch: "Am holding the line and could do so indefinitely."

A lieutenant of that battalion wrote of the valor needed to hold that line:

Soldiers wounded in the early morning remained at their automatic rifles or in their rifle pits unflinchingly until killed. One man of Company G was found lifeless with his rifle and pistol empty, and in front of him a heap of twelve dead Germans. Another private's body was found surrounded by five of the enemy, all killed by a bayonet, but his own rifle was clutched in his hands.

On General Dickman's right, three German divisions crossed the Marne, pushing back the defending French division and a brigade of the American 3d Division. Dickman sent word that he would counterattack to gain the lost ground. The French commander asked him to wait for "further coordination." With the confidence shared by all his men the general replied:

"We regret being unable on this occasion to follow the counsel of our masters, the French, but the American flag has been forced to retire. This is unendurable, and none of our soldiers would understand their not being asked to do whatever is necessary to remedy a situation which is humiliating to us and unacceptable to our country's honor. We are going to counterattack."

And counterattack the Yanks did, denting the German line and holding the regained ground through the rest of the battle. Staunchly supported by the 28th "Keystone" Division and the 26th "Yankee" Division, the Allied line held at the *Bois de Condé,* and at Vaux. By the morning light the French and their American comrades in arms found that the offensive had spent itself. Hutier dared not risk more of his reserves. Counterattacks found the Germans retreating to their former positions. The staunch defense had won another victory on the Marne, and made possible the engagement that marked the turning point of the war.

Forward to the Attack!

Responding to Foch's order, the American 1st and 2d Divisions roll by train and truck to their rendezvous at the Forest of Retz, called also the *Bois de Villers-Cotterets.* Only then do their commanders and staffs learn the momentous assignment that awaits them. There they receive orders from the small, wiry veteran French army commander, General Mangin:

They are to move up to the line that night, a distance of ten miles, ready for the major attack to begin at 4:35 in the morning. The line of assault will have the 1st Division on the left wing, the 2d Division on the right, while between them will be the 1st Moroccan Division. There will be no artillery preparation to warn the enemy of the attack; only a rolling barrage by divisional artillery, whose guns will move up as fast as the advance proceeds. The objective will be the Soissons–Château-Thierry road, which if taken will command the entire German salient between the Aisne and the Marne

Rivers. The French divisions flanking the attackers will maintain contact by turning on their pivots.

General Summerall orders the 28th and 26th Infantry of his 2d Brigade to take position on the left and the 16th and 18th of his 1st Brigade on the right. General Harbord accepts a slightly smaller front; his 5th Marine Brigade and the 9th and 23d Infantry of his 1st Brigade will take the line, with the 6th Marine following in reserve.

The July night is murky dark as the three divisions leave the wooded area for the long march with full fighting equipment. This is well, for otherwise the moonlight would disclose to German aviators the movement and the plan. The Moroccans move ahead. They are stolid veterans, experienced fighters, shock troops that include the Foreign Legion with its Caucasians of France and many other European countries, and the black natives of Morocco, all hardened by many months of trench warfare. The 1st Division regiments follow, over roads thoroughly congested. A hard rain begins. It is long past midnight when the drenched men of the 1st untangle their mixed units and take their places in the line.

But where is the 2d Division? It is forced to march through dense forest all the way, over muddy roads so clogged with vehicles, carts, trucks, ammunition wagons, ambulances and lost units of troops that it spends most of the night in rainy confusion. The downpour continues to drench everything and adds to the fatigue of soldiers who have not slept for two days and nights, but it prevents what certainly would have been fearful bombardments upon the moving Allied corps. One reason for the late arrival of Harbord's fighting men at the wooded rendezvous has been the insistence of a French subordinate officer that every American soldier transported by the trucks be counted and receipts obtained for everyone so transported, so that his country can be reimbursed. With the life of his country at stake, he demands the receipts!

Not until 3 o'clock have the forward battalions of the 2d Division reached the line. At 4:25 the last of the companies are still two hundred yards away.

"Double time!" sounds the order, and the weary soldiers, loaded with the equipment of battle, break into a run that brings them, gasping and worn, to their comrades just as the artillery barrage roars its fiery salute to the enemy.

Forward, eastward in the early light under the barrage, move the 67,000 officers and men of the attacking corps, out over a wide plain checkered with gardens and grain fields and dotted with farms. In the American divisions are 48,000 men, soldiers of the regular army, national guardsmen and marines, with drafted replacements—men from many communities of their homeland. Forward the attacking tide rolls, the infantry and machine gunners staying closely abreast in two files, the tanks clanking along just behind. The field artillery at the rear pounds out its steady tattoo, while already in the dawn several aviators circle about, ready to wireless their messages to men of the Signal Corps working in liaison with the artillery.

The German first line is reached—a series of foxholes and machine-gun stands which offer resistance but are rapidly overcome by the attackers. "*Kamerad!*" cry the survivors of these emplacements as they face the overwhelming odds. It is clear that surprise has caught the Germans unprepared. Nevertheless, the defenders fight bravely, with rifles, and even when surrounded, with their bayonets. Hidden in the tall wheat are countless German machine-gun nests, while every cluster of houses is a German rifle and machine-gun fortress. These take the greatest toll of the advancing Americans and French. Toward the farmhouses and the caves the tanks zig and zag, blasting away the resistance, bringing out the survivors in surrender, moving on with the foot troops again.

The machine guns at the mouth of one large cave cut down every American of the 26th Infantry approaching it. A tank is brought up, and after firing its explosive shells into the cave, six hundred German officers and men, among them a colonel, emerge with their hands over their heads, utterly astonished to find their captors are Americans.

The field artillery moves along a rural roadway here, over grainfields there, into a ravine, over a crest, the horses being led away when a stand for firing is made and returned at a gallop when the order "Forward the guns!" sounds again from battery commanders.

By noon the advance of all three divisions has covered nearly half the distance to Soissons. A steady stream of disarmed prisoners moves through the lines and to the rear, there to be treated if wounded, and questioned. One German sergeant, informed by an American major that under the rules of war he need give only his name, rank and serial number, readily answers an additional question:

"Why have you not dug trenches during the month?"

"We expect soon to be in Paris, Herr Commandant!"

The afternoon's advance brings the 1st Division to the town of Missy-aux-Bois and a ravine extending to the left. The French "pivoting" division on the left flank of the Yanks is stopped at the ravine by strong artillery emplacements. Units of the 1st's infantry regiments move in to help the French, and clear the ravine of the enemy with the capture of thirty German cannon. The 2d Division also meets strong resistance and engages in fierce hand-to-hand encounters to take the village of Vauxcastille and the town of Vierzy. The Moroccan Division has moved abreast, capturing the town of Chaudun. All three divisions are advancing against stiffening defenses.

General Mangin, in his field headquarters within the Forest of Retz, moment by moment checks the course of the battle as couriers dash in and out. He is gratified by the progress, but hopes to speed the advance by a grand cavalry charge. He sends two battalions of French cavalry from the woods, the troopers resplendent in new blue uniforms with polished buttons, buckles and spurs, riding their steeds proudly. On they come across the newly won plateau, through the artillery lines, through the infantry reserves, past the front line of the American 1st Division. When the two columns approach the hill which marks the German front line their colonel raises his sword and orders *"En avant!"* for the charge. All draw sabers and gallop toward the hill. A storm of machine-gun bullets cuts their line to pieces. Horses and riders fall like grain before a scythe. A few ride back, survivors of a cavalry charge destined to be one of the last of its kind, the beginning of the end to centuries of cavalry warfare.

Meanwhile the new war of the air brings German aviators to strike at the French and American reconnaissance planes. The attackers fly the red-nosed Fokker fighters of Baron Manfred von Richthofen's command, while the Allied planes are Spads, the Americans sporting the "Hat in the Ring" insignia of Captain Edward V. Rickenbacker. Numerous duels are fought above the lines, and foot soldiers glance up briefly as one plane or the other falls as result of mortal combat in the sky.

By evening, the 1st Division has established its line east of Missy-aux-Bois to end the day's fighting; the 2d has moved farthest, nearly four miles. Outposts are stationed along the new line, while the men of the ranks fall to the ground to rest where they have stood. The medical corpsmen, busy all day gathering up the wounded, still work diligently at their merciful tasks, augmented by hundreds of volunteer stretcher-bearers. Some of the wounded, American, Moroccan and German, have lain for hours in the warm July sun, among the dead that dot the wheat fields and ravines. All are taken to safety as night approaches.

Up from the rear amble the horse-drawn carts with the hot meal of the day—goulash, potatoes, bread and coffee. Again the German aviators appear, circling in the darkness, releasing flares attached to parachutes to light up the roadways and fields, and dropping small bombs toward the moving targets. Still the food carts plod on. The soldiers are fed and then they sink into the sleep of exhaustion.

Worthy Sons of a Great Country

During the night the Germans work desperately to reinforce their line with artillery and machine guns. At dawn the cannon of the attacking Americans and French roar again, and the front lines, formed by the reserves of the day before, move forward.

In the lead of the 2d Division is the 6th Marine Regiment, moving swiftly along until within sight of Tigny, lying just west of the Soissons–Château-Thierry highway. Here the determined German lines hold. Marine units that have actually reached the road are thrown back. Harbord sets his line at the edge of Tigny and by nightfall his guns control the town. The division has captured seventy-five guns, and more than 3,000 prisoners—among them personnel of four German divisions—in the two days' fighting, but at the heavy cost of 5,000 casualties. Later on that night of July 19, it is relieved by two French divisions. The Moroccan Division also is relieved.

The 1st Division, moving ahead of the pivoting French meanwhile, exposes its left flank to raking German fire. Summerall rushes tanks and artillery to the defense, holding the Germans until the French units catch up. Then forward, slowly, fighting for every yard of ground, the advance is made —less than one and one-half miles for the day. While casualties of the 1st are comparable to those of the 2d, General Summerall and his staff ask to remain in the battle, for the next day may well spell victory or defeat for the whole offensive in the approach to the Soissons "hinge" of the German line, where strongly fortified Berzy-le-Sec guards the highway.

On the morning of July 20, the 1st Division can count an advance of little more than one mile, as the German reserves pour into Berzy-le-Sec. Early in the afternoon Mangin orders Summerall to take the town. The 1st Brigade under General John L. Hines moves forward to the task, but murderous fire forces a retreat to a railroad where survivors of the two Yank regiments dig in for the night. Summerall surveys the plight of his badly reduced regiments and the remaining strength of his division.

"We will capture Berzy-le-Sec in the morning," he calmly tells his staff. He orders his 2d Brigade, under Brigadier General Beaumont B. Buck, to bring up all available men and equip them for the battle. Detachments of engineers, quartermasters, military police, clerks—even cooks, kitchen details and orderlies are rounded up. By dawn they all stand ready for the assault. The divisional artillery rains havoc upon the town and its environs. Then Buck leads his infantry regiments through a veritable hail of bullets into Berzy-le-Sec. By evening the Yanks have reached their objective, the highway to Château-Thierry, and their guns command Soissons.

While the 1st and 2d Divisions are writing this glorious chapter of the great war, to the south their American comrades are adding determined footnotes as they assist the French to press the whole salient. One brigade of the 4th Division strikes quickly to capture Noroy, while another brigade assists in the capture of Hautevesnes, Courchamps and Chevillon. The Yankee Division and the French 167th Division take Torcy and Belleau. Nearby is an eminence known as Hill 193. Attempts by the French to take this hill fail, but on July 20 the New Englanders secure a foothold on its western edge, and next day they sweep over it, cross the Soissons–Château-Thierry highway and move on to Epieds. Eastward, the 3d Division pursues the Germans retreating across the Marne.

On the same day, General Pershing tours the front from Château-Thierry to the Forest of Retz. Behind the attacking 1st Division he comes upon General Mangin, trudging along on foot, personally directing the battle. The French commander speaks in highest praise of the Americans. When on July 22 the "Fighting First" is relieved by a Scottish regiment, Mangin writes his praise in glowing words:

American Comrades: You have shown yourselves worthy sons of your great country and you are admired by your brothers-in-arms. . . . I am grateful to you for the blood so generously spilled on the soil of my country. I am proud to have commanded you during such days, and to have fought with you. . . .

Back in the Forest of Retz, units of the 1st muster to count their survivors and losses. The casualties total 8,365, of which 1,252 have given their lives. Three regiments have lost all the officers above the rank of captain except for one colonel. Every battalion commander is a casualty. Some companies have lost all their officers and are commanded by sergeants and corporals.

The Allied offensive south of Soissons renders the whole salient untenable for the German forces, and their great retreat begins. During all the rest of July and into the early days of August, skillful rear-guard defenses are used to save most of the weapons and the vast stores of munitions and supplies, but pressure from the French and their American comrades is unrelenting. The battle of movement involves the 1st, 2d, 3d, 4th, 26th, 28th, 32d, 42d and 77th Divisions, a force of nearly 200,000 officers and men. Steadily Ludendorff's armies are pushed back from all the gains of the spring offensives, back to the Aisne and the Vesle. When the movement halts on August 6 the front line runs almost straight from Soissons to Rheims.

The bravery of all the fighting Yanks will be reflected from the citation presented to General Buck:

BEAUMONT B. BUCK: Before and during the attack on Berzy-le-Sec, France, July 21, 1918, he displayed conspicuous gallantry and heroic leadership of his command. When most of the officers of his brigade had fallen, General Buck, in contempt of personal danger, and in spite of heavy artillery bombardment and machine-gun fire, traversed the front of his advancing forces, gave correct directions to his organization commanders, and led the first wave of the culminating attack which stormed and captured the town.

"Finie la Guerre!"

More than a salient on the battle line was gained by the Allied victory of the Second Battle of the Marne. As General Pershing so succinctly wrote in his memoirs:

"We had snatched the initiative from the Germans almost in an instant. They made no more formidable attacks, but from that moment until the end of the war they were on the defensive."

Every day, every hour, brought to the German officers and soldiers the bitter realization that the growing American strength could not be overcome. This stark fact sapped the will to win that had sustained the Kaiser's legions through four years of stalemated conflict. The Yanks formed an inexhaustible Allied reserve, insuring that blows could be struck effectively at any point of the line.

Marshal Foch lost no time unleashing Haig for the first blow. On the morning of August 8, in an area shrouded in mist and fog, the British began action to wipe out the salient of the Somme. All along the sector, German defenses crumbled and German troops surrendered in droves. Their officers were astonished to hear many of their soldiers call out to fresh troops thrown in to relieve them:

"Blacklegs! You are only prolonging the war!"

Ludendorff was to call this the "black day of the war." He resigned himself to the defensive, while the strategy of Foch and the Allied command was to "pick the German pockets" by attacks against the most vulnerable salients, using up German men and materiel until victory. Hardly had the British campaign flattened the Somme pocket when Foch sent Mangin's army attacking between the Oise and Aisne rivers. On September 1 the Australians captured Mont St. Quentin, and on the following day the Canadians took Drocourt.

Victory, in the minds of Foch and his European staff members, was scheduled for the summer of 1919, or spring at the earliest. But Pershing felt that the Americans, having turned the tide, could make that tide an overwhelming flood by the creation of an American Army under his personal command, facing a sector all his own. On August 31 the general dispatched a long memo to Foch, containing these words:

I can no longer agree to any plan which involves a dispersion of our units. American officers and soldiers alike are, after one experience, no longer willing to be incorporated in other armies, even though such incorporation be by larger units. . . . The danger of destroying by such dispersion the fine morale of the American soldier is too great, to say nothing of the results to be obtained by using the American Army as a whole.

By firm arguments, Pershing won the man who had become his close comrade in arms, General Pétain, to his view. Then, reluctantly, Foch accepted the plan. The American 1st Army was formed, and staged two brilliant offensives—the reduction of the St.-Mihiel salient and the clearing of the Meuse–Argonne sector.

For four years the city of St.-Mihiel had remained in German hands, forming a bulge south of Verdun, holding the heights of the Meuse and the Woëvre Plain. Pershing assembled his 1st, 42d, 89th, 2d, 5th, 80th and 82d Divisions, in that order from left to right of his line, facing the Woëvre

Plain. Colonel Mitchell was on hand with an aviation force of 821 airplanes, more than six hundred manned by American aviators. On September 12 the commanding general sent his army in an assault against the strong enemy positions. Next day the Germans gave up St.-Mihiel to the French troops flanking the Americans, and four days later the entire salient was in Allied hands. The Americans captured around 16,000 prisoners and 450 guns, suffering 7,000 casualties.

The great Battle of the Meuse–Argonne began on September 26 and lasted forty-seven days, the most prolonged battle in American history to that day. It involved a million American troops, who cleared the Argonne Forest and broke the strongest of the German defenses, proudly called the "Hindenburg Line." The battle brought out the determination of the American soldiers to keep pushing until the war ended in victory. In its pages are written the story of the 77th's "Lost Battalion," cut off for five days in the forest, but refusing to surrender; that of Sergeant Samuel Woodfill who single-handedly attacked three machine-gun nests, killing or capturing all their personnel; that of Corporal Alvin York who led a patrol of seven men, engaged the enemy with rifle and pistol, killed fifteen and captured 132 prisoners; and that of Captain Eddie Rickenbacker, foremost American ace who brought down his twenty-sixth enemy plane.

Pershing now held a sector longer than that held by the British, and commanded about 1,700,000 Americans of the line and auxiliary services. Their presence in France was a striking tribute to the valor of the officers and men of the United States Navy who transported these troops and their equipment through submarine-infested waters, and to the efficiency of the Service of Supply which General Harbord headed in the closing months of the war.

Grasping the opportunity and responsibility of international leadership, which the war had placed upon the United States,

President Wilson offered to the Allies and to Germany his historic "Fourteen Points" to be used as the basis for a future peace, further weakening the will of the Central Powers to continue the war. Like leaves following one another downward in an autumn wind, in rapid succession the three allies of Germany—Bulgaria, Turkey and Austria-Hungary—collapsed and left the war between September 29 and November 4. No longer able to stem the black tide of defeat, the Kaiser abdicated.

On the night of November 10, in a small railway car used as Marshal Foch's traveling headquarters and pulled onto a siding in the Compiègne Forest, the German representatives signed an armistice agreement. The German envoys realized the terms were harsh, but there was the even more compelling fact that their nation was beaten. The agreement called for all fighting to cease at 11 o'clock the next morning. So, at exactly that hour, a great stillness descended over the blasted, pock-marked terrain over which the spiked-wheeled chariots of war had ridden for more than four years, while all the world rejoiced, the people of the victorious nations jubilantly, the people of the vanquished countries quietly but fervently.

"Finie la guerre!" "No more war!" *"Nie wieder Krieg!"*

For this was the war to end war, and now that peace had come, there would never be another war. So they hoped.

CHAPTER FOURTEEN

The Navy Triumphs in the Pacific

"No more war!" said the people of the world, when the armistice ended World War I, the greatest war of history up to that time. Then followed two decades of aspiring, hoping, improvising and blundering, with events crowding one another logically and inevitably to another great conflict. Statesmen were attempting to carve new orders with obsolete tools. They tried to build an enduring peace upon the shifting sands of political alliances, limitations of armaments, treaties and agreements, rather than upon enforceable world order. And they failed.

On November 4, 1918, the Allied powers had agreed to an armistice based upon Woodrow Wilson's Fourteen Points. The President took this as a mandate to lead the victorious Entente to seek no territorial aggrandizement, to exact no punitive reparations, and to permit self-determination of peoples in the formation of new nations. Few men in history worked harder to achieve an idealistic peace. Wilson came personally to France to meet with the heads of state of the other great Allied powers—David Lloyd-George of Great Britain, Georges Clemenceau of France and Vittorio Orlando of Italy—and to head the United States delegation to begin work on a treaty. On January 25, 1919, the President addressed the Peace Conference, proposing the formation of a League of Nations to prevent war in the future.

Then came his shocking discovery that European statesmen were more interested in the spoils of war and maintaining balances of power than they were in building a peace with justice for all. They agreed to self-determination, particularly with respect to the Austro-Hungarian Empire, largely because it shattered into fragments what had been a stable union under the dual kingdom. They restored Poland and the Baltic states, on the theory that this would weaken both Germany and Russia. They returned Alsace and Lorraine to France, set up such international irritants as the Polish Corridor and the occupation of Germany's Rhineland, and in a spirit of short-sighted vengeance they assessed heavy reparations and refused to permit even a customs union between Germany and the now shrunken Austria.

The League of Nations was formed. But at home, Wilson found that the people were weary of war and in no mood to join such an "entangling alliance." Unskilled in the art of political compromise, the President saw his country reject his cherished plan.

Still, people of goodwill pursued the quest for peace. One of these was President Warren G. Harding's Secretary of State, Charles Evans Hughes, who sponsored a Conference on the Limitation of Naval Armaments, meeting in Washington on November 12, 1921—one day after the Unknown Soldier was laid to rest "in honored glory" in Arlington Cemetery. Great Britain, Japan, France, Italy and the United States agreed to Mr. Hughes' plan to declare a ten-year "holiday" for construction of fighting ships, during which a naval power ratio of five for the United States, five for Britain and three for Japan would be established. The plan resulted in scrapping many of the United States naval vessels in being or under construction. The Japanese delegates, realists that they were, gladly signed, knowing that when the idealists of the western world became engrossed in other matters, the

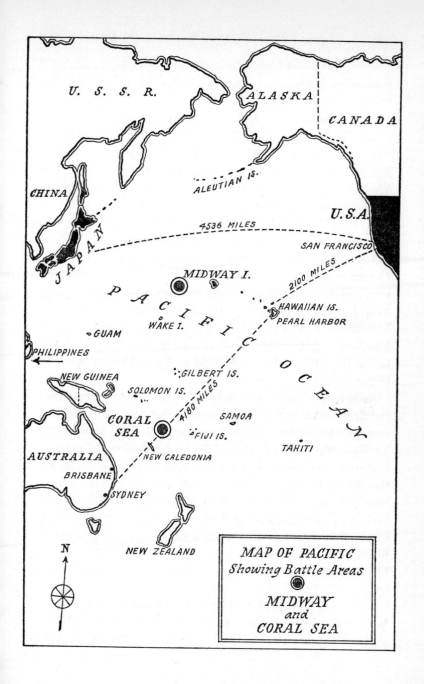

U. S. S. R.

ALASKA

CANADA

CHINA

ALEUTIAN IS.

JAPAN

4536 MILES

U.S.A.

SAN FRANCISCO

MIDWAY I.

2100 MILES

P A C I F I C

HAWAIIAN IS.

WAKE I.

PEARL HARBOR

GUAM

O C E A N

PHILIPPINES

GILBERT IS.

NEW GUINEA

SOLOMON IS.

4180 MILES

SAMOA

CORAL SEA

FIJI IS.

TAHITI

AUSTRALIA

NEW CALEDONIA

BRISBANE

SYDNEY

N

NEW ZEALAND

MAP OF PACIFIC
Showing Battle Areas

MIDWAY
and
CORAL SEA

Kingdom of the Rising Sun could ignore such unsupervised limitations and proceed unhindered with armaments on sea or land.

The enthusiasm for trying to construct world peace upon promises and plans reached full flowering in the signing of the Pact of Paris, in August 1928, whereby fifteen nations agreed to "renounce" war as an instrument of national policy. The treaty gave people temporary hope for peace, with no means for its realization.

Meanwhile, the traditional role of navies was changing with the development of air power. Brigadier General William Mitchell demonstrated that airplanes could sink warships. Commercial airlines began to crisscross the nation with airmail and passenger routes, under the leadership of such World War I flying veterans as Captain Eddie Rickenbacker. On May 20–21, 1927, a courageous young airmail pilot, Charles A. Lindbergh, guided his small monoplane *Spirit of St. Louis* across the Atlantic in a solo flight to Paris. The Air Age had begun.

As hereditary monarchs marched steadily into eclipse after the first world war, a new type of ruler, the party dictator, more ruthless and dangerous than former despots, began stalking upon the stage of national leadership and world politics:

Russia, after deposing the Czar, established a republic, but the Bolshevist leaders, Nikolai Lenin and Leon Trotsky, beat out the brains of this infant, seized control of the government, and began compressing the Russian masses into the bleak mold of communism. In the struggle for power their clever lieutenant, Joseph Stalin, emerged at the top of the snarling heap, and by terror and mass murder made his dictatorship secure.

Italy sank into chaotic social and economic conditions, and in 1922 found a World War I soldier, Benito Mussolini, marching on Rome with his legion of fanatic "Blackshirts." Taking over the government, Mussolini established a Fascist regime based upon his absolute power.

Germany set up the Weimar Republic, whose weak leaders were unable to cope with postwar unemployment and inflation. An Austrian paperhanger living in Munich, Adolf Hitler, wrote a book entitled *Mein Kampf* (*My Struggle*) in which he expressed contempt for democratic processes. He gained a formidable following for his National Socialist (Nazi) party, and when conditions worsened beyond the control of aging President Paul von Hindenburg, *der schoene Adolf*, as Hitler's admirers called him, was made chancellor. Seizing virtually all powers of government, this *Fuehrer* (leader) stabilized the German economy, and created a new, goose-stepping military machine. Hitler put through a crash program to build a *Luftwaffe* (air force) and placed in charge a favorite henchman, Hermann Goering.

Japan in the Far East became an empire in fact when in 1931 its warlords invaded and annexed Manchuria. With Manchuria added to Korea, Okinawa and Taiwan (Formosa) under the Japanese flag, the militarists of Emperor Hirohito built a powerful army, navy and air force—using to best advantage the huge imports of scrap metal from the United States.

The Dictators Call the Shots

In due course, the dictators began the moves inevitably made by those who possess civil and military power with no control by the people they govern: they embarked upon naked aggression, to expand their rule and power. In 1935 Mussolini sent his black-shirted legions into Ethiopia in a quick conquest of this African kingdom, while the League of Nations helplessly wrung its hands.

Hirohito's warlords considered the mainland of China the logical area for further expansion, and in July 1937 Japanese forces occupied Peking and Tientsin. Within a month the invaders controlled the northern Chinese provinces and all the coastal region of the Indochinese border.

In 1938 Hitler's modernized forces were strong enough to invade Austria, which the *Fuehrer* annexed to his realm. Then he seized the Sudetenland of Czechoslovakia, inhabited mainly by people of German descent. Alarmed at last, Prime Minister Neville Chamberlain of Great Britain, umbrella in hand, with Premier Edouard Daladier of France, met Hitler at Munich and agreed to give over to him parts of Czecho-slovakia in the hope that this appeasement would satisfy the German leader.

In August 1939 Hitler and Stalin signed a "non-aggression" pact, which insured the German dictator against opposition from the Soviet dictator while the two aggressors divided Poland and Stalin took also the Baltic states of Estonia, Latvia and Lithuania. War was now inevitable—unless Britain and France, both of which had guaranteed the autonomy of Poland, desired to follow further the futile path of appeasement.

And war promptly came on September 1, when Hitler sent his forces crashing into Poland, his *Luftwaffe* blasting the way by strafing the defending troops and bombing Warsaw into submission. Britain and France declared war. Within two weeks, western Poland was subdued by the mighty Nazi air and land forces. The Soviet Union's Red Army troops moved in from the east for their share of the kill.

In November 1939, Soviet Russia launched an unprovoked attack upon another small neighbor, Finland. The tiny Finnish military forces defended their country bravely, inflicting repeated defeats upon the aggressors, but in late winter the Red hordes broke the back of Finnish resistance and forced an armistice which granted all Soviet demands for territory.

In the United States, sentiment was overwhelming for staying out of this new European war spawned by centuries-old rivalries for trade, territory and power. The biggest veterans' organization at its national convention in September 1939 passed a resolution stating that "The American Legion has always strenuously advocated that this nation pursue a policy of neutrality and peace."

Nevertheless, President Franklin D. Roosevelt moved promptly to put the nation on a war footing. He secured an appropriation of one billion dollars for military expansion, called the National Guard into federal service, secured a Selective Service Act for conscription. The Army, which included the Air Corps, grew from 172,000 men as of September 1939 to 1,500,000 in shortly more than a year. Abandoning all semblance of neutrality, the President presented Great Britain with fifty "over-age" naval vessels, and after bitter debate in Congress secured authorization in March 1941 to "lend-lease" all types of military equipment to nations whose defense he might consider necessary for the defense of the United States.

In Europe a "phony war" with little activity followed the initial Nazi-Soviet aggressions, until in May 1940 the Nazi military juggernaut rolled westward into the Netherlands, Belgium and France. With its major cities bombed, the Netherlands surrendered. Belgium was quickly overrun. By mid-June, half of France was conquered and Hitler triumphantly entered Paris.

The Japanese navy was commanded by Admiral Isoroku Yamamoto, a tough warrior and jingoist who believed firmly in naval air power and who backed his belief by building nine aircraft carriers. In addition, by early 1941 he had at his command eighty-seven cruisers of all types and about three hundred other vessels. A forced-draft program of military aircraft production had equipped thousands of bombers and fighters, and pilots had been trained to fly them.

The policy of the United States was one of steady economic pressure. Shipments of oil to Japan were embargoed, and

Japanese assets in America were frozen. On October 14, 1941, the ministry of Prince Konoye, who was a moderate and friendly to the United States, fell. It was replaced by powerful militarists led by General Hideki Tojo. His avowed policy was to expand the Japanese "co-prosperity sphere" into all the countries of southeast Asia, by aggression if necessary and even if it meant war with the hated peoples of the white nations.

Hawaii, with its excellent base at Pearl Harbor, was the stronghold of American defenses in the mid-Pacific. At Honolulu, Major General Walter C. Short commanded the Army forces, and Rear Admiral Husband E. Kimmel was in command of the Navy base. In late November, orders were issued for the major strength of the Pacific fleet, except for the aircraft carriers, to assemble at Pearl Harbor. Into that fateful rendezvous came ninety-six American warships. There were eight battleships—the *Arizona, California, Maryland, Nevada, Oklahoma, Pennsylvania, Tennessee* and *West Virginia*—with sixteen cruisers, twenty-four destroyers and auxiliary ships. During that first week in December they rode lazily at anchor, like huge ducks dozing on the water.

During the previous July, American cryptographers had deciphered the secret code used by the Japanese government for diplomatic and military messages. Thus, during the fall of 1941, every message to the Japanese embassy in Washington and directives to military units all over the Far East clear enough to be caught were deciphered. From this information, the President, the Secretaries of War and the Navy and their chiefs of the services learned that on the night of November 29 a Japanese task force under Admiral Chuichi Nagumo, including six airplane carriers, had set out from the Kurile Islands. This could mean only one thing: a surprise attack by air.

Although for decades the war plans of the United States

Navy had taken into account the possibility of such an attack, the defending forces at Honolulu were all but asleep. For reasons that may never be known, General Short and Admiral Kimmel were not given adequate warning of the task force's sailing and its likely objective.

The Japanese War Ministry and the officers of that carrier force knew the size of the United States fleet, and even the names of the battleships and cruisers berthed idly at Pearl Harbor. They understood the great risk of detection and interception in the forthcoming assault, but because of the high stakes involved they were more than willing to take the chance.

The Fleet Is Humbled—and the Nation United

The Zero airplane was Yamamoto's pride. It was capable of more than three hundred miles an hour, with a fast climb, long range and good maneuverability. It carried two 20-millimeter cannon and two machine guns, with equipment for bombs or torpedoes. Now in the early morning light of that December 8, 1941, five waves of Zeros were roaring over the Pacific waters. They crossed the international date line into Sunday, December 7, to within sight of Pearl Harbor, without interception or opposition whatever. Their approach was detected by a soldier manning an Army radarscope, but his warning of "a large flight of planes" was ignored by an officer who expected a squadron of American planes to arrive that morning and who told the soldier "Don't worry about it." At 7:55 in the morning, the leading Japanese pilots saw below them the American ships, arranged as though for convenience in bombing, exactly as Nagumo's intelligence officers had told them in their final briefing.

The first wave of attackers struck Fort Island, the naval air base, to immobilize the planes in the hangars or lined up in neat rows outside. Then the bombs fell on the ships, and as their explosions roared and rumbled the proud United States Pacific Fleet was almost annihilated. One bomb fell squarely into the smokestack of the *Arizona*, exploding the forward magazine and sending the battleship to the bottom, carrying 1,102 officers and men to their watery tomb. The *Oklahoma* capsized, disabled beyond repair. The *West Virginia* and *California* were sunk at their berths. The *Nevada*, attempting to flee, was so badly damaged that she was beached to prevent sinking. The three other battleships were disabled, as were eleven other lesser warships.

Seaman Second Class William N. Martin, a gunner on the *Nevada*, gave a vivid account of the surprise attack and the attempts at defense, including the following:

> Several of us were on deck, ready to go on Sunday leave. We could scarcely believe our eyes and ears, as the first wave came in. Had we been at our battle stations, and had our ships and planes been in battle positions, we could have given the attackers a real fight. As it was, I got to my station, a five-inch antiaircraft gun, and threw shells at the masses of Japanese planes in the later waves, until I was knocked unconscious by a bomb and then strafed by machine-gun bullets in face, chest and arms.

Several squadrons rained bombs on nearby Hickam and Wheeler airfields, destroying 188 Army planes. Of the 202 Navy planes ready for action on that morning, only 52 were able to fly after the raid. Antiaircraft accounted for fifty-nine Japanese planes. The heaviest cost was in the tally of 2,403 American officers and men dead, 1,178 severely wounded —more than the United States Navy lost in the Spanish-American War and World War I combined!

Since the raid had succeeded far beyond the hopes of Admiral Yamamoto and his superiors in the War Office, Japanese leaders expected that America would decide not to challenge again the sea and land forces of their empire. Exactly the opposite occurred. The needless tragedy of Pearl Harbor shocked and aroused the nation. Congress passed a declaration recognizing the state of war next day. On December 11, Nazi Germany and Fascist Italy declared war on the United States, countered by declarations of war by Congress.

The Japanese lost no time moving toward their southeast Asian objectives. On the day after Pearl Harbor they launched their first attack against the Philippines. Captain (later Brigadier General) Joseph H. Moore, standing by his fighter plane at Clark Field, near Manila, saw the swift approach of an enemy bombing squadron. Only he and two other pilots got their planes into the air as their field was bombed into shambles with the destruction of about half their 123 combat aircraft, but Captain Moore bagged the first Japanese plane to be shot down in aerial combat.

Later that same day units of the Japanese army appeared in the streets of Bangkok, and Thailand surrendered. On the next day, December 9, the invasion of Malaya began. On December 10 Japanese forces made their first landings upon Luzon of the Philippines, while a naval force assaulted the American garrison on the far outpost island of Guam, and received the surrender of its 365 Marines and 308 native Chamorros.

The news of these disasters was brightened somewhat by a victory of the defenders of Wake Island, another lonely sentinel of the Pacific, under command of Marine Brigadier General James P. S. Devereux (later a congressman from Maryland), when his artillery and bombers beat off an attack and sank the destroyers *Hayate* and *Kisaragi*. But the victory was short-lived, for on December 23 the Japanese with reinforcements overwhelmed the island and hauled down the Stars and Stripes. Hong Kong, for a century ruled by the British, surrendered on Christmas Day.

Still darker days lay ahead for the United States, Great Britain, the Netherlands and Australia—now allies against the relentless Japanese advance. During January 1942, the invading tide pounded at the shores of New Britain, overwhelmed the port of Rabaul, surged through Thailand and into Burma. The British began their retreat into India. On January 24 the Japanese entered Makassar Strait and landed on Borneo. During February they captured another great prize, the city of Singapore. They sent heavy raids upon Darwin, Australia, invaded Timor, and surrounded Java. In a desperate attempt to break their grip on Java, American and Dutch naval forces attacked a convoy of Japanese troopships and their warship escorts, and were soundly defeated with the loss of the *Langley,* oldest American aircraft carrier, the heavy cruiser *Houston* and the destroyer *Pope,* and eleven British, Dutch and Australian warships. During March the Japanese occupied all of Java and extended their expansion with the capture of Lae and Salamaua in New Guinea.

President Roosevelt chose Admiral Ernest J. King, a veteran naval flyer, to be Chief of Naval Operations, and Admiral Chester W. Nimitz to command the Pacific area from Hawaii. These two capable officers decided upon a line of defense which the fleet would try to hold at all costs: from Hawaii northwestward to Midway; and from Hawaii southeastward through Samoa and Fiji to Brisbane, Australia. With that general objective, the resolute Nimitz assumed his command at battered Pearl Harbor. The growing American naval strength began to challenge the invaders with raids by planes from the forces under Admirals Frank J. Fletcher and William B. Halsey, restoring somewhat the sagging Allied morale.

Further aid for Allied hopes came with a daring exploit—the raid over Tokyo, led by Lieutenant Colonel James Doolittle (later Lieutenant General), commanding the Army Air Corps on Hawaii. On April 16 Doolittle and seventy-nine other intrepid airmen took off from the carrier *Hornet,* in heavy seas and still 688 miles from Japan, on their perilous mission.

At noon they were dropping their bombs upon Toyko. Their original plan called for the planes to proceed after the raid to Vladivostok, Siberia, but Stalin personally refused permission for them to land. So the raiders turned toward China to find landing fields or to bail out, and seventy-one of the eighty survived.

Darkest days before the dawn came with the American loss of the Philippines. General Douglas MacArthur, ordered to proceed to Australia and to assume command of the Allied forces in the southwest Pacific, left with the terse warning "I shall return." General Jonathan M. Wainwright took command, with headquarters on Corregidor, while his subordinate, Brigadier General Edward P. King, Jr., remained at Bataan. On March 31 the Japanese under General Masaharu Homma began a heavy assault upon the American positions. On April 9 King found his situation hopeless. With his lines penetrated, his ammunition gone, his hospitals under fire, he sent forward a flag of surrender. His survivors were herded into columns and in one of the cruelest death marches of any war were forced to tramp sixty miles to concentration camps. About one thousand officers and men perished on the way. For a month longer, Wainwright and his beleaguered forces on Corregidor held out, and their heroic resistance stands as an epic of military history. On May 6, just before he surrendered, the general penned these words:

"It is unreasonable to expect that we can hold out for long. We have done our best, both here and on Bataan, and although beaten we are still unashamed."

Determined to prevent any loss of the vast regions they had seized, the Japanese began a many-pronged campaign to cut the long supply lines from Hawaii to Australia and to advance until the continent itself was in their grasp. Specific objectives were twofold: First, to dominate the Coral Sea, and thus secure the Solomon Islands to use as bases and control the passage from north to south through the reefs at the south-east tip of New Guinea. Second, to capture Midway Island, one thousand miles west and north of Hawaii, and to hold this as the eastern corner of their huge offensive wedge. Their campaign brought on the two decisive engagements that together changed the course of the war in the Pacific. In both, the use of naval aviation was the major factor in victory. As Admiral King wrote in his official report:

"It should be noted at this point that during the first five months of the war, nearly every engagement with the enemy had demonstrated the importance of air power in modern naval warfare."

One Flattop under the Coral Sea

It is late April, 1942, and the Japanese plans for conquest of the Coral Sea are complete. They call for the control of the Solomon Islands, the northern border of that sea, and the capture of Port Moresby at the southern edge of New Guinea, closest point to Australia.

Two carrier task forces are assigned the honor of the campaign. The first is commanded by Admiral Takagi, with the biggest of his country's carriers, *Zukiaku* and *Shokaku*, of 30,000 tons each, and the protecting accompaniment of four heavy cruisers and fourteen destroyers. The second is under command of Admiral Inouye, aboard his flagship, the 12,000-ton carrier *Shoho*, with sixteen auxiliary warships. They are to join forces in the Coral Sea, sweep away any Allied resistance and prepare the area for the invasion of Australia.

Takagi moves southward from his huge base on the island of Truk, about seven hundred miles north of Rabaul, while Inouye skirts the Solomons and heads westward. In the warm sunshine of the morning of May 3, Takagi's force reaches Tulagi, Florida Island. From their ships the Japanese warriors pour ashore and within minutes control the city. Australian patrol planes spot the landing of the enemy troops and soon have the news crackling into Nimitz's headquarters at Pearl Harbor and into the receivers of Admiral Fletcher's carrier force in the southern waters of the Coral Sea.

Realizing the importance of the control of this sea for the defense of Australia, Nimitz orders Fletcher to take the offensive. Fletcher moves with the *Yorktown* northward to fly strikes against Tulagi. Soon after dawn the captors of the port city are surprised by the thunder of bombs from the American naval planes. Several waves of bombers severely damage the harbor and a few of the warships.

The *Shoho* task force is moving steadily toward Port Moresby. On the morning of May 6 the light carrier's planes spot the American tanker *Neosho,* that has refueled Fletcher's ships, and its escorting destroyer *Sims* heading back to Australia. Coming in for this easy kill, Japanese torpedo bombers sink both these vessels.

This victory is dearly paid for when *Lexington's* search planes spot the *Shoho.* The American admiral dispatches ninety-four attack planes with the order: "Sink the *Shoho!*"

Roaring down on the task force, the Navy planes center their attack in wave after wave upon the hapless carrier. In five minutes their crews count hits of ten heavy bombs and fifteen torpedoes. The *Shoho,* its ammunition exploding, its oil burning furiously, slides beneath the waves.

"Dixon to carrier! Dixon to carrier!" exultantly calls the commander of the attacking force as his squadron returns to the *Lexington.* "Scratch one Jap flattop!"

Dawn on May 8; the *Yorktown* and *Lexington* forces have joined. From the decks of both big carriers, torpedo and bombing planes take to the air to find the Japanese carriers. As though some ghostly referee of the deadly contest has ordered both dualists to fire, the planes from the *Shokaku* and *Zuikaku* are zooming away to find the *Lexington* and

Yorktown. Admiral Tagaki's order doubles that which sent the *Shoho* to the bottom: "Sink both American carriers!"

A total of 103 Japanese planes take part in the attacks. As they approach the American vessels, one after another falls disabled from the accurate gunfire of the defending cruisers and destroyers; but many get through to their targets. The *Lexington* sustains three severe torpedo hits, the *Yorktown* one serious blow amidships from a maximum bomb.

Meanwhile the American naval dive bombers and torpedo bombers have come down below the clouds and spotted their quarry. They score three direct bomb hits upon the *Shokaku,* setting fires in the stern of this flattop and disabling her, while bombs upon the *Zuikaku* demolish most of the planes remaining on her deck. The American torpedo crews are distressed to find that many of their missiles run badly or fail to explode on contact.

The United States Navy plane crews, returning to their carriers, are surprised to find that enemy planes have attacked their floating bases in their absence. The *Lexington* is listing and smoking ominously. Gasoline fumes are pouring from tanks punctured by torpedoes. Suddenly there is a tremendous roar as the fumes explode between decks. Men and planes are blown into the water. Fires spread uncontrollably, and black smoke billows into the sky. Still the proud carrier, called affectionately "Lady Lex" by officers and men, stays afloat. Captain Frederic C. Sherman (later Vice Admiral) then gives the command: "Abandon ship!"

All the escort vessels stand by to rescue. Crewmen swing down ropes and drop into the sea. A total of 2,735 are pulled to safety. When the muster rolls are made, 216 have given their lives, along with 79 others of the aviation crews lost in the attacks. As "Lady Lex" sinks, her officers and crewmen watch from the rescue ships, many weeping unashamedly.

Crippled from their wounds, *Shokaku* and *Zuikaku* limp

back to Japanese ports for long months of repairing. Although the Americans have sunk a carrier and six warships, Admiral Takagi reports a victory. Still his actions deny his words, for he withdraws all his naval forces from the Coral Sea. Port Moresby is saved, and the danger of invasion of Australia is averted.

Yamamoto Seeks Another Victory

Now the plan of the Japanese high command to seize Midway Island goes forward with increased energy. To Yamamoto, the disgrace of the loss of a carrier and the disabling of two others is unendurable and must be avenged. From the time this ranking officer reluctantly agreed to the bombing of Pearl Harbor, he has planned for the steady elimination of both the surface and air power of the United States Navy. To hold a base in striking distance of Hawaii is essential to his plan. That means Midway must be captured and garrisoned. With that accomplished, the emperor's fleet commander expects—and earnestly hopes—that Nimitz will sally forth from Hawaii and engage in an open sea battle, in which the overwhelming superiority of the Japanese fleet could crush what remains of the American sea power in the Pacific. For Yamamoto has eleven battleships to employ in his campaign, while Nimitz has none available. The Japanese admiral has six serviceable aircraft carriers; with "Lady Lex" gone Nimitz can count only three, including *Yorktown*, given fast repairs at Pearl Harbor after the Coral Sea. The Japanese fleet has at least forty heavy cruisers and twice that many destroyers. Nimitz can spare only eight cruisers and fifteen destroyers to protect his carriers. All his other warships are in use for convoy duty as American troops move in a swelling stream to Hawaii and Australia.

But Yamamoto does not depend upon superior strength alone. He plans a clever ruse. He has made one bomber strike against Dutch Harbor, Alaska, and will make another, followed by transports with troops to garrison the base. Surely, the admiral reasons, the American command will send its strongest force hurrying northward to defend Alaska and the Aleutians, making the capture of Midway quite easy.

The admiral does not know that the messages outlining all his plans have been intercepted, decoded and placed on the desks of Nimitz and the task force commanders. The Americans have no intention of being decoyed; rather, Nimitz makes a decision of historic importance. Despite the tremendous odds against him, he accepts the enemy challenge to Midway, and prepares to make the best possible use of his naval air power. On May 28 he orders Admiral Halsey's Task Force 16, with the carriers *Enterprise,* Captain George D. Murray, and *Hornet,* Captain Marc A. Mitscher, commanding, to proceed from Pearl Harbor to a point east of Midway to intercept the enemy fleet. Halsey has fallen ill, and as if by a design of fate, his command has been assumed by calm, clear-thinking Rear Admiral Raymond A. Spruance. At 9 o'clock on the morning of May 31, Admiral Fletcher also leaves with his task force, accompanying the lone carrier *Yorktown* to rendezvous with Spruance on the afternoon of June 2. There in the wide Pacific they await whatever forces Yamamoto will lead against them.

On his huge flagship *Yamato* with its sixteen-inch guns, accompanied by six other battleships and a flock of destroyers, Admiral Yamamoto moves toward Midway. He has dispatched Rear Admiral Kakuta with two light carriers and several troop transports to make the Alaskan-Aleutian attack. To the southwestward the faithful Admiral Nagumo is sailing for the Midway attack, with four of the six carriers that took part in the Pearl Harbor assault—*Akagi, Kaga, Soryu* and *Hiryu,* and a score of protecting warships. To the southwest of his force

Vice Admiral Kondo is converging upon Midway with two battleships, eight heavy cruisers and a dozen destroyers, escorting twelve transports carrying 5,000 selected Japanese warriors who are to assault the Midway beaches and occupy the island and atoll.

On June 2 Kakuta's two carriers are in striking distance of Dutch Harbor, and the next morning each launch their planes, which break suddenly through the clouds and fog to bomb the American base. The defenders are ready and suffer only slight damage, but the Japanese lose several of their Zeros. As they return to their carriers, the attackers are themselves attacked by Army fighter planes and sustain even heavier losses. Surprised by this turn of events, as well as the refusal of the American fleet to follow him up so that Yamamoto could destroy it, Admiral Kakuta moves southwestward and occupies the uninhabited islands of Kiska and Attu.

Now it is early morning on Thursday, June 4, and Admiral Nagumo's task force is 186 miles southwest of Midway. The admiral rises early, sips his rice gruel with his staff and in stiff formality mounts the bridge of his flagship, the carrier *Akagi*. Since midnight, 216 of his planes have been ready for the Midway strike, their motors tested, their pilots dressed in their equipment. Nagumo reserves ninety-three planes in below-deck hangars, with torpedoes and bombs for attacking American warships. The first light discloses a few thin clouds, and the winds are easy.

Through the misty dawn Admiral Fletcher's search planes sight the Japanese task force, and call out the message: "Enemy carriers!" More detailed information follows, giving the position; it is relayed to the American commanders of the joint task force and the Midway Base. Now Fletcher makes a fortunate decision. He gives to his subordinate Spruance the initiative for the battle in the order:

"Proceed southwesterly and attack enemy carriers when definitely located. I will follow as soon as my search planes are recovered."

Almost at that moment, Admiral Nagumo, entirely unaware that American carriers are in his area, orders the assault on Midway to begin. With shouts of *"Banzai!"* from all the crews of his carriers the Zeros roar off, zoom up and circle into formation. Two waves of 108 planes each take to the morning air within an hour.

Immediately, the radar watchers at Midway sing out, "Enemy planes aloft!" Pilots and crews of every plane on the island hurry into fighting equipment and roar down the runways. Patrol planes, useless in this engagement, turn eastward and head for safety of Hawaii. Navy torpedo planes, a squadron of twenty-seven marine aviators, and fighter planes of both Navy and Army speed westward for the battle.

First to meet the enemy planes are the marines, flying twenty obsolete Buffalo-type aircraft and seven Wildcats. The Americans, hopelessly outclassed by the Japanese "Zekes," sacrifice themselves bravely and seventeen of their planes are shot down into the sea. The Japanese bombers thunder on, swinging down their target runs upon Midway, laying their missiles upon the facilities of the base. Except for the destruction of one hangar and a fuel tank, damage is slight, while twenty enemy planes are brought down by ground fire. Monitors hear the Japanese flight commander radioing to his ship that another attack will be necessary.

Now follow, one after the other, the tragic failures and losses of the counterattacking American flyers. Moving in together, seven Navy Avengers and four Army Marauders attempt to bomb Nagumo's force, with not one direct hit and with the loss of all but three of the planes. A few minutes later sixteen Marine bombers, led by Major L. R. Henderson, arrive at the scene. They score no hits and eight are shot down. Another attacking wave enters the air battle over the watery arena, as Lieutenant Colonel Walter Sweeney leads his Army bombers 20,000 feet above the Japanese force but scores no damaging hits. Finally another squadron of marine flyers in slow Vindicators make their challenge, but the "Zekes" shoot down several and the survivors turn back toward Midway.

Nagumo is well satisfied with the defense his force has made. Still he knows that another attack must be made upon Midway before it can be conquered. Accordingly he makes a fateful command decision. Still unaware of the proximity of Fletcher and Spruance and their carriers, he orders the armament on his ninety-three planes in reserve changed from bombs and torpedoes to fire and blasting bombs for the second assault on Midway. His officers and men fall to the task, which takes more than an hour, and just as it is completed, at 8 o'clock, a message comes from one of his search planes that the American carriers have been sighted.

The Japanese admiral and his carrier captains must wait for the return of the planes from their mission. By 9 o'clock all are recovered and the admiral orders:

"Proceed to the northward. We will attack and destroy the American carrier force!"

"Peel Off and Strike!"

As the four Japanese carriers and their huge flock of defending vessels of war move north by northeastward over smooth waters and under a clear sky, Nagumo's seamen fall to again, changing the armament of their recovered planes to anti-ship missiles to be ready to deal with the American fleet.

Admiral Spruance is a cruiser officer, with no experience in carrier warfare, but with a logical mind that now rises to the supreme test of battle decisions. He knows his only chance of averting the capture of Midway lies in the destruction of Japanese air power. He consults his chief of staff, Captain

Miles Browning, who advises that the strikes be launched at 7 o'clock. Spruance's thinking is seen in these words:

"It was my reasoning that if we gave the enemy planes time to return from their Midway mission, the carrier decks would be filled with them being armed for another strike, and that by attacking at that moment we could accomplish the maximum destruction."

In about one hour, all the planes selected for the mission from Spruance's two carriers have been launched: from the *Hornet,* fifteen planes of Torpedo 8 Squadron, and a squadron of dive bombers. From the *Enterprise,* fourteen planes from Torpedo 6 Squadron, and sixty-seven planes in two squadrons of Dauntless dive-bombers. Near 8 o'clock *Yorktown*'s search planes are all recovered, and Fletcher launches Torpedo 3 Squadron of fourteen Devastators.

Since no intelligence has been received of Nagumo's swing to the northeastward, the American naval aviators seek out the original enemy position and find nothing below but the broad expanse of the Pacific. *Hornet*'s dive bombers proceed far westward and miss action completely. *Hornet*'s Torpedo 8 Squadron becomes separated from the other units, but its commander leads the search northward and at 9:30 sights the enemy force.

"Form for the attack!" Waldron orders.

As the TDBs come in low to launch their torpedoes, with no fighter protection, Japanese fighters converge upon them with deadly fire. Every one of the fifteen American planes is shot down, with the loss of all the crew members except one. Ensign George Gay saves himself after bailing out over the water by seizing a rubber raft, and from his floating perch this junior officer witnesses the rest of the flaming air battle at sea.

Now the planes of Torpedo 6 attack, and of the fourteen aircraft, eleven are destroyed by the vigilant Zero fighters.

Finally, at 10:15, *Yorktown*'s Devastators come in under cover of six Navy fighters—the only squadron to be so favored. Again the Zeros attack furiously, downing ten torpedo planes and three American fighters, but not before several hits are made on the carrier *Soryu*.

Meantime *Enterprise*'s Air Group 6, led by Lieutenant Commander Clarence W. McClusky, has searched the area of the Japanese force's last known position. Flying in widening circles, McClusky sights on the horizon a Japanese destroyer that for some reason has lagged behind Nagumo's fleet. It is heading northeastward. The American commander rightly assumes the enemy ship is on its way to join its task force, and sets the course of his squadrons accordingly. *Yorktown*'s dive bombers, led by Lieutenant Commander Maxwell F. Leslie, pick up the *Enterprise* squadrons' signals and turn to the same course.

It is 10:20 A.M., and the smoke of the slaughter of the American torpedo planes swirls skyward, mingling with the clouds that now cover the Japanese force. The carrier *Hiryu* has pulled away from the battle as a reserve. The three other carriers, which have been maneuvering to lessen the danger of the torpedo hits during the attack, are turning to windward in preparation to launch their strikes as McClusky's air group swing high into view. The eager American pilots sight the three enemy carriers surrounded by their warships, and note that, just as Admiral Spruance has surmised, the carriers are loaded, their decks bristling with planes like wasps swarming on floating logs. The *Akagi* is already to windward and one plane has been waved aloft. As if to complete the favorable situation for the Americans, nearly all the Japanese fighters are at low level as result of their battle with the torpedo planes.

"Peel off and strike!" McClusky commands.

At a seventy-degree angle, in an evenly spaced line, the

Dauntless pilots dive toward the *Akagi*. As they zoom up over the big carrier their bombs fall. The first three miss the target. Then the hits begin—direct hits exploding with tremendous, staccato-like thunder upon *Akagi's* deck or in her hangars below. In a Japanese officer's vivid account are these words:

"We are caught by surprise and there is big destruction. Huge holes are blown in our deck, our elevator is twisted and drooping, our planes flattened or standing on end and burning fiercely."

Meantime *Kaga* (the name means "more joy") suffers the same fate from McClusky's second squadron, with four direct hits in vital areas. As though from a giant with an enormous torch lighting a hundred bonfires, the carrier literally bursts into a mass of flame and billowing smoke. Several hits are made upon the Japanese cruisers and destroyers. The 13,000-ton *Mikuma* is wrecked by bombs, flames spurting amidships, while a battleship and destroyer also are disabled.

Now Commander Leslie arrives with his seventeen TDBs from *Yorktown,* armed with thousand-pound bombs—heaviest of the mission. Three of these explode squarely upon the *Soryu*. Again explosions and flames sweep a proud vessel and it becomes a shambles.

Kaga and *Soryu* are abandoned by most of the surviving crews immediately. Officers and seamen are picked up from the water by boats from the warships. As fires continue to spread over the *Akagi,* Nagumo's chief of staff begs him to abandon the vessel. After some hesitation, the admiral bids Captain Oaki a formal farewell, leaves the listing, flaming carrier and hoists his flag over the light cruiser *Nagara*.

Search planes from the *Hiryu* have located the American task force. At noon about sixty of this carrier's torpedo planes and dive bombers take off for the attack. Finding the *Yorktown* at a distance from the other carriers, the Japanese bombers make three direct hits upon this veteran of the Coral

Sea, disabling her engines and opening seams. All the anti-aircraft guns of the American force in range open upon the attackers, bringing down half their number. *Yorktown* begins listing so seriously that Captain Buckmaster orders her abandoned.

Revenge moves swiftly in for the crippled *Yorktown*. At 2:45 P.M. one of her search pilots sights *Hiryu* and reports the position. Admiral Spruance promptly orders twenty-four SBDs prepared for the strike. No fighter escort can be provided, but at 3:30 the squadron takes to the air. At 5 o'clock they are diving down upon the *Hiryu*. Four hits and the resulting below-deck explosions and fires curl up the vessel's flight deck as though it were tin. Shortly after midnight *Hiryu* slides beneath the surface, its heat sending up geysers of steam.

Meantime, at 6 o'clock, Captain Oaki and his remaining crew abandon *Akagi*. "May I sink the crippled flagship?" he asks of Nagumo. The admiral refuses permission unless given by Yamamoto. The commander-in-chief grants permission, and at 4 o'clock the next morning, four destroyers deliver the *coup de grâce* and hasten *Akagi* to the bottom.

At 7:25 P.M. *Kaga* goes down. *Soryu* is sinking. Her Captain Yamagimoto refuses the pleas of his officers to leave his ship. As the Pacific waters close over it, he grips the rail outside his bridge, singing his national anthem *"Kinigayo."*

Before dusk, Army bombers from Midway make hits on three enemy warships. June 5 is beset by poor visibility, but again the bombers, joined by aircraft from *Enterprise* and *Hornet*, seek out the enemy and cripple three cruisers. June 6 is clear and once more American planes from the *Enterprise* and *Hornet* press the search, attacking and damaging four cruisers and a destroyer.

Admiral Fletcher is trying to save *Yorktown* and has the carrier in tow. The destroyer *Hammann* comes alongside to put a salvage crew aboard. Suddenly the carrier is hit by two torpedoes, and the *Hammann* by one, launched from an enemy submarine. Within minutes the destroyer sinks. At morning's light the *Yorktown* joins all ships that lie on the bottom of the seas—in honored glory, as befits a fighting craft whose work has been well done.

Admiral Yamamoto, scarcely able to believe the reports of the astonishing reversal of his victory tide and the loss of his carriers, moves eastward in the hope that the American fleet will still meet him for the sea battle. But Fletcher and Spruance have drawn back to near Midway. The Japanese admiral knows that American submarines are moving into the area in increasing numbers, so sadly he bows to the defeat. "The Imperial naval task forces will move westward," he orders.

Three Years to Victory

Thus ended the Battle of Midway, the battle that saw the sharpest and quickest turn in the fortunes of the antagonists that engaged in the struggle for the Pacific. In the five minutes of naval dive-bombing operations against the enemy carriers, that turn was accomplished. In the whole engagement, the Imperial Japanese Fleet lost four carriers, six other warships, and most of its naval aircraft. Losses in personnel totaled about 2,500; most important of all, among these were about three-fourths of the best-trained pilots. The American losses were 512 lives, one carrier, one destroyer, and 49 planes.

The battle added to the proud traditions of the United States Navy the valor of carrier-borne aviators. It established air power as an indispensable arm of naval warfare. It brought to light the necessity of fighter protection for carrier or land-based bombers and torpedo aircraft. As the engagement in the Coral Sea stopped the Japanese advance upon Australia, so the engagement of Midway halted the Japanese threat to the central Pacific. As Admiral King said in his summary report:

"The Battle of Midway was the first decisive defeat suffered by the Japanese Navy in 350 years. Furthermore, it put an end to the long period of Japanese offensive action, and restored the balance of naval power in the Pacific."

There still lay ahead three years of intense, bitter struggle, in which the armed services, each with its complement of airpower, shared in the sacrifices and the honors. There were the marines at Guadalcanal in August, 1942, initiating the first Allied offensive movement in the southwest Pacific. There were the sharp battles for the Solomon Islands. There was the battle of the Bismarck Sea, in which General George C. Kenney's Army Air Force planes smashed a large Japanese convoy headed for New Guinea. There was the continuing battle led by General Claire L. Chennault and his flyers to regain China. There was the Battle of Leyte Gulf, the greatest naval battle of them all, and possibly the last great battle of the Navy line in history. There was the tragic sinking of the *Indianapolis,* all alone in the Philippine Sea, with the loss of more than eight hundred brave men of the sea.

There was the successful "island hopping" strategy of General MacArthur, which regained, by unrelenting pressure of the power of land, air and sea forces, the territories overrun by the Japanese early in the war. It was the strategy that fulfilled the commander-in-chief's prediction to return to the Philippines, and to move on to Tokyo.

The military, industrial, economic and political strength of the Japanese warlords ebbed away; by early June 1945 the emperor and his advisers knew the end was in sight. They sought a graceful way to halt the destruction of their realm by an armistice, approaching (ironically, as later developments disclosed) the representatives of dictator Joseph Stalin of Soviet Russia. The leaders of that nation were determined there should be no Japanese surrender until they could get into the war and reap the benefits of the victory so dearly won by the valor and power of the Allied forces.

August 6, 1945, ushered in a new epoch of history, for at 8:15 o'clock on that morning an atomic bomb, launched by order of President Harry S Truman upon the unsuspecting people of Hiroshima, almost totally obliterated the city and more than 100,000 of its inhabitants. Two days later another atomic bomb was dropped over Nagasaki, with almost as great destruction. The atomic bombs hastened, but did not bring about, the Japanese surrender. Japan was already defeated—conquered by the destruction of her capacity to make war.

CHAPTER FIFTEEN

Air Power Spearheads Defeat of Germany

On August 17, 1942, a flight of United States Army Air Force planes took off from an airfield north of London, on the first heavy bomber mission by American personnel against the war facilities of Nazi Germany. The planes smoothed out into formation, and like ponderous gulls they skimmed over the English Channel and headed toward Rouen, France.

Leading the roaring four-engined Liberators was Brigadier General Ira C. Eaker, veteran of the Army Air Force since World War I days. The target was the railway depot of Rouen, with its marshalling yards and repair shops, a key center of transportation in the area of France occupied by Hitler's forces. Moving without interception or interference across the Channel, over the coast and directly to the French city, Eaker and his squadron struck a surprise blow, blasting the tracks and yards with their 500-pound bombs.

Such was the beginning of the American air effort in Europe, which grew to a mighty crescendo of power. Coordinating all its campaigns with the valiant officers and men of Britain's Royal Air Force, the United States Army Air Force gave the needed power to curtail the production and fighting strength of the German Air Force, or *Luftwaffe,* so that the way for an invasion by land forces was prepared and the whole nation under the Nazi regime was brought to its knees in defeat.

From small beginnings, the Army Air Force had grown to

327

a lusty striking arm by the time of this its first major bombing raid over European soil. Until World War I, army aviation was a small, experimental branch of the Signal Corps. In January 1918 it became the Army Aviation Section, with its own proud insignia—the wings and propeller. During the years of expansion of civilian aviation, the military air arms of both Army and Navy kept pace with the progress of the air age, and often led the way. In 1923 an army aviation officer of World War I, Lieutenant Colonel E. L. Hoffman, won the Collier Award for the most distinguished contribution to aviation, his work in perfecting the parachute.

In 1935 the General Headquarters, Air Force, was established to command the combat elements of the Army Air Force, under Brigadier General Frank Andrews. A program of research was intensified, centered at Wright Field, Dayton, near the home of the first men to fly in a self-propelled heavier-than-air machine. At Wright and at a few other fields scattered over the country, training of pilots and technicians leaped forward, emphasizing the techniques of flying in all conditions of weather, precision bombing of targets, tactical operations with ground troops and services of aviation supply—all in anticipation that some day these factors would be used in actual warfare.

In 1936 the first B–17 bombers, called "Flying Fortresses," were put into operation at Langley Field, Virginia. In 1938 a squadron of these planes demonstrated their power, stamina and range by flying to Buenos Aires, Argentina, with only one stop at Lima, Peru. By mid-1938 the Army Air Force had 1,300 offcers and 180,000 men, with 2,800 reserve officers and 400 enlisted reserve, and 1,600 aircraft.

This was only the beginning. In 1939 Congress appropriated 300 million dollars to expand personnel, materiel, equipment, training programs and bases of the Army Air Force. Mass production of both bombers and fighters began. The les-

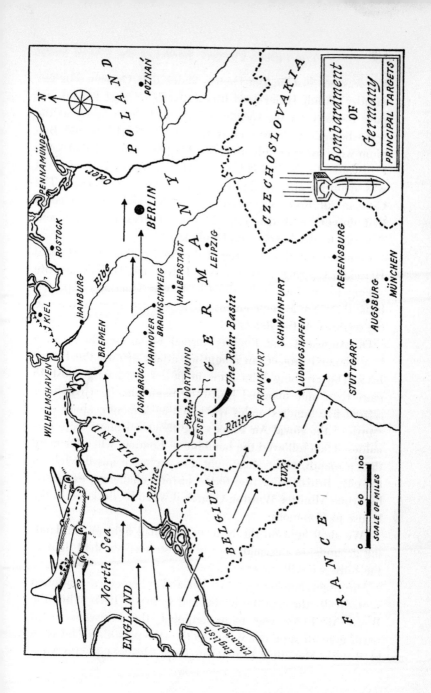

Bombardment OF Germany PRINCIPAL TARGETS

son was not lost on the United States that German *Fuehrer* (leader) Adolf Hitler used his Luftwaffe to blast Poland and pave the way for the speedy reduction of that country at the war's beginning. It was clear that the Netherlands and Belgium were overrun only after bombing by planes of that same Luftwaffe. In April 1940, when Hitler attacked Norway, it was again his air arm that opened the path for invasion. The German Air Force supported the mechanized armored corps that drove the British Expeditionary Forces in France and Belgium to the beaches of Dunkirk.

Commanding the air force of the Nazi regime was Marshal Hermann Goering, a World War I flyer and Hitler's favorite among his military subordinates. It was Goering's repeated boast that "Not a single enemy plane will get through to bomb the territory of the *Reich!*"

On August 3, the Fuehrer turned his airmen loose on a long-planned project, an all-out air attack against the British Isles. The crushing blitz grew in power until on August 15 more than nine hundred Luftwaffe planes made strikes over a front five hundred miles wide. Within a month, about one-fourth of the Royal Air Force's one thousand pilots were casualties. Then followed the bombing of London, when for more than a month, night after night, the explosive missiles fell on the city. British valor rose to the historic challenge, expressed by Prime Minister Winston Churchill when he declared in the House of Commons:

"We shall fight on the beaches, we shall fight on the landing grounds, in the fields and in the streets; we shall fight in the hills; we will never surrender!"

The night bombing of London and other cities continued sporadically through the winter and spring of 1941. While the Royal Air Force was badly crippled, the Luftwaffe could never gain air supremacy enough to make possible an invasion of Britain. Meantime the Italian *Duce* (leader) Benito Mussolini, forming the small end of an axis with Hitler, had struck at Greece from Albania, which he had occupied in 1939. The resolute Greeks struck back. British forces occupied the island of Crete, and in North Africa under General Archibald Wavell, they soundly defeated the Italians with the capture of whole divisions of troops.

In June 1941 Hitler's eastern partner in the enormous crime of plunging the world into war, Soviet Dictator Joseph Stalin, began one of the cruelest programs of genocide in history—the systematic reduction of the populations of the Baltic states of Estonia, Latvia and Lithuania, by mass deportations to slave-labor camps in Siberia.

Communist agents in the United States had been dutifully beating the drums for the party line, which was to urge America not to become involved in the war in Europe. During the days of late May and early June, pickets representing the Communist leadership in the United States paraded in front of the White House in Washington with signs reading "KEEP OUT OF WAR!" and "THE YANKS ARE NOT COMING!" On the morning of June 18 the pickets failed to appear. They had received word of an impending change in fortunes. On June 22 the Nazi war machine rolled eastward in an attack upon the forces of the Soviet Union. Immediately, the American Communist party line switched to urgent pleas for all-out war in support of Soviet Russia.

At that moment, the opportunity presented itself to the Allies to permit these two major aggressors to exhaust each other in a finish fight, with the inevitable depletion of the military and political strength of each. While this self-destruction was going on, the free nations could have established more firmly the principles of liberty, justice and mutual security in the countries outside the control of the dictatorships. This course was advocated by numerous students of communism and its kindred totalitarian ideologies, fascism and nazism, but the strategy of assisting one dictator to crush the other was embraced, and it shaped and colored all decisions of the United States government, military or political, to the end of the war and far beyond.

"Only in America——"

With the passage of the Lend-Lease Act in March 1941 the United States had become in fact an ally of the powers at war with Nazi Germany. The major production of military aircraft of all kinds began flowing to Great Britain, and after June 22, to Soviet Russia. The B–24 Liberator and the B–17 Flying Fortress bombers, and the Lockheed Lightning and North American Mustang fighters, were among the planes that went into mass production. In April, 1941, the Army Air Force was expanded into the 1st, 2d, 3d, and 5th Army Air Forces, with General H. H. "Hap" Arnold in command.

At the time of the Pearl Harbor attack by the Japanese, the Army Air Force had about 3,000 planes of all types, with only 1,157 suited to combat service. Of these, 159 were four-engined bombers and 913 were fighter planes. At least one-fourth were destroyed in the first Japanese attacks. Said General Arnold: "We are entering this struggle with few planes, but many plans."

In Hitler's blueprint for speedy victory were plans to complete the Russian campaign in ninety days, to secure and hold all of North Africa, and to build up his Luftwaffe to invincible strength. The Fuehrer presumed that the American Air Force would never delay the Nazi triumph. This proved to be his fatal miscalculation. With the United States officially at war, the air arm began a vast program of expansion. Hundreds of hotels, garages, warehouses, hangars and even theaters were leased as Air Force schools and facilities. Numerous new airfields were obtained for the training program. The Air Transport Command was set up. Thousands of firms were converted to air war production. As General Arnold said in his first summary report:

Only in America would a piano company believe that it could convert to building airplane wings in a few months, and do it. A tire manufacturer built fuselages and tail surfaces. A former pickle plant turned out airplane skis and floats, and a manufacturer of girdles and corsets began making parachutes.

In January 1942 General Eaker arrived in England with five other officers, the first unit of what became the mighty Eighth Air Force. The first five months were spent in rapid construction of the runways, hangars and other facilities of the assigned areas. One runway, begun by British engineers with a target date for completion in six months, was built by American engineers and machinery in two weeks' time. In June, General Carl Spaatz arrived in England from the Pacific area and took command of the Eighth Air Force.

Hitler had sent his best combat general, Marshal Erwin Rommel, to command the *Afrika Korps,* and this "Desert Fox" drove along the coastal region to Tobruk, captured about 30,000 British troops, crossed into Egypt and reached El Alamein, only sixty-five miles from Alexandria.

In July, General George C. Marshall and Admiral Ernest J. King, top officers of the American Army and Navy staffs, met with the British chiefs of staff in London to plan the grand Allied strategy of war. They made it clear that the primary concern of President Franklin D. Roosevelt and his advisers was to assist to the greatest possible extent the armies of Soviet Russia. As reported by General Marshall:

"After prolonged discussions, it became evident that the only operation that could be undertaken with a fair prospect of success that year was (Operation) Torch, the assault on North Africa. Landings there would be a long way from

Germany, but would serve to divert at least some pressure from the Red Army."

Despite American aid to Soviet Russia, that nation's dictator and his underlings made no moves to assist in a common victory except those whereby the Soviet Union stood to gain. On June 17, 1942, President Roosevelt sent a message of "great urgency" to Stalin, suggesting that Russian airfields be made available for Allied bombers. The dictator did not even reply.

Lieutenant General Dwight D. Eisenhower was appointed commander-in-chief of the American and British forces entrusted with Operation Torch. Taking General Spaatz with him to command the air operations, Eisenhower established headquarters at Algiers and directed the campaigns that regained the whole of North Africa. The French government, moved to Vichy and under control of the Nazi conquerors, put up some resistance to British and American invasion of its African area, but a combination of gunfire and diplomacy overcame the objections. A dynamic American commander, General George Patton, assisted by United States warships, captured Moroccan port cities. British and American forces took Oran and other Algerian strongholds. Combined operations of the Navy and air forces cut off Rommel from reinforcements and supplies. A new British commander, General Bernard Montgomery, routed Rommel at El Alamein and sent him retreating westward into Tunisia. In all the fighting of the Torch campaign, Allied airpower proved the decisive factor by its tactical support of the ground and sea forces.

By the end of 1942 the expected Nazi victory over the Russians had failed to materialize. Winter, that unconquerable enemy of Napoleon's invading armies a century and a quarter before, again picked up his fearful weapons and took the field against the Germans. War materiel from the United States, shipped at tremendous hazard and expense, gave substance to the valor of Soviet troops. At Stalingrad the German tide was turned.

The year 1943 opened with grim determination on the part of the Allies to destroy as much of the Nazi war machine as possible, both in the field and at centers of production. Broad outlines of the massive campaign were drawn up in January, when President Roosevelt, Prime Minister Churchill and their chiefs of staff met at Casablanca, Africa. There these Allied leaders planned Operation Husky, to take Sicily, in preparation for a greater campaign against the Italian peninsula; also to begin bombing raids against the oil fields of Rumania and to step up the bombing of German military targets; to accomplish, as the conference directive said, "The progressive destruction and dislocation of the enemy's military, industrial and economic system, to a point where his capacity for armed resistance is fatally weakened."

The agreement involved settling a point of difference between British and American leaders. It was the general policy of the R.A.F. to engage in night bombing. British flyers had tried daylight missions and had given them up as too costly. The American command held that while daylight missions offered more hazards, they provided such accurate bombing that results justified losses. It was a determined American officer, General Eaker, who prevailed upon Prime Minister Churchill to agree to both night and day bombing. With the approval of his superiors, Eaker told the British statesman:

"If you will agree to a campaign of daylight bombing by our American planes, and you British continue with the night missions, we shall be pounding the enemy around the clock."

In his report to the House of Commons the Prime Minister declared: "By His Majesty's Royal Air Force attacking by night, and the Americans attacking by day, we shall be bombing the enemy continually, around the clock."

The Army Air Forces Come of Age

Thus, the combined air forces of two great nations developed strategy and tactics of their own, cooperating with all other forces. The wisdom of the policy became immediately apparent in the campaigns of North Africa, where American bombers shattered enemy airfields and knocked down enemy transports. Rommel's *Afrika Korps* was driven into prisoner-of-war camps and the area was cleared of enemy forces.

The saga of air power, coordinated with the forces of armies and navies, continued its story of victory through Operation Husky as Sicily was taken by British and American troops under air support of the R.A.F. and the A.A.F. Immediate result was the fall of Italy from partnership with Hitler. On September 8, 1943, General Eisenhower announced Italy's formal surrender.

German military power in Italy still had to be conquered, and essential to that operation was the defeat of its air arm. On October 1 the Twelfth Air Force, a tactical arm under General John K. Cannon, assisted the heavy bombers in clearing the way for the capture of Naples. One month later, the Fifteenth Air Force was activated. Integrating all their operations with the ground troops, both strategic and tactical air units supported the advance of Allied armies northward toward Rome. During some periods of the campaign, U.S. Army and Air Force engineers smoothed out and made usable an airfield every second day, with bulldozers and wire-mesh coverings.

Since July 1943, Generals Spaatz and Eaker and their fellow air commanders had brought enemy targets under terrific bombing attacks. They gave highest priority to the destruction of the basic industries vital to the Nazi war machine:

Oil, anti-friction bearings, rubber, steel, chemicals, transportation and utilities.

Much of the oil for the Hitler regime came from the Ploesti refineries in Rumania. In the early dawn of August 1, 177 bombers took to the air from a base in Libya, in groups of about forty each. On over the Mediterranean, across Albania and Yugoslavia, the bombers roared. One group reached Ploesti ahead of their comrades and found the whole area completely unaware of their approach. Turning back, the group met and joined the mission. Down the bombers swooped, dead on their targets. Now the alerted defenders were ready. Tremendous flak hit the American formations. As related by one of the B–17 pilots, Captain (later Colonel) David W. Alexander:

We came in low—just over the chimneys of the plants, so low that my antenna picked up weeds and a Rumanian sunflower. Our bombs blew the refineries apart, setting fires that shot flame and smoke sky-high. But the antiaircraft gunners were ready for us, and about half our bombers, with their brave crews, failed to join us for the return.

Heavy bombing raids were made on plants turning out anti-friction bearings, such as the one at Schweinfurt, Bavaria. There, on August 17, in one attack two hundred Flying Fortresses dumped more than four hundred tons of high explosives —but at the cost of thirty-seven planes and their crews. Then followed a series of raids on similar plants in Germany, Austria, France and Italy, accounting for a total of 11,000 bombs and causing the first serious disruption in the war economy of the Reich.

A second raid on Schweinfurt was made on October 14 by a force of 228 heavy bombers. Every bearing plant of that area was heavily hit; but again the cost to the American raiders was shockingly high. Wave after wave of Luftwaffe fighters met the formations, flying recklessly into them under orders to destroy the American aircraft whatever the cost. Sixty-two of the bombers were lost and 128 others damaged, with loss of 599 lives and 40 other airmen wounded.

Such were the costly lessons learned in the early years of strategic bombing. The heavy casualties of the Schweinfurt raids stunned the Air Force command into realization that daylight bombing without fighter escort for the bombers demanded too high a price. The range of the fighters was stepped up by tanks for increased fuel, and in December 1943 the P–51 made its appearance, with sufficient gasoline capacity to range all over Germany. These improvements prompted a change in tactics. The mission of the fighter plane was no longer restricted to escorting and protecting bombers. It assumed also the task of pursuing and destroying enemy fighters, wherever sighted.

The B–17 Flying Fortresses carried the major share of the bombing of Germany, aided, from mid-1943, by the heavier B–24 Liberators. Both bombers carried two pilots, a navigator and six other crewmen, with oxygen for high flights and four 20-millimeter guns for defense. By the end of 1943, with increased fighter protection, these aircraft, based either in England or Italy, were ranging as far as Berlin and return. Plants producing aircraft, rubber, motor vehicles, explosives, tanks, machine tools—all industry geared to the German war effort—felt the crushing, relentless weight of systematic strategic bombing, by ever-increasing numbers of planes and of trained pilots, bombardiers and other crewmen. To counter the steadily increasing Allied air power with its destructive operations, Hitler, Goering and their staffs concentrated on the production of fighter planes for defense. Airdromes and antiaircraft guns rimmed all areas turning out war materiel.

President Roosevelt, Prime Minister Churchill and Marshal Stalin met at Teheran, Iran, in November 1943 to plan the defeat of the Nazi regime. The Soviet dictator strenuously opposed Mr. Churchill's plea for an invasion of Germany through what the British leader called "the soft under-belly" of Europe—the Balkan countries. The President sided with Stalin, and agreement was reached that the attack on the *Reich* would be made through France. The assault for a foothold on the Continent was named "Operation Overlord," and the President personally informed General Eisenhower of his appointment to command the vast operation, set to begin in early June, 1944. From that moment, all campaigns were pointed toward the launching of Overlord.

To coordinate the operations of both the Eighth and the Fifteenth Air Forces, a unified command of the United States Strategic Air Forces in Europe was formed, headed by General Spaatz. Under him were America's most experienced and able air generals and officers: Generals Eaker and James Doolittle of the mighty Eighth Air Force, with its three air divisions; General Cannon, commanding the Mediterranean-based Twelfth Air Force and General Nathan F. Twining, the Fifteenth Air Force; General Hoyt S. Vandenberg, commanding the Ninth Air Force, a tactical group of fighter planes and medium, attack and fighter bombers; General Lewis H. Brereton, heading the First Allied Airborne Army, attached to Supreme Allied Headquarters. An average of 120,000 men, pilots and their crews, were in the air in training or combat every hour of the day and night, supported by two million more in the uniform of the A.A.F.

On the home front, as 1944 dawned, was the backing of a huge industrial empire, its machines now geared to produce 10,000 aircraft a month. More than 1,400,000 men and women were employed in building and assembling the engines, propellers and airframes required for this colossal output. By the persistence and foresight of General Arnold and his associates, the Army Air Force had developed its own aviation engineers, its improved medical and hospital services, its weather findings and reportings, and the production of planes that could function under all weather conditions. Most important, the A.A.F. had hammered out a successful policy: to use highly trained crews, each working as a team; precision bombing in daylight, on targets selected as vital to the enemy war effort; and integration with ground troops and all other branches of the service, through staff planning and tactical field operations.

The Army Air Forces were poised and ready for their decisive battle of World War II in Europe.

A Mortal Blow for the Luftwaffe

It is late January 1944, and the very weather of western Europe speaks of uncertainty. The cold of normal winter is punctuated by continual dampness, overcast with a fog that seldom lifts and then only to admit more rain or snow. The officers and men of the United States Army Air Force and the British Royal Air Force, poised for a heavy assault on vital military targets in Germany, can do little but wait. On into February the dreary weather persists, as air combat operations congeal into stagnant idleness.

Saturday February 19, and the bulletin boards at the information centers of the Eighth Air Force display the terse announcement, "WEATHER OPERATIONAL FOR TOMORROW." The favorable word is relayed by code to commanders of airdromes in Italy and at scattered points where Allied airmen wait. All understand the meaning.

As Sunday morning dawns clear, the greatest air battle of history begins. For nearly a week it will rage in full fury, then continue on many fronts until the foothold of Overlord in France is secured and the mighty invasion has begun. For the Allies, its general objective is the destruction of the German Air Force.

As though answering the signal of one gigantic pushbutton pressed by General Doolittle, more than nine hundred bombers of the Eighth Air Force take off in the early light and thunder toward their appointed targets. Objective of this day's operation is to strike plants supplying the Luftwaffe's equipment and facilities.

About one-third the invading force converge upon the assembly factories of the Messerschmitt 109's near Leipzig. During the night before, R.A.F. bombers have appeared over this same target, and now the plants are alerted and their defending fighting planes ready. In full force the Luftwaffe pilots rise to do battle. They meet the American bombers head-on. As one Eighth Air Force pilot wrote:

"We caught flak, rockets and trailing attacks. Twenty-millimeter shells came zinging past with our names and rank on them—everything but our serial numbers!"

Many American planes fall before those deadly shells. Some bomber formations are beset with fighter attacks during three hours of their missions. American fighter planes never leave the battle, while the bomber formations close ranks and fly on. The heavy explosives rain down upon the aircraft plants of Leipzig, Bernberg, Brunswick, Oschersleben and Munich. The factories making a third of all Luftwaffe fighter planes are put out of production for from four to sixteen weeks.

With each dawn of five more days, all of them bright with unclouded sunshine, the A.A.F. bombers attack. Relentlessly they pound the aircraft factories, all previously bombed but never with such destructive force as now. More than five hundred bombers and three hundred fighters take part in the missions of Monday. On Tuesday the Eighth Air Force raiders are joined by bombers of the Fifteenth Air Force based in Italy, in the Strategic Air Forces' first coordinated attack. On Wednesday the commands go their separate ways, to join again on Thursday. Again on Friday the Eighth and the Fifteenth formations converge with more than 2,000 planes, in a mighty series of repeat and mopping-up attacks upon Stuttgart, Regensberg, Augsburg and Furth.

With each successive day, Luftwaffe resistance declines. Quick replacement of men and planes is impossible. Goering anxiously counts his losses for the six days: 692 aircraft shot down in air combat, many more destroyed on the ground. At least one-fourth of his best pilots are casualties. Most serious of all, much of the *Reich's* capacity for aircraft production is destroyed or seriously crippled. Price of the American victory: 244 heavy bombers, 33 fighter planes, and 2,200 pilots and crewmen lost.

These six days have proved conclusively the wisdom of daylight precision bombing of industrial facilities. The blow forces the Luftwaffe command to convert almost completely to a defensive arm, its fighters rising to battle only when they have local superiority or when protection of the target is urgently vital. In March the German Air Ministry receives its first consignment of jet aircraft, the Messerschmitt 262 twin-engined fighter—too late to come into quantity production or to permit training of pilots and crewmen for effective combat.

For the next three months the air battle is pressed relentlessly. "Around the clock" the Allied bombers roar with their fighter escorts, huge knights in armor with their swift and deadly champions. The morning light of March 4 shines upon the first big daylight attack upon Berlin. In the capital city are the principal plants for the production of one-third of the nation's railway locomotives and cars, three-fourths of the tanks, and substantial quantities of bearings, cables, instruments, parachutes, torpedoes, mines, radios and small arms. Production of all such vital items in the Berlin area is cut in half during those decisive weeks of March, April and May.

Between April 20 and June 6, bombers and fighter bombers

of the Eighth Air Force make fifty-five attacks upon the railway marshalling yards of France, Belgium and Germany. Typical of the scores of targets hit in history's first war of attrition by air power is the aircraft equipment depot near Augsburg, struck by waves of one hundred and sixty Eighth Air Force bombers on April 24. On the morning of May 12, two hundred and twenty Eighth Air Force Flying Fortresses and their escorts attack the hydrogenation plant at Leuna, employing 35,000 men and producing aviation gasoline. The bombs wreck the big facility and production is halted completely. Under forced labor, repairs are made which permit a limited operation by May 28, when the A.A.F. bombers strike again. On May 15, bombers of the Eighth Air Force fly the 1,200-mile round trip to raid the factories of Môst, Czechoslovakia. Working now in complete coordination, the Eighth and Fifteenth Air Forces on May 28 blast into twisted metal and glowing rubble the aviation fuel plants at Magdeburg, Lutzkendorf and Zeitz. During that critical month of May, formations of heavy bombers are dispatched on missions from the Eighth during twenty-five days and from the Fifteenth during twenty-one days. On June 2 the strategic forces join in a tremendous raid upon Hamburg, striking all seven oil refineries of that area.

Thus, the air battle is carried to all plants sustaining the Nazi war effort, including every one of the twenty-six plants engaged in production of trucks, other motor vehicles, and their parts; to the eighteen hydrogenation plants from the Ruhr to the Sudetenland and to Neechhammer in Silesia; to the chemical works centered in the Rhine Valley, along the Swiss and Austrian borders and near Leipzig, cutting in half their production of nitrogen and ethylene; to the powder and other munitions plants, bringing their output down to one-fourth the needed amount.

Meanwhile, American fighter wings have become more

numerous, their pilots better trained and their weapons more effective. The Ninth Air Force under General Vandenberg has become the greatest tactical air arm in the world. Its fighter and fighter bombers now range from England to Berlin, escorting, strafing, bombing selected targets. The pilots have developed special techniques of their own, such as swooping low to cast a bomb squarely into the entrance of a railway tunnel, to demolish bridges, to cut railroads, highways and canals.

During March the tactical group commanded by Colonel Donald J. Blakeslee, flying Mustang fighters, destroys 156 enemy aircraft. During April the A.A.F. counts 1,300 victories over Luftwaffe planes in aerial combat. For the month of May and the first six days of June, Ninth Air Force fighters and fighter bombers make 35,000 tactical sorties, an average of a thousand a day. The names of American aces emerge from the reports: Gabreski, O'Donnell, White, Sanders and many more. Luftwaffe pilots, in their ME–109's and FW–190's, brave as their opponents, engage the Americans and the British in life-or-death combat. But German valor is not enough: day by day the Luftwaffe becomes more helpless to prevent raids on any part of Germany.

In early June, Production-Minister Albert Speer reports to the *Reichschancellor* on the effects of the air attacks upon aircraft and fuel-oil production: "The strictest orders will have to be issued to start limited flying. . . . The strictest measures in the consumption of motor and diesel fuel will have to be taken. . . . I regret having to inform my Fuehrer of these tragic developments." Now Hitler storms at his Luftwaffe and accuses Goering of cowardice!

Air Power Supports the Greatest Invasion

Like rays of the sun brought to a point through a burning glass, plans for Operation Overlord now converge in heated preparations. The month of May sees the greatest accumulation of military equipment in history gorging the coastal areas of southern England. On the green waters of the Channel opposite Portland, Weymouth and Poole floats a mighty and varied armada of 2,493 vessels and landing craft, manned by 124,000 officers and men, ready to transport a million fighting men to their decisive engagement.

Normandy, in northern France, is enclosed in a huge triangle formed by the Seine from Paris to Le Havre, and by the Loire from Orléans to Nantes. Its Cotentin Peninsula is crowned by the city of Cherbourg. General Eisenhower and General Montgomery with their staffs choose the eastern beaches of this peninsula as best suited for the hazardous assault. They agree that the American 1st Army under General Omar E. Bradley will form the right wing of the invasion force, while the British 1st Army will form the left. "Utah" and "Omaha" are the names given the beaches the Americans must take. June 5 is set for "D-day"—the critical battle of combined sea, air and land action for a foothold on the Continent.

The German high command is aware that the invasion is prepared and its launching imminent. In fact, for months Marshal Rommel has been strengthening the coastal defenses in Belgium and northern France in the hope of repelling any attempt at invasion. Marshal Karl Gerd von Rundstedt, directing the ground forces in the west, sends this word to all his commanders:

"We must stop the assaulting forces in the water, not only delaying, but destroying all enemy equipment while still afloat."

German officers and men understand the importance of their general's directive. They have massed artillery, antiaircraft guns and machine-gun pillboxes along the coasts of Normandy. But they know also that these defenses can do little more than delay the landing unless the Luftwaffe can be revived to such strength as will match that of Allied air power. In late May they see the planes of the Ninth Air Force begin systematically destroying railway and highway bridges behind the Normandy beaches, while R.A.F. and A.A.F. bombers split the English Channel skies and roam over the ports of France, striking and strafing their targets almost at will. Crippled by lack of planes, with most of its veteran pilots gone and its new crewmen scarcely trained, the Luftwaffe flits impotently from one defensive nest to another. Anxiously the German troop commanders and their men scan the skies and ask: "Where is our Luftwaffe?"

Not an officer or man among the Allied forces, whether of land, sea or air, but realizes the tremendous responsibility his unit carries. All know that if the initial assault is successful, the foothold on the Continent can lead to defeat of the enemy; if it fails, long months may pass before it can be tried again.

Upon the supreme commander, General Eisenhower, rests most heavily the burden of the vital command decisions. A factor of greatest uncertainty is the weather. For success of the great amphibious operation, sea and winds must be favorable. On June 1, the D-day date still stands for June 5. The embarkation of the invasion force begins; but by June 3 storms are blowing and there is prospect for worse weather still. In a decision destined to avert probable disaster, Eisenhower postpones D-day until June 6.

The plan calls for dropping two airborne divisions—the 82d under General Matthew B. Ridgway, and the 101st, commanded by General Maxwell D. Taylor—on the peninsula south of Cherbourg, to seal off the area from reinforcements by ground troops and from outside communications. Several officers of Eisenhower's staff call the airborne operation a "suicide mission" and beg the general to call it off. Again the commander makes a firm decision: the air drop will be made.

Now all the machinery of the greatest invasion of all time moves into gear. As darkness closes in, three small motor launches slip away from shore and take up positions in a line across the Channel, floating beacons to guide the planes with their airborne troops. The hundreds of naval craft put out into heavy water, breasting six-foot waves from winds of twenty knots.

Shortly before one o'clock the paratroopers of the 101st take off into the murky, blustery night, followed by the second waves with the 82d an hour later. Taylor's units drop back of Utah Beach near the town of Ste.-Mère-Église, while Ridgway's men land astride the Merderet River west of the town. British paratroopers meanwhile are dropping to the eastward before the town of Caen. In this operation the 9th Troop Carrier Command sends 1,662 aircraft aloft, with 512 gliders—landing 17,262 troops, 504 artillery weapons and a thousand tons of equipment and supplies behind the enemy lines. There are the expected casualties among individual parachutists and from crack-up of gliders, with the loss also of forty-one powered aircraft. But at the glow of morning's light, the first of the Americans and British to make the invasion begin their mission of destroying communications and forming a defensive line.

At 2:30 A.M. the first waves of bombers take off and begin dropping their missiles at daybreak just back of the beaches, to knock out the defending units and their artillery bastions. At 5:50 the escort naval vessels are in range of the coast and begin their thunderous bombardment. A strong tidal current carries the first assault wave over a mile to the south of the designated beach, but luck is with the invaders for the defenses are weaker there than at the area of the intended landing.

The cloudy daylight discloses the forms of hundreds of ships nearing the Normandy coast. There are the crowded troop transports, the LST's packed to the edges with artillery, tanks and other weapons, the cruisers and destroyers hotly bombarding the areas back of the beaches; the landing craft, ready to disgorge their fighting men.

Here is the greatest opportunity of the entire war to show what defensive bombing and strafing can do. If only a thousand Luftwaffe bombers were ready to strike at the Allied armada, and only half survived fighter planes and ships' guns to reach their targets, they could make a shambles of the transports and barges crowded with troops, and turn the waters and sands of the Normandy coast red with the blood of the attackers. But only a few intrepid German fighter-bombers are on hand, and most are quickly downed by Allied aircraft.

At 6 o'clock the Air Force strikes begin in heavy volume, ranging far into the triangle between the Seine and the Loire, blasting bridges, highway hubs, canals and communications lines. During two and one-half hours of the D-day morning, Allied bombers fly a total of 2,362 sorties, and fighters a total of 1,813 sorties, effectively sealing off Paris from contact with the area and making difficult any reinforcement of the Nazi troops. A total of 7,616 tons of bombs are dropped during the day in support of the assault.

In the leading waves of the landing forces at Omaha Beach are the veteran 1st Division and the untried 29th Division. At Utah Beach is the 4th Division, while on the extreme left, opposite Caen, are two British and one Canadian divisions. As the heavily armed soldiers leap from their landing barges and slosh ashore, they find that the early bombing assault has been made too far inland, due to lack of visibility, and Rommel's coastal batteries are quite intact.

The German defenders fight bravely, pouring all their available artillery, shells and machine-gun bullets upon the landing craft, and taking a heavy toll of the attackers, of the weapons and supplies, especially at Omaha Beach. But they look in vain for their Luftwaffe. The attrition of the air battle which began in February has rendered Nazi air power helpless. By nightfall 21,328 troops, 1,742 vehicles and 1,695 tons of supplies have been landed. The beaches are secured.

During the next two days the weary invaders begin offensive campaigns. The VII Corps, under General J. Lawton Collins, fights its way to Cherbourg. Soon all the Cotentin Peninsula is cleared of the enemy.

The shock of the realization that their air arm has been knocked out strikes a mortal blow at the morale of the German troops. A lieutenant who survived Omaha Beach wrote:

We see the enemy that have dropped among our lines. We move forward toward the coast and see the hundreds of transports. What targets the transports and landing craft would make! We look up and see the formations of American planes. We keep saying "Where is our Luftwaffe?" Without the Luftwaffe, we lose the defense of Normandy. We lose our confidence—and finally, the war.

Now the Air Forces assume a new and major role in combat, that of interdiction—to stop the movements of enemy troops, to make advance impossible or costly and to make retreat extremely difficult. By the continued pounding of bridges, railways and highways, German reinforcements are effectively cut off. By mid-July a million Allied soldiers with their combat equipment have reached Normandy. On July 25 more than 2,500 planes of the A.A.F. take part in a tremendous bombardment of St. Lô. The German ground troops are stunned. The principal defending panzer forces suffer 70 per cent in casualties, with half of these killed. Surging through the breach made by air power the 1st Division, and the 2d and 3d Armored Divisions, advance. Six panzer divisions are hurled into a counterattack, but without air support their operations are hopeless. On July 31 Marshal Gunther von Kluge reports to the German high command:

"Yesterday's heavy fighting was successful for the enemy only because he paralyzed all our movements by employing fighter-bombers on an unprecedented scale. . . . Every movement of the enemy was prepared and protected by its Air Force. Our losses are extraordinary."

On August 1 General Patton's Third Army swings down from the Normandy beaches, his VIII Corps racing toward Brest, the other units moving south and westward, overcoming all opposition as thousands of German officers and men surrender. By mid-August the Nazi forces are routed from all Normandy and the Allies are moving toward Paris.

The Mission Is Accomplished

Thus was the final victory assured in World War II by the might of the Air Forces in history's longest decisive battle. With the success of D-day for the Allies, even before the breakthrough of St.-Lô, responsible German leaders, military and civilian, knew that the war was lost for them. Several attempts were made upon Hitler's life. Enraged, he purged, by torture and death, hundreds of his best officers, and began his descent into madness, holding his power by the thin unity of a people hounded by the fear of "unconditional surrender."

Through the remainder of the struggle, the Air Forces effectively carried out two missions of top importance: maintaining tactical support for the ground troops, and continuing the attacks upon the oil industry of the Reich until all its military machines, from Luftwaffe to trucks, came to a halt.

Coordination of tactical air power with ground troops proved uniformly workable and effective. As Patton began the advance eastward with his Third Army, this capable and daring general moved so rapidly that he was forced to leave his right flank exposed. To General Vandenberg he sent this message: "I am counting on the Ninth Air Force to protect my flank." And for the first time in history an air arm filled in the gaps between armies in hostile territory. Also for the first time, ground troops surrendered to units of an Air Force.

By late summer of 1944, the continued bombing of war facilities in Germany had tied down a labor force of 4½ million men and women. Shifts worked feverishly around the clock in a losing battle to replace destroyed factories that had produced military items and civilian goods. Engaged in debris clearance alone were more than two million persons. Accompanying the loss of equipment and crewmen by the German Air Force was the inevitable deterioration of the quality of its pilots. By August 1944 the average training period of American and British pilots was four to five times as long as that of the German pilots. Short of both machines and fuel, the Luftwaffe could not waste them on training operations.

Marshal Goering had one fantastic experience which gave him a close view of the effectiveness of American air missions. In the co-pilot's seat of his private four-engined plane, Goering was hopping toward Passau one day in late 1944. His plane was warned that American aircraft were approaching the area. Guenther Fechner, the air marshal's navigation and radio man, later wrote:

Suddenly we found ourselves surrounded by American bombers. Nobody said a word. We just held our breath. I think that we went unnoticed because we were flying a four-engined plane, too. At any rate we had a grandstand seat for the bombing of Passau. Goering just sat there, pale and quiet. Finally we hit a cloud formation and managed to slip away.

The Allied operations were not without some tragic errors. Soon after D-day a wave of planes miscalculated its target and rained bombs upon American troops, killing Lieutenant General Lesley McNair, chief of U.S. ground forces, and eighty-eight men of the 30th Infantry Division.

As though to substitute for the dying Luftwaffe, the self-propelled V–1 bombs and the V–2 rockets came whining out of the Nazi arsenal and down upon British ports and cities from bases in Normandy, Belgium and the Netherlands. Despite the resulting casualties, these weapons did little but fan the determination of civilians in the British Isles and in European Allied countries to support the war to a finish.

On December 12 Hitler met with his principal generals in an underground room at Zeigenberg to map a grand scheme to break through the Allied lines, and—as incredible as it must have sounded to his hard-bitten, practical military men—to end the war in victory. The plan led to the Battle of the Bulge, which lasted three weeks—the last great offensive of the forces that had already lost the war. Fog and rain prevented effective operations of air power during the first half of the battle, and the American forces were pushed back for twenty miles. With better weather, the Air Force played havoc with Nazi ground positions, ammunition depots and supply routes. Goering assembled all his available planes for an air offensive, and on New Year's Day, 1945, came *der grosse Schlag* (the great stroke), when the Luftwaffe flew more than eight hundred sorties, hitting principally at Allied airfields. It was the final effort of the dwindling German Air Force, and it cost the Luftwaffe the best of its remaining planes.

By January 15 the Allies had hammered the enemy back into the old positions, and soon afterward the Nazi armies were in full retreat. When the great crusade across Germany got underway, the results of the Allied air victory became apparent. Replacements for German planes, weapons and vehicles of all kinds were impossible to obtain, while the condition of oil facilities was graphically reported by General Bradley:

"When the Allied breakthroughs followed west of the Rhine in February and across the Rhine in March, and through Germany in April, lack of gasoline in countless local situations was the direct factor in the destruction or surrender of vast quantities of tanks, guns, trucks, and thousands and thousands of enemy troops."

As seven great Allied armies pushed eastward, relentless hammer blows of the Air Forces supported their every operation. On February 21 the A.A.F. and the R.A.F. began a month-long bombing of the great industrial area of the Ruhr. More than 9,000 Allied aircraft took part in the pounding of Dusseldorf, Essen, Bochum and other cities producing the major output of coal and steel in Germany. The industrial heart of the *Reich* all but stopped beating.

The sweep of American and British advances could have been made complete by the capture of all Germany, but everywhere the victorious western Allies were halted at "restraining lines," previously determined as the borders which the forces of Soviet Russia desired to reach. Brigadier General John Pierce's 16th Armored Division raced one hundred miles from Nuremberg to Pilsen in twenty-four hours of May 5 and 6. An Associated Press dispatch from the headquarters of the Third Army on May 10 related:

While Pilsen was being liberated by the Americans, May 6, patriots who seized the Prague radio kept sending out appeals to the Americans. . . . But the 16th stayed at Pilsen—because it was told to stay, and not because it could not get to Prague. It failed to make sense to the doughboys and tankmen.

On April 30 the crazed Nazi *Fuehrer* took his life in a bunker in the heart of Berlin, while cannon of the Red Army reduced the once-proud capital to hollow stone walls and dusty rubble. On May 7, in a small schoolhouse at Rheims, France, an armistice was signed, based upon the fact of unconditional surrender of all German military forces.

The Allied Air Forces had delivered 1,440,000 bomber, and 2,680,000 fighter, sorties in the Great War, loosing a total of 2,700,000 tons of bombs. The A.A.F. lost 79,265 and the R.A.F. 79,281 personnel in action. Together the air arms lost about

40,000 aircraft in combat and attacks upon almost countless targets in thirty-one major German cities.

The Army Air Forces had proved to be the indispensable partner of all the other services in modern warfare: partner of the Navy in clearing the seas and their lanes, and of the Army in ground engagements from skirmishes to grand campaigns; partner with both in preparing and clearing the way for invasions; faithful ally of every branch of the armed services as reconnaisance photographer, mover of troops, transporter of critical supplies, and attacker of the enemy's vital strength far behind the battle line. At the war's end, without detracting from the credit of its comrade services, the Air Forces could write:

"Mission Accomplished."

Bibliography

For those who desire additional reading on the Decisive Battles of American History, there is offered the following:

For General Background Reading—All Chapters

DUPUY, COLONEL R. ERNEST. *The Compact History of the United States Army.* New York: Hawthorn Books, Inc., 1956.

ESPOSITO, COLONEL VINCENT J. (chief ed.). *The West Point Atlas of American Wars.* New York: Frederick A. Praeger, 1959.

MITCHELL, COLONEL WILLIAM A. *Outlines of the World's Military History.* Harrisburg, Pa.: Military Service Publishing Co., 1929.

PRATT, FLETCHER. *The Compact History of the United States Navy.* New York: Hawthorn Books, Inc., 1957.

SPAULDING, OLIVER LYMAN. *The United States Army in War and Peace.* New York: G. P. Putnam's Sons, 1937.

Chapter One: Oglethorpe Defends His Colony

BRUCE, HENRY. *Life of General Oglethorpe.* New York: Dodd, Mead and Co., 1890.

CHARLTON, WALTER GLASCO. *The Making of Georgia.* Savannah, Ga.: Georgia Society of Colonial Dames, 1900.

KIMBER, EDWARD. *James Edward Oglethorpe.* Boston: C. E. Goodspeed and Co., 1935.

MARSHALL, JOHN. *American Colonies.* Philadelphia: Abraham Small, 1824.

Chapter Two: Wolfe Vanquishes the French at Quebec

DOUGHTY, ARTHUR GEORGE. *The Siege of Quebec.* Quebec, Can.: Dussault and Proulx, 1901.

HENTY, GEORGE A. *With Wolfe in Canada.* New York: A. L. Burt Co., 1900.

PARKMAN, FRANCIS. *Montcalm and Wolfe,* Vols. II and III. Boston: Little, Brown and Co., 1897.

PUTNAM, DONALD F. (ed.). *Canadian Regions.* New York: Thomas Y. Crowell Co., 1952.

Chapter Three: Canada Remains British

ADAMS, CHARLES FRANCIS (ed.). *The Works of John Adams,* Vol. II. Boston: Little, Brown and Co., 1856.

DEARBORN, CAPTAIN HENRY. "Benedict Arnold's Expedition," *Magazine of History,* Vol. 34, No. 3 (Tarrytown, N.Y., 1928).

Letters of Benedict Arnold. Collected by the Maine Historical Society. Portland, Me.: Fraser and Co., 1831.

ROBERTS, KENNETH L. *March to Quebec.* New York: Doubleday, Doran and Co., Inc., 1940.

SMITH, JUSTIN H. *Arnold's March from Cambridge to Quebec.* New York: G. P. Putnam's Sons, 1903.

Chapter Four: Burgoyne Surrenders at Saratoga

BOWEN, CATHERINE DRINKER. *John Adams and the American Revolution.* Boston: Little, Brown and Co., 1950.

BRANDOW, JOHN HENRY. *The Story of Old Saratoga.* Albany, N.Y.: Fort Orange Press, 1900.

FISKE, JOHN. *The American Revolution,* Vol. I. Boston: Houghton Mifflin Co., 1901.

HAZELTON, JOHN H. *Declaration of Independence, Its History.* New York: Dodd, Mead and Co., 1906.

Chapter Five: Washington Leads to Victory at Yorktown

FITZPATRICK, JOHN C. (ed.). *George Washington Diaries,* Vol. II. Published for the Mount Vernon Ladies' Association of the Union. Boston: Houghton Mifflin Co., 1925.

FITZPATRICK, JOHN C. *George Washington Himself.* Indianapolis, Ind.: The Bobbs-Merrill Co., 1933.

FREEMAN, DOUGLAS SOUTHALL. *George Washington,* Vol. V. New York: Charles Scribner's Sons, 1952.

SIMMS, WILLIAM GILMORE. *The Life of Nathanael Greene.* New York: Derby and Jackson, 1861.

Chapter Six: Perry Meets an Enemy on Lake Erie

ADAMS, HENRY. *History of the United States during the Administration of James Madison,* ed. HERBERT AGAR. Boston: Houghton Mifflin Co., 1947.

BANCROFT, GEORGE. *The Battle of Lake Erie.* New York: R. Bonner's Sons, 1891.

———. *Oliver H. Perry and the Battle of Lake Erie*. Providence, R.I.: State Department of Education, 1913.

DUTTON, CHARLES JUDSON. *Oliver Hazard Perry*. New York: Longmans, Green and Co., 1935.

PARSONS, USHER. *Battle of Lake Erie*. Newport, R.I.: The Mercury Publishing Co., 1912.

PRATT, JULIUS W. *Expansionists of 1812*. New York: The Macmillan Co., 1925.

ROOSEVELT, THEODORE. *The Naval War of 1812*. New York: G. P. Putnam's Sons, 1910.

Chapter Seven: Jackson Defeats the British at New Orleans

BASSETT, JOHN SPENCER. *The Life of Andrew Jackson*. New York: The Macmillan Co., 1931.

BEIRNE, FRANCIS F. *The War of 1812*. New York: E. P. Dutton and Co., 1949.

BUELL, AUGUSTUS C. *History of Andrew Jackson*. New York: Charles Scribner's Sons, 1904.

JAMES, MARQUIS. *Andrew Jackson, The Border Captain*. Indianapolis, Ind.: The Bobbs-Merrill Co., 1933.

PARTON, JAMES. *Life of Andrew Jackson*. New York: D. Appleton and Co., 1897.

Chapter Eight: Houston Wins Independence for Texas

CREEL, GEORGE. *Sam Houston: Colossus in Buckskin*. New York: Cosmopolitan Book Corp., 1928.

DAY, DONALD, and ULLOM, HARRY H. (eds.). *Samuel Houston, an Autobiography*. Norman, Okla.: University of Oklahoma Press, 1954.

JAMES, MARQUIS. *The Raven: A Biography of Sam Houston*. New York: Blue Ribbon Books, Inc., 1936.

LESTER, CHARLES EDWARD. *Samuel Houston*. Philadelphia: Davis, Porter and Coates, 1866.

WILLIAMS, ALFRED M. *Sam Houston and the War for Independence in Texas*. Boston: Houghton Mifflin Co., 1893.

Chapter Nine: Taylor Stands Fast Near Buena Vista

DYER, BRAINERD. *Zachary Taylor*. Baton Rouge, La.: Louisiana State University Press, 1946.

FROST, JOHN. *Life of Major-General Zachary Taylor*. New York: D. Appleton and Co., 1847.

Letters of Zachary Taylor (edited from originals). Rochester, N.Y.: The Genesee Press, 1908.

THORPE, T. B. *Our Army on the Rio Grande*. Philadelphia: Carey and Hunt, 1846.

Chapter Ten: Grant Besieges Vicksburg

CATTON, BRUCE. *U. S. Grant and the American Military Tradition*. Boston: Little, Brown and Co., 1954.

GARLAND, HAMLIN. *Ulysses S. Grant, His Life and Character*. New York: The Macmillan Co., 1920.

GRANT, U. S. *Personal Memoirs of U. S. Grant*, Vol. I. New York: Charles L. Webster and Co., 1885.

LOSSING, BENSON J. *A History of the Civil War*. New York: The War Memorial Association, 1912.

PORTER, HORACE. *Campaigning with Grant*. New York: The Century Co., 1897.

WOODWARD, W. E. *Meet General Grant*. New York: Horace Liveright, 1928.

Chapter Eleven: Lee Meets Defeat at Gettysburg

BROCK, R. A. *General Robert E. Lee*. Atlanta, Ga.: H. C. Hudgins and Co., 1897.

COMMAGER, HENRY STEELE. *The Blue and the Gray*. Indianapolis, Ind.: The Bobbs-Merrill Co., 1950.

DOUBLEDAY, ABNER. *Chancellorsville and Gettysburg*. New York: Charles Scribner's Sons, 1882.

FREEMAN, DOUGLAS SOUTHALL. *Lee's Lieutenants*, Vols. I, II, and III. New York: Charles Scribner's Sons, 1944.

————. *R. E. Lee, A Biography*, Vol. III. New York: Charles Scribner's Sons, 1935.

HENRY, ROBERT SELPH. *The Story of the Confederacy*. Indianapolis, Ind.: The Bobbs-Merrill Co., 1931.

HITCHCOCK, ETHAN ALLEN. *Fifty Years in Camp and Field*. New York: G. P. Putnam's Sons, 1909.

HORN, STANLEY F. (ed.). *The Robert E. Lee Reader*. Indianapolis, Ind.: The Bobbs-Merrill Co., 1949.

LONGSTREET, JAMES. *From Manassas to Appomattox*. Philadelphia: J. B. Lippincott Co., 1896.

Chapter Twelve: Dewey Conquers the Spanish Fleet

HALSTEAD, MURAT. *The Life and Achievements of Admiral Dewey*. Chicago: Our Possessions Publishing Co., 1899.

JOHNSON, ROSSITER. *The Hero of Manila.* New York: D. Appleton and Co., 1899.

SARGENT, NATHAN. *Admiral Dewey and the Manila Campaign.* Washington, D.C.: Naval Historical Foundation, 1947.

WOOLFALL, F. HARTLEY. *Life and Letters of Admiral Dewey.* New York: The Woolfall Co., 1898.

Chapter Thirteen: The Americans Turn the Tide

PALMER, FREDERICK. *Our Greatest Battle.* New York: Dodd, Mead and Co., 1919.

REPINGTON, LIEUTENANT COLONEL CHARLES À COURT. *The First World War, 1914–1918.* Boston: Houghton Mifflin Co., 1920.

SULLIVAN, MARK. *Our Times.* New York: Charles Scribner's Sons, 1933.

THOMAS, SHIPLEY. *The History of the A.E.F.* New York: George H. Doran Co., 1920.

VAN EVERY, DALE. *The A.E.F. in Battle.* New York: D. Appleton and Co., 1928.

Chapter Fourteen: The Navy Triumphs in the Pacific

CHURCHILL, WINSTON, and the Editors of *Life. The Second World War.* New York: Time, Inc., 1959.

MARSHALL, GENERAL GEORGE C.; ARNOLD, GENERAL H. H.; and KING, FLEET ADMIRAL ERNEST J. *The War Reports.* Philadelphia: J. B. Lippincott Co., 1947.

Chapter Fifteen: Air Power Spearheads Defeat of Germany

The Air Power Historian, Vol. VI, No. 1 (January, 1959). Montgomery, Ala.: Maxwell Air Force Base, Air Force Historical Foundation.

Command Decisions. Compiled from official reports of the U.S. Army by KENT ROBERTS GREENFIELD. New York: Harcourt, Brace and Co., 1959.

GOLDBERG, ALFRED (ed.). *A History of the U.S. Air Force, 1907–1957.* Princeton, N.J.: D. Van Nostrand Co., Inc., 1957.

GUNTHER, JOHN. *D Day.* New York: Harper & Brothers, 1944.

MARSHALL, GENERAL GEORGE C.; ARNOLD, GENERAL H. H.; and KING, FLEET ADMIRAL ERNEST J. *The War Reports.* Philadelphia: J. B. Lippincott Co., 1947.

Index

(Boldface references are to maps.)

360